Through the Money Maze

Through the Money Maze

The Essential Guide to Finding the Right
Financial Advisor
and Reaching Your Financial Goals

Mounir R. El-Ayari

Published in 2007 by
StrawberryFrog Press Ltd.
92 Glenview Avenue
Toronto, Ontario
M4R 1P8

www.StrawberryFrogPress.com

Canadian Cataloguing in Publication Data

El-Ayari, Mounir R., 1970-
Through the money maze: the essential guide to finding the right financial advisor and reaching your financial goals / Mounir R. El-Ayari. -- 1st StrawberryFrog Press ed.

ISBN 978-0-9781919-0-0

1. Finance, Personal--Canada. 2. Financial planners--Canada. 3. Investment advisors--
Canada. I. Title.

HG179.E43 2007   332.02400971   C2006-906017-7

Although the author has exhaustively researched all sources to ensure the accuracy and completeness of the information contained in this book, we assume no responsibility for errors, inaccuracies, omissions, or any inconsistency herein. Any slights of people or organizations are unintentional. Readers should use their own judgment and/or consult a financial expert for specific applications to their individual situations.

All characters in this book are fictitious. Any resemblance to actual persons, living or dead, is purely coincidental.

Cover Design: New Design Group

This book is lovingly dedicated to my beautiful wife and children.

Preface

A well thought-out financial plan and a realistic investment strategy are integral to achieving your financial goals. Unfortunately, many families spend very little time organizing their finances even though there are many talented and honest financial professionals available to help. Some individuals feel that a financial plan isn't necessary, and others simply lack the motivation to start the planning process. I have always believed that many people simply find the process overwhelming.

Even more interesting, many individuals who do work with a financial professional aren't always sure of the actual services he or she offers. I am a portfolio manager, but I have often been asked if I can help clients prepare their tax returns or even advise them on writing their wills. Although I have a general understanding of these things, I am not qualified or licensed to give tax or legal advice.

The purpose of this book, therefore, is to clarify the differences between the services offered by various professionals and help you find the right financial advisor to assist you in reaching your long-term financial goals. If you have yet to start the financial planning process, are in the early stages of implementing the various parts of your plan or feel that the relationship between you and your current financial advisor isn't working, then this book is for you. Along the way, I also refer to various aspects of the financial services industry, and I hope that after you've finished reading the story you'll have a clear understanding of what the Canadian financial services sector is all about.

For the sake of clarity, I have drawn distinct lines between the various financial professionals as they are introduced. In today's ever-changing financial landscape, however, many people offer a variety of services as opposed to just one. If a financial professional has the experience, educational qualifications and personality you are looking for, then he or she is likely to be a good candidate for your consideration. Just make sure the person you choose offers the specific services you need. For simplicity's sake, I have also kept the solutions presented in the book relatively straightforward. In practice, this is rarely the case.

Finally, I hope you enjoy the story in which the information is presented. One of the challenges in writing a personal finance book is presenting the material in a lively but accurate manner. By embedding the financial information in a story that follows the fictional Connor family from the beginning of the financial planning process to the very end, I am hoping the book will be useful to a large audience.

Table of Contents

| 1 |
Sleepless Nights

For the second time in a week, Rachel was awake, tossing and turning and trying desperately to fall back asleep. Eventually, frustrated, she nudged her husband, Thomas. As usual, he was sleeping like a hibernating bear. Nothing ever seemed to worry him. After a few unsuccessful attempts at trying gently to wake Yogi Bear, Rachel decided to go downstairs to make some herbal tea. As she climbed out of bed, she noticed the clock radio said 3:00am.

After boiling the kettle, she went into the living room to find the business section of yesterday's newspaper in order to have another look at the article that she'd read that morning. When she found what she was looking for, it was obvious why she was having so much trouble sleeping. The headline said, "The Coming Retirement Crisis."

Over the last few months, this was just one of dozens of articles that had made her worry. This one claimed that many Canadians are inadequately prepared to retire comfortably. Due to longer life expectancies, the author argued, a large number of individuals would outlive their retirement savings. All in all, it painted a very bleak picture of the future, which made Rachel feel very uneasy about her family's financial well-being.

Lately, because of articles like this, she had been giving their financial situation a lot of thought. Rachel realized how little time she and Thomas had devoted to planning for their future. Unlike many of their close friends, who already had sound financial strategies in place, Rachel didn't know where to begin. She had always been the one who took care of the family finances because Thomas didn't want to think about the "money stuff," as he liked to call it. In fact, they never really discussed it. This also worried Rachel.

At last, she had taken the initiative and started some preliminary research on her own. After speaking with several people, her fears about their inadequate financial strategy were confirmed. Neither she nor Thomas had an accurate idea about how their investments were performing. They had also neglected to update their wills and life insurance policies following the births of their children. And they definitely didn't know how much they needed to save in order to retire comfortably. Everyone else seemed to have a sound plan in place— why didn't they?

Drinking her tea, Rachel vowed that this would be the last time that this 3:00am ritual would take place. She didn't want to neglect their financial affairs any longer. She would finally make Thomas discuss their overall financial situation. The thought of this was enough to make Rachel feel a little bit better. Hopefully, she could still get a few hours sleep before heading to work. As soon as she finished her tea, she headed upstairs to join Yogi. He was still sleeping as soundly as a bear.

Key Point

When evaluating your financial health, you should consider all your income (employment and investment); debts and future debts.

| 2 |

We Don't Really Need Help, Do We?

Three hours later, when Thomas went downstairs to the kitchen, he found Rachel reading some brochures on retirement and financial planning. "Good morning!" Thomas said. "What are you doing up so early?"

"Worrying about money," she said. "We need a financial strategy, Thomas. I couldn't sleep again last night. I feel like we're sleepwalking and one day we'll wake up ready to retire but we won't be able to afford it," she said sternly.

"Honey, why do you keep worrying about this? We both earn a decent living. In fact, we make about twice as much as both of our parents did in their best years, and we're only in our late thirties. Besides, all of this financial planning stuff is just a passing trend. Our parents didn't need a financial plan and they are doing fine," Thomas said, with a hint of doubt in his voice. "Besides, it's six in the morning. Do we really have to talk about this—?"

"Money stuff?" Rachel quickly interrupted. She smiled at him wryly.

"Thomas, every time I want to talk to you about this, you immediately want to get off the subject. You can't always compare our situation to that of our parents. Things have become more complicated since our parents were young. Everyone is living longer, the cost of post-secondary tuition is outpacing the level of inflation and many companies have inadequate pension plans for their employees. Do you have any idea of how much income your company pension plan will pay you when you retire? Do you even know if your company has a pension plan?" Rachel asked with frustration in her voice.

"To be honest, honey, I don't," Thomas confessed. "We are in the fortunate position of not having to worry about money. Our combined household income is well into six figures. As far as I am concerned, we are doing pretty well. If we weren't making good money I would understand your concern. Don't worry about it," Thomas said trying to sound confident. "We'll be fine."

"Thomas, please listen to me. Listen very carefully. If we're in such fine shape, as you like to claim, why do Patrick and Cindy never worry about money, even though they make about half of what we do? They have very little debt, live in a nice house, which is mortgage-free, and seem to be well on their way to financial prosperity. Why is that?" she asked.

"Well, that's because…it's because…I don't know. Are they really in such good financial shape?" Thomas asked somewhat surprised. "How do you know?"

"They also each have a will, are saving a fixed percentage of their gross income every month and have a fairly good idea of how much retirement income they are eventually going to need. They have life insurance policies, disability insurance and they maximize their Registered Retirement Savings Plan (RRSP) contributions at the beginning of every year. To top it all off, they have also started making annual contributions to a family Registered Education Savings Plan (RESP) so they can help their kids with the cost of university. Did you know that the federal government actually pays a grant to a child's RESP when contributions are made by the subscriber?"

Needless to say, Thomas was taken aback. All these years he'd been feeling somewhat guilty for making more money than their friends Patrick and Cindy. He hadn't realized that they were both so financially astute. For the first time in many years, Thomas felt as though he had really let Rachel down. He felt irresponsible and even a little embarrassed.

Rachel was surprised by Thomas's reaction. He had never taken their financial affairs seriously, figuring that the more money they made, the less they had to worry about implementing a financial strategy.

"Thomas, I didn't want to scare you. I just wanted to make sure that you know how important this is. I have been worried about this for months and I just don't want to have to think about it any longer."

"I guess that I should have taken this more seriously a long time ago," said Thomas. "We should probably tackle this sooner rather than later. Maybe we should continue this conversation tonight after work. I always thought that we were in control. Obviously we're not," Thomas said, before planting a kiss on his wife's forehead.

Later that morning, at her office, Rachel saw Megan, one of her closest friends. She couldn't wait to tell her the good news about her conversation with Thomas.

"Judging from the dark rings under your eyes, you must have had a long night," Megan said, thinking her friend had been worrying about work.

"Actually, I did have a long night," Rachel replied. "But it's not what you think. Do you remember a few months ago, when I told you that I was having trouble sleeping because I was worried about our finances?" Rachel asked.

"I thought you were going to talk to Thomas about this," Megan said sternly. "I've told you how important it is to get your financial house in order. Why haven't you talked to him yet?" she demanded.

"I did, first thing this morning," Rachel said proudly. "As usual, he tried to wriggle out of it. I wouldn't let him off the hook, though."

"Good for you!" Megan shouted, giving her a friendly nudge. "How did you finally get him to listen?" she asked curiously.

"Well," Rachel explained. "I told him how Patrick and Cindy are in such great financial shape even though they earn less money than we do. He couldn't believe how well they seem to be able to plan and save. I didn't even give him the full story because I wanted to go easy on him," she said. "He was a little bit embarrassed after he admitted how naïve he's been about planning for our future. The whole conversation is, of course, thanks to you."

"You don't have to thank me," Megan insisted. "All I did was emphasize the importance of knowing where you are, financially, and making proper retirement plans. You still have a lot of work to do. Realizing that you have to get your finances in order and deciding to do it is the first step. The next step is finding a financial professional who can help you achieve this. It isn't as easy as it sounds. The process of choosing financial advisors can often be confusing and overwhelming. I'll be able to give you some guidance, but the final decision will be yours."

"Megan, I wasn't quite finished basking in this morning's glory and now you already have me thinking about the next step. You don't waste any time, do you?" Rachel asked.

"Not a chance," she answered. "I want to keep you on your toes at all times. One day you'll thank me for this."

"That's why you're my best friend," Rachel told her, as they walked towards the elevator.

In the elevator, Rachel thought about her next challenge: trying to convince Thomas to hire the services of a financial professional.

"This could prove to be difficult," she thought.

Thomas is a proud, self-proclaimed do-it-yourselfer. He has always been wary of hiring professionals. He proves this every year during the tax season when he pulls an all-nighter trying to figure out the difference between a tax deduction and tax credit. Although she knew that she still had her work cut out for her, Rachel was looking forward to taking the next step.

Key Point

Earning an above-average income does not guarantee financial security. Individuals from all income levels can benefit from a detailed financial plan.

| 3 |

What Are Friends For?

Despite their very different backgrounds, Megan and Rachel had become instant friends when they met during their first week at university. Megan, who grew up in the city with very wealthy parents, was pursuing a Bachelor of Commerce degree. Rachel grew up in a small rural community and was working towards a Bachelor of Arts.

The two grew to rely on each other, even though their interests and talents were very different. Megan, for instance, had always been knowledgeable and interested in business and the economy. She followed the stock market, and if anyone needed to know how a particular company or mutual fund was performing, she was the person to ask. It was almost like having a financial encyclopedia right at your fingertips.

Initially, Rachel thought that Megan's interest in the financial markets stemmed from the fact that she was studying commerce. It wasn't until later that Rachel learned that Megan's father was the CEO of a major public company and, as she was growing up, he had taught her a lot about investing. What was most impressive was that Megan didn't find the financial markets intimidating; she found them intriguing. Rachel knew very little about the world of finance. Her passion was politics.

After university, the two friends ended up working for a small management consulting firm in Toronto and they had stayed friends ever since.

The ring of Rachel's telephone suddenly interrupted her brief moment of reminiscing.

"Hello, Rachel speaking," she said into the receiver.

"Hi Rachel, it's Cindy," the voice on the other end said. "Do you have a second?" she asked.

"Of course, how are you?"

"I am doing very well. Business is a little slow this morning. I guess people aren't in the mood to buy antiques today," Cindy answered. "But on the whole, business has been extremely good. It was a little slow at one point, which is never a good thing. Patrick and I have been able to manage, however. We still love running our own business."

Several years ago, Cindy and her husband Patrick had found themselves in a difficult situation after Patrick unexpectedly lost his job. Having been put in this unfortunate position, they decided to turn a setback into a unique opportunity by taking out a small loan and starting an antique furniture business. It took a while, but eventually, after several years of hard work, they managed to earn a decent living from it. Rachel told Cindy about her conversation with Thomas and their plans for financial stability. Cindy listened sympathetically.

"I know what you mean," she said. "At first we thought our work was done just by admitting that we needed some help. This wasn't the case at all. It took a lot of work to find the right financial advisor. There are so many people out there calling themselves 'investment professionals', and many of them aren't qualified to provide sound financial advice. It's actually quite confusing and overwhelming. It was a long and tedious process, to say the least. With that said, though, once we found the perfect advisor, the rest was easy. Without her, we never would have achieved our financial goals."

"I don't know how I can convince Thomas to employ the services of an investment professional," Rachel said in despair. "As you know, he's a proud do-it-yourselfer. Six years ago he was trying to convince me that we didn't need a lawyer to close the purchase of our house because he was convinced that he could get any information he needed off of the Internet. That's what I'm dealing with!"

"Well, how about telling him that if he doesn't co-operate you will gladly take care of it by yourself. Let him know that as the chief financial officer of the family corporation, you will start by reducing any unnecessary expenses. Tell him that the first thing to go will be his hockey season's tickets. I think he'll get the picture pretty quickly," Cindy said laughing.

"That is excellent advice!" Rachel said.

"I'm glad I could help," Cindy laughed. "The reason why I'm calling is to see if you wanted to have lunch this afternoon. We haven't seen each other in a while."

"That sounds good," Rachel replied. "How about at one o'clock at our regular place?"

"Perfect! See if Megan would like to join us. We can give you some ideas about where to go next with Thomas," Cindy said.

"Okay. I'll see you then."

After Rachel put the telephone back in its cradle there was a knock on her door. It was Megan.

"Is there any way that we can go over our presentation before lunch? Something important has come up and I'd like to make sure that we are ready as soon as possible."

"No problem," Rachel said. "I don't have as much to do as I thought. Speaking of lunch, I just got off the phone with Cindy. She'd like to get together this afternoon."

"That would be great," Megan said. "I haven't seen Cindy for ages and it would be nice to catch up."

"Great! Let's go over the presentation now so that we don't have to worry about it later," Rachel said. "That way we won't feel guilty if we take a little longer for lunch."

Key Point

The process of finding the right financial advisor entails a great deal of work. In order to find an investment professional whom you trust to manage your finances, you must be willing to go through the process in its entirety.

| 4 |

Who Needs a Financial Advisor Anyway?

From the moment he had left the house that morning, Thomas couldn't stop thinking about the conversation he had with his wife. He was still having a hard time believing that Cindy and Patrick were in such great financial shape given their moderate income. Despite having a combined household income that was well into six figures, he and Rachel still seemed to have difficulty saving money on a regular basis. This fact alone baffled him.

It was now apparent to Thomas that simply earning more money wasn't the answer. If it were, Rachel probably wouldn't be so concerned about their financial future. Since she was the one who took care of their finances, she probably had reason to worry. Maybe sitting down and implementing a retirement strategy was the answer. It would certainly make her feel better, which was as good a reason as any to do it.

Before he got himself worked up into a frenzy, Thomas decided to call the one person to whom he always turned for support—Patrick. They had been friends for a long time and he was always the first person Thomas would talk to whenever he needed some friendly advice. Thomas dialled the number at the antique store.

"Hello, Antiques On King," a female voice answered.

"Hi, Cindy. It's Thomas. How have you been?"

"Hi, Thomas. I'm doing well. I'll be doing even better after I have lunch with Megan and your wonderful wife this afternoon. I spoke to Rachel this morning," she said.

"Just make sure that you don't spend the entire afternoon gossiping about us men," Thomas said sarcastically. "We're sensitive about that kind of stuff."

Cindy could sense Thomas smirking through the phone.

"I'd better pass you over to Patrick before I get myself into trouble. I'll talk to you soon," she said, before handing the phone over to her husband.

"How are you doing?" Patrick asked.

"I'm okay," Thomas answered. "The reason I am calling is that I wanted to talk to you about financial planning. Rachel confronted me early this morning. She hasn't been sleeping well because she is worried about our financial situation. Do you have a few minutes to talk?"

"Of course I do. Let me go into the office where it's a little quieter," Patrick said. A few moments later Patrick was back on the phone. "That's better. How can I help?"

"As I was saying, Rachel approached me this morning and wanted to discuss our financial future. As usual, I was somewhat reluctant because I've always assumed that we were in good shape and didn't need a financial plan. After talking to her, I started to have some doubts. She mentioned that you and Cindy are in great financial shape. Do you mind if I ask how you managed this?"

"Well, the first thing that we did was accept the fact that we needed a financial strategy. Before I was laid off, I wasn't in the least bit worried about our retirement. I assumed that because I had a company pension plan, we would both retire comfortably. Cindy was constantly trying to convince me of the merits of implementing a formal financial strategy, but it wasn't until after I was out of work that I realized how important this was. Fortunately for us, it wasn't too late."

"What did you do then? It's one thing to acknowledge that you need a plan, but it's an entirely different ball of wax to actually implement a strategy. Did you do it on your own?" Thomas asked.

"No," Patrick replied. "Cindy and I needed a professional. We wanted to make sure that we did everything properly the first time around. It wasn't until after we had a plan in place that we realized we had done the right thing. We needed advice on estate planning, retirement planning, insurance and portfolio management. It was far too complex for us to handle on our own."

"Patrick, you know I like to take matters into my own hands. I have always done everything on my own. Rachel sometimes thinks that I'm being stubborn, but I'm really not. I just don't like spending money on something that I can do myself."

"It's not always about saving money," Patrick replied. "It's about feeling confident that everything is being properly looked after. As you know, Cindy and I don't earn anywhere close to what you earn. If anyone should be concerned about saving money, it should be us. We realized early on that proper financial advice is indispensable. Neither of us have the time or interest to keep up with the changes in the investment industry or financial markets. A truly skilled investment professional stays current on the latest changes in tax law, estate law and insurance and investment products. We would rather focus on growing our business."

Thomas was still worried. "What if I can't find somebody that I trust? For me, it just isn't about saving money," Thomas emphasized. "It's about finding someone who is honest, trustworthy and who will act in our best interests. The newspapers make it seem like most investment professionals lack integrity. I don't really have a good impression of the financial services industry as a whole."

"There are bad apples in any profession," said Patrick. "There are bad doctors, dentists, lawyers, accountants and even kindergarten teachers. The most important thing to remember is that you have to be diligent when hiring any professional. Do your homework. Most people seem to forget that a professional works for you. You can fire them if you're not happy with their work."

"I don't know if I'm totally convinced," Thomas said. "I still think that I can do my own financial planning. That way I won't let a stranger into our personal financial affairs. I am a fairly private person."

"Let me ask you this," Patrick said. "Do you know how much insurance you currently have or need, how much money you need to retire comfortably or that dividends are taxed at a much better rate than interest earned from term deposits and guaranteed investment certificates (GICs)? These are just a few of the many things that you would need to know to effectively manage your finances. Although it's possible, it would eat up a lot of your time to stay on top of everything in a timely manner. Wouldn't it be nice to be able to call your financial advisor and have all of these answers right at your fingertips?"

"I do have all this information at my fingertips," Thomas insisted. "You may have heard of a little invention called the Internet," he said sarcastically.

"Just because you are a vice-president at a software company doesn't give you the right to pick on the technologically inept," Patrick laughed. "I know exactly what the Internet is—it's that plastic cover that you put over your computer to keep the dust off."

Thomas mentioned his new Internet investing strategy but Patrick reminded him that using a financial advisor involved more than stock trading.

"I think you have missed my point entirely," he said. "Buying and selling investments is only a small part of financial planning. There is so much more to it than that. It's about professional advice. More importantly, it has been proven that people who use the services of an investment professional are better prepared for their retirement than those who don't. Skilled financial advisors will encourage their clients to be disciplined savers and stick to a long-term investment strategy. Those investors who go it alone often lose focus and make bad decisions. All it takes is one or two bad decisions to throw you off track. To prove my point, let me ask you a question. Do you know who Mohammed Ali is?" Patrick asked in a serious tone.

"Of course I know who Mohammed Ali is," Thomas replied.

"Is it fair to say that he's probably one of the greatest boxers in history?" Patrick asked.

"Absolutely," Thomas replied.

"If he was so talented, why did he need a trainer? For that matter, why does any professional athlete need a coach or trainer? The reason is very simple—a trainer provides discipline, focus and direction. Although professional athletes have the necessary skills to play the game, they often have trouble setting realistic goals and working towards achieving these goals. In many ways, investors are the same. They may know what they would like to achieve financially, but most of them don't have the discipline to implement and stick to a long-term strategy. A financial advisor helps them do this."

"Okay, you've made your point," Thomas said. "But how do I know who to choose?"

"Well, this is where you have to do your homework. One way is to ask friends and find out whom they work with. This is a common approach. I could, for instance, refer you to the person we work with. She has done an exceptional job and we trust her completely. In fact, we wouldn't know what to do without her. One disadvantage with referrals is that financial advisors are not 'one size fits all.' Cindy and I may have a great working relationship with our advisor but that doesn't mean that you would have a good relationship with her. Your financial needs are different from ours. Although it is time consuming, the best strategy is to go through the entire process on your own. You'll learn a lot about the financial services industry in general. You'll also find that most investment professionals are honest and ethical. Everyone's needs are different. You have to find a financial advisor that has a good understanding of your specific investment objectives, not mine."

"That makes sense. But wouldn't it be smart to start by meeting your financial advisor, given that you speak so highly of her?" Thomas asked. "It certainly would save a lot of time."

"Yes, it makes complete sense," Patrick responded. "And you will meet her. As I said before, it's important that you go through the process on your own because you will learn a lot more. You should also commit to interviewing several people, no matter how highly someone is recommended. It could save potential problems later on. Imagine if you begin working with our financial advisor and she was the only one that you interviewed because I referred her to you. Let's pretend that the relationship eventually soured for one reason or another. If this happened, my relationship with her might become strained or you might get upset with me because she didn't meet your expectations. Problems like this can be avoided by interviewing several candidates and making sure that the financial professional you hire is a perfect fit for you, based on your own unique needs."

"That makes a lot of sense. How did you learn so much about all of this stuff?" Thomas asked.

"We have Megan to thank for pointing us in the right direction. She's fairly astute when it comes to financial matters. She's also one of those rare individuals who has had a financial plan since she was in her early twenties and has worked with the same financial advisor for years. Megan is responsible for getting us on track, but she was adamant that we do our own homework. She insisted that this would be the only way that we would learn for ourselves, and she was right."

"Megan does seem to have everything neatly in place. I have a feeling that she's responsible for encouraging Rachel to talk to me about all this. I am going to have to thank her," Thomas said. "I think you've convinced me to look into using the services of an investment professional. I now understand why it makes more sense to work with a professional instead of doing everything myself. It will take some work but I think it'll be worth it in the long run," Thomas said.

"Rachel is going to be thrilled when she sees that you're taking your finances seriously. She'll be even more thrilled knowing that you don't want to go through this process on your own. She told us about what happened when you tried to fix the roof last spring. We couldn't stop laughing," Patrick said, teasing his friend.

"That wasn't my fault," Thomas said defensively. "How was I supposed to know that the entire roof was rotten? Besides, I could have seriously hurt myself. You shouldn't laugh so hard."

"You were lucky that you didn't go through to the basement. If you ever leave the software business, you should start your own general contracting business. You'd make a fortune!"

"Very funny," Thomas said. After a few minutes' discussion of their hockey team's prospects for the next season, they ended their conversation with a promise to get together for dinner soon.

Thomas realized that everything Patrick had said made a lot of sense and that the next logical step was finding a qualified investment professional. He was surprised to find that he felt a bit relieved that he had made this decision. In the back of his mind he knew that they should have worked out a financial strategy years ago. He had always been reluctant to take the first step, however, because he found the entire process a little overwhelming. He had never told Rachel this because he was embarrassed to admit that he was somewhat intimidated by the investment industry, but he now realized that this was absurd.

He also knew that Rachel would be excited by his decision. She was constantly worrying about their financial affairs, which made him uncomfortable. It wasn't fair that he left all the worrying up to her because they were both equally responsible for their financial well-being. From now on, he was going to make sure that there would be no more sleepless nights. He couldn't wait to tell Rachel that he was ready to begin the search for someone to help them with their finances, so he called her at work to let her know.

Key Point

It's worth hiring a professional to manage your money. It takes a great deal of time to stay on top of developments in the financial services sector and to acquire and update the background knowledge necessary to make sound investment decisions. You trust your dentist to look after your teeth; trust your financial advisor to look after your money.

| 5 |

A Penny Saved Is A Penny Saved

It was shortly before noon when Megan and Rachel wrapped up their presentation in the main boardroom. It was such a tremendous success that they landed the client on the spot.

"I can't believe how well our presentation went," Rachel said shutting down her laptop.

"I'm not all that surprised," Megan insisted. "I knew we would do well, but it's nice that the client seems excited about our future working relationship. It makes all of the long hours we put in worth it."

"Wait until we tell the partners. They are going to be absolutely thrilled. I think that we deserve an extra long lunch. What do you think?" asked Rachel.

"Absolutely!" Megan agreed.

"We should get going; it's almost noon," said Rachel. "Cindy will be expecting us."

"Should we take your car or mine?" Megan asked when they met at the elevator.

"Let's take your car. After a presentation like that we deserve to ride in style. Nothing short of a Honda Accord will do," Rachel joked.

"I agree," Megan said smiling. "We deserve nothing but the best."

Megan was taught from an early age that you should try to avoid spending too much of your disposable income on items that depreciate substantially in value. This is especially true of cars. Being someone who practised what she preached, she prided herself on the fact that she drove a pre-owned Honda. Why would anyone want to allocate a significant portion of his or her savings to something that eventually becomes worthless?

"I have to give you some credit," Rachel said as they approached Megan's car. "You are one of the few people I know who put their money where their mouth is. Out of all of our friends, you are the one person who can easily afford an expensive sports car without worrying about the cost, yet you still drive your Honda."

"I'm sure a lot of people think I'm being stingy," Megan laughed. "I think they would be pretty impressed if they knew that I invested the money that I saved and nearly doubled the original amount since I bought 'Old Faithful'. I then used that money to pay off the balance of my mortgage. Besides, I love my car!" Megan said proudly.

"I wish Thomas and I had our mortgage paid off," Rachel sighed. "Despite the fact that our monthly net income is almost five times higher than our monthly mortgage payment, we still haven't been able to pay off the mortgage early. That doesn't make sense to me. Where does all the money go?"

"Well, now that you have decided to get some financial advice, you won't have to worry about it much longer," Megan replied. "A good financial advisor should be able to help you with your cash and debt management. After analyzing your overall situation, he or she will be well positioned to advise you on how to properly allocate your net income."

Rachel and Megan were looking forward to seeing Cindy. They rarely had the opportunity to go out for lunch unless it was with an important client. Although they tried to get together at least once a month, it had been quite a while since they had seen her. Lunch with their old friend would be fun.

Key Point

Just because you can afford an expensive car or other large-ticket discretionary items does not mean you should purchase them. Rather than spending money on consumer goods that will decrease in value, wise investors will first pay off debts like mortgages, personal lines of credit or credit card balances.

| 6 |

Would You Like to Start with a Hot Tip?

As Megan and Rachel pulled into the parking lot of the restaurant, they saw Cindy getting off the bus. They both waved at their friend. As they parked the car, she walked over to greet them.

"Shouldn't you guys take the bus? It's cheaper than owning a car, you know," Cindy chirped.

"We know, we know," Megan replied. "But with the heavy traffic we never would have made it on time. And who wants to take the bus when you can take this baby for a spin?" Megan replied as she motioned towards her beloved Honda.

"You have a point," Cindy responded with a smile. "Anyway, I'm not in a rush today. We sold a dining room table and a cabinet this morning, and I was hoping that you guys could take an extra-long lunch."

"You took the words right out of my mouth. We landed a big project on the spot today and were hoping we could all take a long lunch together. Rachel wants to talk about getting her financial house in shape. She finally convinced Thomas that it couldn't wait any longer."

"You did?" Cindy asked. "How did you ever manage that? Thomas hates talking about money. Everyone knows that!"

"I just put my foot down and insisted," said Rachel. "Once I told him how worried I've been, he realized that he was being unfair leaving me to do this alone. Plus, I pointed out that our friends have financial plans and their lives are less stressful because of it. He's all in favour of anything that cuts down on stress."

Rachel was glad she had these women as her friends. She knew she could depend on the girls for unconditional support. This thought was extremely comforting.

Inside, the host greeted them warmly. "It's always a pleasure to see my silent partner," he said, embracing Megan.

Several years before, Megan's accountant had encouraged her to diversify her investments. At the time, she had already increased her portfolio to over seven figures. In addition to this sizeable nest egg, she also owned several income-producing properties that she managed herself. When her financial planner told her he had a client who was interested in selling his successful restaurant, she looked into the opportunity. After careful analysis of the business and its books, she decided to become the majority owner in a renowned bistro. In hindsight, it was an excellent decision.

As the women were shown to their table, Rachel couldn't help but feel proud of her two friends. Even though Megan came from a wealthy family, she had managed to build a significant nest egg without the help of her parents. She had achieved this through many years of saving and investing her money intelligently. Cindy, on the other hand, had gone through a very difficult period after Patrick lost his job. Despite this, they still managed to work through a very tough time and fulfill their dream of establishing a profitable antique store. How did they do it?

Waiting for the waiter to bring their drinks, the women continued their discussion of Rachel and Thomas's financial plans. Rachel asked Cindy what her secret formula for financial success was.

"I'll sum up how we did it in four words: living below our means," Cindy responded. "As you know, Patrick and I live very modestly. When I saw you in the parking lot, for instance, I commented on how you should have taken the bus because it's cheaper than driving a car. I wasn't kidding! We have only one car and, although it is difficult at times, we manage. Although having two or three cars may be easily affordable for some, for us it meant whether or not we could open our antique store. After careful financial planning, it became apparent that we could save more than six hundred dollars a month on insurance, parking, maintenance and gas. That is more than half of our monthly mortgage payment for the store."

"You mean you own the store?" Rachel asked. "I always thought that you rented it."

"No, we actually bought the building. I know it's not the Eaton Centre, but it's an excellent piece of property. When we started looking for a location, we were initially interested in leasing a space. It never really occurred to us to actually buy a store. After talking to our financial planner, we learned that buying and quickly paying down the mortgage was an excellent investment decision. The benefits were that we were building equity for our future and we never had to worry about our lease expiring. Also, the interest on our mortgage payments is tax deductible."

"That's amazing!" Rachel said. "Congratulations," she proudly said to her friend.

"Tell Rachel about the apartment above the store," Megan encouraged. "That's the best part!"

"Well, when we were looking for a spot, we thought it would be nice to buy a building that had an apartment above the shop. We planned to use it for storage, or maybe to show people what furniture looked like in a room. When we discussed it with our financial planner, she gave us a better suggestion. She told us that we might want to consider renting out the apartment in order to generate a monthly income. This would help us supplement our personal income. We took her advice and we now rent out the apartment for nine hundred and fifty dollars a month."

"Nine hundred and fifty dollars per month!" Rachel exclaimed. "I can't believe it."

"It couldn't have worked out better. We put a little money into the apartment to modernize it and we now have a great young couple living there. They have a nice, safe, affordable place to live and we have some very decent tenants providing us with a little extra money. It's the best of both worlds. More importantly, it gives us room to breathe from an income standpoint. We could go six months without selling a piece of furniture before needing to access our emergency fund. Nowadays, though, it's rare to go three days without selling some major pieces."

"And you," Rachel said, looking at Megan. "You have your own restaurant. Who would have thought that one day we'd all be dining at Chez Megan?"

"None of us would ever have guessed it. I have to say, though, it's nice to have your own restaurant. You never have to pay to eat out," Megan joked.

"Of course, with your family money you can buy almost anything that you want," Rachel said, poking fun at her friend. "It must be nice being rich!"

"I know you're just teasing me. You're lucky that I have a good sense of humour. But seriously, so many people think my parents give me everything. I'm an adult, for heaven's sake. They haven't supported me for years. I guess it's inconceivable that I've managed to save, invest and build wealth all on my own, the old-fashioned way. It gets quite frustrating at times," Megan said.

"Okay," said Rachel. "So far I've learned that you have to live below your means and that you have to work hard at saving and investing your money. This all makes sense. The problem is, how do you know what to do, how much to save and how to invest it once you've saved it? That's the bit that's overwhelming," Rachel admitted.

"I'll give you the same advice my father gave me," said Megan. "As the CEO of a multinational corporation, he knows all the ins and outs of business and running a company. Even though he has a lifetime of business experience, he still relies on the help of a small group of investment professionals. In fact, he has a very tight-knit group of advisors upon whom he relies. For as long as I can remember, he has always told me that my financial security would greatly depend upon the quality of the people I worked with. So far, he has been right."

"Are you telling me your dad doesn't do his own investing?" Rachel asked.

"Yes, that's what I'm saying. Even with all of his business experience, he still has to rely on someone who has a great deal of expertise in managing money, much in the same way as he has expertise in running a multinational corporation."

"Are all CEOs the same?" Cindy asked.

"Yes, most of them are," replied Megan. "In fact, most wealthy individuals and families rely on several investment professionals for advice. The ultra-wealthy, for example, often create their own investment holding companies that employ portfolio managers, investment bankers, lawyers and accountants. These individuals are responsible for making almost every investment decision. They will often invest in private and public companies to ensure that they diversify across various asset classes."

"Isn't that exactly what you do?" Rachel asked. "I mean, you're always talking about how important it is to diversify your assets."

"Yes, it's very similar. The only difference is that I rely on only a few professionals as opposed to the big team that would be employed by a private investment holding company. The process is the same. Even the ultra-wealthy have investment objectives, just like you and me. As a result, they rely on someone to advise on and address these objectives. Most people seem to think that the more money you accumulate the less you have to worry about it. In fact, the exact opposite is true. The reality is that as an individual begins to build significant wealth, he or she needs to rely on individuals that are much more experienced."

"What do you mean?" Rachel asked with a hint of confusion. "Aren't all investment professionals the same?"

"Actually they're all very different," Cindy said. "I used to think exactly the same thing until Megan taught me that various professionals offer various services. There are so many different job titles out there that it took Patrick and me a while to learn about the various services that are available."

"It sure isn't as simple as I thought," Rachel said with a sigh. "When I convinced Thomas that we needed to get our financial house in order, I thought the rest would be a piece of cake. I guess I should have listened to Megan when she said the easy part was over and the biggest challenge was finding a professional. I assumed I would just look in the Yellow Pages."

After ordering the roast duck, garlic mashed potatoes and green beans, she looked at her friends and asked, "Would you guys mind sitting down with Thomas and me so we can all talk about this together? I'd like him to be there so he takes the process seriously."

"Of course we don't mind," Cindy said.

"Don't be silly," Megan said. "We'd be glad to help. What are friends for? Plus it'll be quite fun to watch Thomas squirm as we walk him through everything. He won't know what hit him."

For the rest of the meal the women talked about everything under the sun other than their finances. Although they got together fairly often, it was usually just for a quick cup of coffee, or Rachel's and Cindy's children were there too. Everyone always had such busy schedules. Rachel really appreciated that Megan and Cindy were so willing to help her regarding her finances. Friends like this were hard to find and Rachel felt very fortunate to have them. Despite what many people think, there are some things that are more important than money.

Key Point

Not all investment professionals are the same. Choose a financial advisor whose expertise matches your needs. Even if you have a great deal of business experience, chances are that you won't have the time to do it all yourself.

| 7 |

The Turning Point

When Rachel arrived at home after her relaxing afternoon, Thomas was already there. As soon as she walked in the front door she could smell dinner cooking.

"Ah, the sweet smell of my man making dinner," she laughed as she walked in the kitchen. "How are you?" she asked.

"Good," Thomas responded. "Aren't we in a good mood?"

"Well, I had the perfect day. Do you know that huge project that we bid on? We landed it on the spot. The client had heard so many positive things about our work that they had already decided to hire us before the presentation. They told us afterwards that it was just a formality."

"That's great, honey. Good for you," he said proudly to his wife.

"And that's not all," she said. "Megan and I decided to celebrate, so we met Cindy for lunch at the restaurant. We were there for ages."

"It must be nice to be semi-retired!" Thomas teased.

"Yes it is. What are we having for dinner?"

"I am making my famous lasagna, accompanied by a loaf of homemade garlic bread and a nice Caesar salad."

"I can hardly wait," Rachel said enthusiastically. "It smells great."

"Anything for my pretty wife. Why don't you go upstairs and get changed and say hi to the kids. They're outside playing in the tree house. We'll be ready to eat in a few minutes."

As Rachel made her way upstairs she had a quick peek outside. Sure enough, all three girls were playing in the tree house. After quickly changing out of her suit, she went back downstairs to help Thomas set the table. Even though she had had a big lunch she was looking forward to eating with the family. Thomas had always been good about making sure that dinner was ready if Rachel wasn't home in time. This made it possible for the family to eat together, which Rachel treasured.

As soon as Rachel walked into the backyard she realized that poor Dexter, the dog, was in desperate need of her help. One of the girls' favourite games was playing dress-up. Unfortunately, when the girls were bored with dressing each other up, they volunteered Dexter to model their latest fashions. If it weren't for the big rubber boots he had on all four paws, he probably would have made a clean getaway. Due to his inability to escape, however, the boots were accompanied by a pink dress, a white straw hat and a pair of sunglasses. He looked almost good enough to be on the cover of Vogue, Rachel thought.

"Hi girls!" Rachel said. "How are you?"

"Hi Mom," they all said in harmony.

Ashley, the six-year-old, walked up to Rachel and gave her a big hug and kiss.

"How do you like Dexter's outfit?" she asked. "Isn't he pretty?"

"Yes he is. Don't you think that he might be a little too hot though? He doesn't look very comfortable."

At that moment Dexter barked, almost as if to convince the girls that Mom had hit the nail right on the head.

"No, he likes it." replied Anna, who was the youngest of the girls at three years old. "Look, he's smiling," she added.

At that moment Dexter let out a groan, almost as if he thought he was losing Rachel's support.

"I'll tell you what. Why don't we get Dexter out of his clothes and we'll let him go and help Dad with dinner. Dad hasn't made dessert yet, so maybe Dexter can help him make some chocolate chip cookies? What do you think?"

"Okay, Mom," Ashley said. "But just so you know, Dexter's a dog and he can't cook," she said proudly, as if she had taught her mom something new.

"He can't?" she asked playing along. "Who do you think makes your lunch every day?" she teased.

The girls giggled at the thought of their furry friend standing in the kitchen making lunch. They then proceeded to strip him out of his clothes. As soon as they got the last boot off his hind leg, he ran towards the house. At least they didn't use the lipstick this time, Rachel thought.

Once the family was seated at the dinner table, they had a chance to hear each other's news.

"How was your day, Ashley?" Rachel asked her eldest.

Ashley spent the morning in an organized play group. She loved telling everyone what she did during the day.

"Today we learned what kind of animals live on a farm. We also learned how to sing a new song!" she said excitedly.

"That's great," Rachel replied. "How about you, Hilary?"

"Well, Grandma took Anna and me to the park," explained Hilary, the couple's precocious four-year-old. "We played on the swings and monkey bars. Then we came home and Grandma made us pickle sandwiches for lunch."

"Pickle sandwiches! Is that really what you had for lunch?" Thomas asked, looking at Anna.

"Yes, they were good," she giggled. "Grandma had one too," she added.

"I might have to have a little chat with Grandma," Thomas said, smirking at Rachel. "One can't live on pickle sandwiches alone," he added.

When Rachel and Thomas decided to have children, they had had to make difficult decisions about Rachel's career. Despite the significant drop in their household income, Thomas had felt that it would be better for everyone if she stayed at home. Rachel, however, wasn't so certain. It had taken her many years of hard work to get to where she was. More importantly, she truly enjoyed her work and the people she worked with. The thought of walking away from it all had scared her. On the other hand, the thought of having a nanny raise her children scared her even more. What if she missed watching her kids grow up?

When Ashley was ten months old, Rachel decided that she couldn't bear to leave her daughter with a nanny and subsequently told her company that she wouldn't be able to return after her maternity leave was over. Thomas knew how difficult this decision was for her and wished that there were another suitable option available to them. Then they received two offers that they couldn't refuse.

The first offer was from Rachel's boss. He valued Rachel as an employee and knew that replacing someone with her dedication and experience would be close to impossible. As such, he was willing to accommodate her needs as a mother. He knew that it wouldn't be long until Rachel and Thomas's children were in school full-time, so he offered her the opportunity to come back to work three days a week until she was ready to return permanently. In addition, he offered her two months' holidays, giving her ample time to spend with the family. Her salary, of course, was adjusted accordingly.

The second offer came from Rachel's parents. They had always been very supportive of her. They knew how hard she had worked to be successful. They also loved kids and wanted nothing more than to be an active part of their grandchildren's lives. As a result, they offered to take care of Ashley during the days Rachel was working. Rachel and Thomas were thrilled at the opportunity and accepted immediately.

After Rachel returned to work part-time everything had fallen neatly into place. Hilary and Anna were born in fairly quick succession, but Rachel knew that she could balance her career and her family. Now, work was going well and the CEO was happy to have retained a key employee. The children seemed very happy to spend three days a week with their grandparents, and Grandma and Grandpa appreciated the opportunity to help raise their grandchildren. Aside from a few too many pickle sandwiches for lunch, it was an ideal arrangement for everyone. It also made Rachel's transition to working full-time much more manageable.

As Rachel passed around the plates of lasagna, she asked Thomas how his day had gone.

"It was actually nice and quiet," he answered. "We've been so busy during the last few months that today was a nice change of pace."

"How about you?" he asked her. "Did anything else exciting happen other than landing that big project?"

"Well, at lunch the girls and I discussed our financial affairs. I learned quite a bit from Megan and Cindy. What I didn't know is that it actually requires a lot of work to go through the entire process properly."

"I do know it's going to take a lot of work. I had a good conversation with Patrick this morning. We discussed everything that we need to do. More importantly, he explained to me why it's important to deal with an investment professional. And to be honest with you, it makes complete sense. For the record, I think that we should hire someone as soon as possible. I think that we will feel a lot better once we have everything in place. That means no more sleepless nights for you, which is important to me."

"That's fantastic, honey. What made you change your mind?"

"Well, for starters, I have to admit that I've never really felt that it was fair that you were the one who had to worry about taking care of our finances. I've felt like this for quite a while. I think that one of the reasons that I don't like discussing money is that I find the whole thing intimidating. It was much easier to let you deal with it. There are so many different aspects of the investment planning process. As Patrick said, there is financial, tax and estate planning, portfolio management and accounting. I can't expect you to do all that."

"I like what I'm hearing, but why the sudden change of heart? Up to a few days ago, you were always so against hiring someone," she asked with skepticism. "This morning, when you agreed that we should consider hiring a professional, I didn't think you were serious. I thought that you were just trying to get me off the subject."

"Actually, you can thank Patrick for making me see the light. As you said, Cindy and Patrick really have their financial house in order. And they did it all with the help of an investment professional."

"What else did Patrick say?" Rachel asked.

"To make a long story short, he said that an investment professional is indispensable in helping people implement a plan and then stay the course. He compared the role of a financial advisor to that of a coach of a professional athlete or sports team. He stressed that investment professionals help their clients achieve their investment goals by providing them with impartial advice. More importantly, they also help to ensure that their clients remain dedicated to their investment strategy."

"And you agreed with all of this?"

"For the most part, everything made complete sense. The most compelling reason for hiring an investment professional is that once the plan is in place, the person that we've hired will help us stay on track. Although we are ultimately responsible for the final decisions, a top professional will make sure that we are headed in the right direction. Currently, we don't even have a direction. We have to change this as soon as we can. So, the first thing we need to do is learn about the investment industry. Then we'll find an investment professional," Thomas concluded

"I guess it's settled then!" Rachel said triumphantly.

After the family finished dinner they cleared the table and moved to the living room. For the next hour they played a friendly game of Snakes and Ladders, after which the girls went to bed. Thomas and Rachel spent the rest of the evening discussing how much work they had in front of them. They decided that the first thing they were going to do was invite Megan, Cindy and Patrick up to the cottage next weekend. The five of them hadn't been up to the cottage together for ages. Thomas knew that everyone would look forward to it and it would be a good opportunity to get more financial advice from their friends.

Key Point

Adhering to and remaining disciplined about your investment plan over the long-term is more challenging than one might think. Try not to get distracted by short-term events and focus on the goals that you initially set.

| 8 |
Information Equals Knowledge

As they crept into their parents' bedroom the three girls looked like a row of baby ducks slowly tiptoeing towards the bed in single file. When they reached Thomas's side of the bed they crouched down and leapt on him like a pride of jungle cats.

"Surprise," they shouted as they landed on their dad.

"Good morning, ladies." Thomas mustered with as much enthusiasm as he could. "Try and whisper so you don't wake up Mom."

"Too late," Rachel groaned. "Why are you guys up so early?"

"We couldn't sleep anymore. It's too bright outside," Ashley answered. "And Dexter was hungry!"

"Dexter is always hungry", Thomas thought.

"Why don't I take care of the kids while you run your errands? I'll take them out for breakfast," he offered.

"The girls are invited to play with Patrick and Cindy's boys this afternoon. What else do you want to do today?" Rachel asked Thomas.

"I thought I'd start my research on the financial services industry. I was going to drop by the library and the bookstore to see if there are any books we can use. I was also going to spend a few hours on the Internet. I should be able to get everything that we need. That way we will be somewhat prepared for next weekend."

"That sounds great. Everyone will be quite impressed with how seriously we are taking all of this."

"I know," Thomas responded. "The things I do for my wife."

An hour and a half later, washed and dressed, Thomas and his daughters headed out the door. On his way out, he picked up the newspaper that was rolled up on his porch. The front page of the business section trumpeted, "Financial Advice and the Fees You Pay." Thomas's curiosity was piqued so he tucked this section underneath his arm and put the rest of the paper inside.

Although it was only eight-thirty in the morning, it was already starting to get warm outside. So far the summer had been particularly dry, which made time at the cottage very enticing. Thomas didn't mind staying in the city on the odd weekend, however. It was nice to catch up on the chores around the house, and it always seemed that there was a never-ending list of things that needed to be done.

As they walked up the street, they could hear the birds chirping in the oak trees that soared above their heads. Thomas and Rachel had moved to the neighbourhood from their pre-parenting high-rise condominium right after Ashley was born. The apartment had been great when they were childless, but after they had Ashley they needed more room.

Before choosing a real estate agent they had sat down over a glass of wine and made up a "wish list" of everything they wanted in a house. Rachel, for instance, wanted a large backyard and private driveway. She also wanted to be within walking distance of good schools. Thomas, on the other hand, was interested in a detached house that was close to public transportation. They both wanted to live in the city, so they could avoid the long commute to and from work. After compiling their wish list they had applied to be pre-approved for a mortgage.

Once they were approved they found a real estate agent and also began looking on their own at listings on the Internet and in the newspaper. Within a few weeks, it became apparent that it would be nearly impossible to find a house they could afford in the area where they wanted to live. One option they had was to move out of the city. After a brief discussion, they had decided that they would rather stay close to downtown and, in order to do so, had to make some sacrifices.

Their agent suggested that they look in neighbourhoods that were "up and coming" as opposed to "already established." She explained that a good strategy was to look in the most expensive neighbourhood that they could afford, even if it meant buying a house that was smaller or needed some work. Once they had widened their target area, within a few weeks they found a house that they immediately fell in love with. It had everything that they were looking for. The street was a quiet cul-de-sac close to one of the city's major arteries. This meant that public transit was just around the corner. They were also within close walking distance to good schools, several cafes and restaurants and a large park. They bought the house immediately, paying about five per cent below the asking price. In hindsight, Thomas and Rachel knew they had made an excellent decision.

When Thomas and the girls made it to the bistro, a friendly, familiar face welcomed them.

"Hello girls! Who did you bring with you today?" Francine asked, teasing them.

"This is Dad," Hilary answered. "He's hungry," she added, "really hungry."

Francine had been a waitress at the bistro since long before Thomas and Rachel moved into the neighbourhood. She was always in a great mood and put a smile on everyone's face. The kids adored her because she paid extra special attention to them.

"How about a booth this morning?" she asked.

"That would be great," Thomas said. "Thank you."

Francine led the four of them to one of the large booths by the window. After everyone sat down she put a menu in front of each of them.

"Would you like the usual round of drinks?" she asked Thomas.

"Yes, please," he said.

This meant a cup of coffee for him and orange juice, apple juice and milk for Ashley, Hilary and Anna.

"What do you feel like having for breakfast this morning?" Thomas asked.

"I want blueberry pancakes!" Hilary shouted, as if she's never had them before.

"What about you, Ashley?"

"I'll have bacon and eggs, Daddy. Can I have my eggs all mixed-up?" she asked.

This meant that she wanted them scrambled.

"Of course. Anna, how about you?"

"Can I have mixed-up eggs too?" she asked.

"Sure. Do you want some toast as well?"

"Yes, please!" she said.

At that moment Francine came back with the drink order. She knew exactly who was drinking what and put each glass in front of the correct person.

"Are you guys ready to order?"

"We're ready. I'll have two eggs, over easy, with bacon and brown toast. Ashley and Anna will each have one scrambled egg with bacon and toast. Hilary will have the blueberry pancakes."

"Great. I'll be back in a few minutes with your food. Can I bring you today's paper?" she offered.

"Actually, I brought a section of my own," Thomas said, pulling it from his lap.

"Okay. I'll be right back," she said.

A minute later Francine returned with some crayons and colouring placemats. This usually kept the kids quiet until breakfast came and gave Thomas the opportunity to read the paper for about fifteen minutes. He opened the paper and began to read the article that caught his attention.

"What are you reading so intently?" asked Francine as she put the crayons on the table. "It must be interesting."

"Oh, Rachel and I have decided to hire a financial advisor. We have to learn as much as we can about the industry so we can make our choice. I'm just doing my homework," Thomas replied.

"That's great, Thomas. It's a lot of work. I went through all that a few years ago."

"You did?" he asked, a little surprised.

"I did. But I'll be honest with you. I never thought in a million years that I would have to hire an investment professional. What I earn here isn't really what I would classify as a fortune."

"What made you decide to hire someone?" he asked curiously.

35

"A few years ago, my uncle passed away. He didn't have kids of his own so he named me the beneficiary in his will. We were very close. Anyway, I ended up receiving a little over a hundred and fifty thousand dollars from him. With my income this was more money than I'd ever seen or expected to see in my entire life. At first, I thought that I could quit work and travel around the world—it seemed like such a lot of money!"

"It's definitely nothing to sneeze at," Thomas agreed. "What happened?"

"I have to be honest. When I found out about the inheritance, I was overwhelmed. I needed some advice, so I spoke with several friends. All of them encouraged me to talk to a professional. At the time, my thinking was that it wouldn't hurt to meet with someone, so I did."

"How did you decide whom to work with?" he asked.

"Like you, I did my homework. The first thing I learned was that different investment professionals offer different services. What I needed first and foremost was to see if I could take an extended leave from work and travel. This meant that I needed to see a financial planner."

"What's the difference between a financial planner and other financial advisors?"

"I didn't think there was a difference, but it's like night and day. In the financial services industry, professional titles are extremely important. What I learned is that a financial planner is someone who will help you with saving, budgeting and retirement planning. What they are very good at is providing you with a complete plan that will tell you whether you are living beyond your means and whether you have enough money for retirement. They will also help you put a strategy in place."

"Will they invest and manage your money?" Thomas asked.

"My financial planner didn't, but some do. You have to be very careful, though, because the financial planning industry is fairly unregulated. Many individuals call themselves financial planners when in fact they're not. My planner charged an hourly fee and then referred me to an investment advisor who advised me how to invest the money. This meant I actually hired two people, not just one."

"So what happened to retiring and travelling around the world?" Thomas prodded.

"To make a long story short, the financial plan showed me that I didn't have enough money for my retirement. My savings were so inadequate that I would have been in really rough shape when I stopped working. I would have had to rely completely on the Canada Pension Plan, which isn't all that much. The financial plan indicated that during retirement my monthly expenses would exceed my pension benefits. So, instead of travelling, I used a portion of the money to pay off the mortgage on my townhouse. It's not much, but now it's all mine. I then invested what was left over. The money is a gift that I will appreciate for the rest of my life and the financial planner helped me to avoid squandering it."

Francine excused herself to go fetch their food. When she came back, she asked Thomas what he'd learned from the newspaper article.

"Well, it was an in-depth look at the various ways in which investment professionals are compensated. This author of this article was very much in favor of fee-based compensation but acknowledged that there were advantages to commission-based compensation. Any advice?"

"From what I learned, it depends on the service. Don't worry about that until the very end of your journey, however. The fees in the financial services industry are very competitive," she said.

"Francine, what do you think we should learn about first?"

"The best advice I can give you is that you should start learning about the different institutions within the financial services industry. There are banks and trust companies, insurance companies, mutual fund dealers, brokerage firms and wealth management firms. Depending on your needs, you'll use the services of one or more of them. Once you know what services each of these institutions offer, you'll be one step closer to deciding on exactly which services you need and where to get them."

"You've been very helpful," said Thomas. "Thanks. I've actually set some time aside to go to the library and bookstore to collect some reference material. At least now I know where to begin."

Breakfast done, with food for thought as well, Thomas and his girls headed down the street to the hardware store.

Key Point

When you come by a large sum of money unexpectedly, take some time to think about how you will spend it. Pay off your mortgage, ensure that your retirement is secure, and avoid spending your capital needlessly.

| 9 |

Ready, Set, Go

It was 9:30 and the neighbourhood was already bustling with activity. Although most of the shops had just opened their doors, they were already filled with customers.

When Thomas and Rachel had first moved to the area it didn't offer as many amenities as they'd have liked, but it had some great potential. At the time there had been only a handful of shops and restaurants scattered along the main street. In fact, for every space that was occupied by a flourishing business there were three stores that remained vacant. In the last three years, however, things had changed for the better.

One of the reasons that they had decided to buy a house in this neighbourhood was that several major movie studios and entertainment companies had established offices in the area. With them came a gradual influx of young professionals who wanted to live closer to work. In order to accommodate all the new residents, the neighbourhood slowly sprouted additional cafes, restaurants, bakeries, a movie theatre and a number of specialty shops. The hardware store was one of the recent additions.

As they entered the store a little bell announced their arrival. As always, Fred, the store's owner, stood behind the counter.

"Good morning. It's a beautiful day isn't it?"

"Good morning, Fred," Thomas answered.

"I'm surprised to see you here. How come you're not at the cottage? Especially on a beautiful weekend like this?" Fred asked.

"Rachel and I have a list of errands we have to run so we decided to stay in town. Whenever we try to get things accomplished during the week we fall behind. These three little tykes keep us pretty busy."

"That doesn't surprise me one bit. What can I do for you this morning?" Fred asked.

"I need to fix our screen door. The hinges are pretty rusty so I'm going to have to replace them. I'll also need some wood filler."

"Have a look halfway down the third aisle. All of our hinges are on the left side," Fred said. "And the wood filler is a few feet further down."

Thomas went to the third aisle and picked up the hinges and wood filler. The girls followed quietly behind him. They were always very well behaved when they went shopping with Dad.

"That will be eight dollars and thirty cents," Fred said, putting the products into a paper bag.

"Don't forget to let the wood filler dry thoroughly. If it isn't completely dry, the screws will just pop out again."

"Thanks, I appreciate it. Rachel has been after me to fix the back door for months. I'm only now getting around to it. The last thing I need is for it to break again right after I tried to fix it. She never lets me live these things down. Remember the episode with my plumbing work?"

"Didn't you have to stay in a hotel for almost a week while the plumber came in to fix everything from top to bottom? That's the story I heard."

"Actually, it was only three days and it wasn't entirely my fault," Thomas said defensively.

"It never is," Fred teased. "That reminds me, have you had a chance to introduce yourself to our new neighbour, Jim? He just opened the bookstore next door."

"No, I haven't. We've been out of town for the last three weekends. I'll drop by and say hello. Thanks for letting me know. Have a good weekend."

"You too, Thomas. Say hello to Rachel," Fred said as the family left.

Walking into Read All Over, Thomas thought, "What a great name for a bookstore."

"Hello," a deep voice bellowed from the back of the store. "I'll be right with you."

Sending his daughters to the children's section to choose a book each, Thomas greeted the man emerging from the back of the shop.

"I'm Thomas. Fred next door told me that you just recently opened the store. I thought I'd take the opportunity to introduce myself. It's always a pleasure to meet new people in the neighbourhood."

"I appreciate it. Fred has been wonderful. He's encouraged so many people to come in and welcome me to the area, which has been great.

"I was wondering, do you have any books on the financial services industry? My wife and I are in the process of hiring a financial advisor and we would like to start by learning about the industry first."

"Well, our finance section is over there in the second aisle. I'm not sure what you're looking for. Why don't you have a look and call me if you need any help."

"That makes sense considering I don't know what I'm looking for either," Thomas agreed.

He walked over to the financial section. There were dozens of titles on topics including budgeting, saving for retirement, investing in the stock market, estate planning, insurance needs and mutual fund selection. The only problem was that nothing was catching his attention. After flipping through a few titles, he knew these weren't the types of books that he was looking for. He walked back to the counter.

"You have a great selection, Jim. Unfortunately, I don't think that you have what I'm looking for. It seems as though most of the books are very specific in terms of their subject matter. I'm looking for something that gives a general overview of the investment industry. Do you know of any books that do that?" Thomas asked.

"Actually, I don't. The investment business is very diverse. In fact, most of the books that you will find focus entirely on one specific subject like mutual funds or stocks or bonds. I think that's why you'll be hard pressed to find something more general. Have you looked on the Internet yet?" he asked.

"No, I haven't," Thomas said. "I was actually planning on spending a few hours on the computer this afternoon."

"One of the sites I would visit first is the Department of Finance Canada web site (www.fin.gc.ca). They have some great information on the Canadian financial services industry. The only problem is that I don't know in which section you'll find what you're looking for. The government sites are usually quite vast so you'll have to do a keyword search."

"I'll take a look," Thomas said, enthusiastic at the thought of making some headway. "I really appreciate it. You have no idea how much help you've been," he added.

"It's my pleasure. Once you've learned a little about the financial industry I'm sure you'll be back in no time to buy a few of the books on my shelf," Jim said.

"You're absolutely right," Thomas said.

Thomas called to his daughters, and each girl came to the counter with a book in her hand. They looked as though they were ready to go home.

"For the time being, I'll take these three," Thomas said, sliding the books onto the counter.

"Thanks for coming in," Jim said, as he rang up the purchase and gave Thomas his change. "I appreciate it. And I'll keep an eye out for something more general on financial planning."

"You've been very helpful. I'll definitely tell people about the store. And welcome to the neighbourhood," Thomas said turning for the door.

On the way home, Thomas thought about the advice Jim had given him. He was glad that he had dropped by the store to introduce himself. Thanks to Jim, he now had a place to start. If he could find the information that he was looking for, he and Rachel would be well prepared for their weekend at the cottage with Megan, Cindy and Patrick.

When he arrived at home the girls plumped down in the living room so they could read their books. This would probably keep them busy for the next half hour or so. Thomas knew that Rachel was probably in the backyard tending to her garden. This was one of her favourite ways to spend a Saturday morning when they stayed in the city.

"How was breakfast?" Rachel asked when Thomas found her outside.

"Breakfast was good," Thomas said, carefully opening the door so it didn't fall off its hinges. "Francine says hello. I had a talk with her about her finances. Did you know that she hired a financial planner a few years ago?" he asked.

"Of course I do," Rachel answered. "She hired him after she received the inheritance from her uncle. I remember talking to her one morning when we were both there for breakfast. If I remember correctly you had your head buried in a newspaper. I told you that you don't listen."

"I know, I know. I listened today though. You would have been very proud of me," he said.

"I'm sure I would have," she replied. "What did you learn?"

"Francine said a lot of interesting things. For instance, I learned that financial planners provide a different service than investment advisors. I didn't realize that there were so many differences between various investment professionals. I also learned that we probably have to save quite a bit of money in order to retire comfortably. The only problem is that I don't know how much we have to save. A financial planner will tell us this."

"It sounds like you made some progress this morning. Who would have thought that it would be over breakfast?"

"And at the bookstore," Thomas added.

"At the bookstore?" Rachel asked puzzled. "What bookstore?"

"After breakfast we went to the hardware store to pick up the hinges for the door. Fred told me I should drop by the new bookstore that's opened up next door to say hi to the owner, Jim. I was asking him about books on the financial services industry, and he recommended that we visit the Canadian government web site first. That'll help us narrow down what we need to know. He seems like a great guy. So, I thought that I would start right away. What are your plans for the next few hours before you go shopping?" Thomas asked.

"Gardening. I'll head out around noon."

"Okay," Thomas replied. "I'm going upstairs to start working on the computer. Let me know when you're ready to go out."

"That sounds good. Can you let the girls know I'm in the garden? Once I'm done maybe we'll play a game together."

"Sounds good," Thomas agreed.

For the rest of the morning Thomas scoured the Internet for information. He was a little surprised at the amount of information that was available with a simple click of the mouse. By the time he finished reading through all the material on the Department of Finance Canada site, he had a dozen pages of information outlining how the industry was structured.

Here is what Thomas learned:

* The financial services sector includes a variety of institutions including banks, trust companies, credit unions and caisses populaires, life insurance companies and Property and Casualty (P&C) insurance companies. Also included are investment counsellors, securities dealers and stock exchanges, mutual fund companies, finance and leasing companies, as well as independent financial advisors, pension fund managers, insurance agents and brokers.

*Large financial groups offer a wide variety of financial services such as deposit taking, insurance and wealth management both directly and through subsidiaries, but boutique companies, which focus on one or a few areas of business, have also emerged.

* Under the Canadian Constitution, the federal government has sole jurisdiction over banks under the Bank Act. Other financial bodies are regulated by the provincial governments. There is also self-regulation by the Investment Industry Regulatory Organization of Canada (IIROC), the Mutual Fund Dealers Association of Canada and the stock exchanges.

*The Office of the Superintendent of Financial Institutions (OSFI) is responsible for supervising federally regulated financial institutions, including the banks, federally incorporated insurance companies and federally incorporated trust and loan companies. The Financial Consumer Agency of Canada enforces the consumer-oriented provisions of the federal financial institution statutes.

*The Canada Deposit Insurance Corporation (CDIC) insures deposits in banks, trust companies and loan companies against loss up to $100,000 per depositor in each member institution. Deposits with credit unions and caisses populaires are protected under provincial regulations.

*Insurance policies are guaranteed up to certain limits by the Canadian Life and Health Insurance Compensation Corporation, and the industry-run Property and Casualty Insurance Compensation Corporation guarantees most P&C insurance policies up to certain limits.

*The Canadian Investor Protection Fund (CIPF), sponsored by the Investment Industry Regulatory Organization of Canada and the stock exchanges, protects securities investors in the event of the insolvency of a member firm for up to $1 million per account.

Key Point

When buying a home, it is extremely important to be realistic in terms of what you can comfortably afford. If you overextend yourself it is likely that you will have difficulty comfortably saving for your retirement.

|10|
The Next Step

After Rachel left to do her shopping, Thomas and the girls headed for Cindy and Patrick's house. Rachel had made a Black Forest cake, which Thomas gave to Ashley to hold for the duration of the drive. Cindy and Patrick lived only fifteen minutes away and he was fairly certain that this wasn't enough time for the girls to sample the dessert. Of course, once in a while they did manage to surprise him.

As Thomas walked up the path, he noticed what great shape his friends' house was in. After opening the antique store on a busy downtown street, Cindy and Patrick had made the difficult decision to move closer to the store, although initially this was the last thing that they wanted to do. But, given their long hours, it didn't make sense to commute from the suburbs, so they bought a semi-detached house just around the corner from the store. Despite having trouble adjusting to a smaller living space, they eventually grew to enjoy living downtown.

Rather than ringing the doorbell, Thomas led the girls around to the backyard gate. He knew that Cindy and Patrick were probably outside enjoying the nice weather.

"Anyone home?" he asked, poking his head over the fence.

"Come on in," Patrick answered. "I hope you guys brought your appetites because there's a lot to eat."

"We brought some cake!" Ashley responded, holding the box over her head.

This made Thomas a little nervous as an image of the box landing upside down on the ground went through his mind. He gently took the cake out of her hands, after which she ran over to the boys, Marc and Evan, who were playing ball in the back corner of the yard. Her sisters immediately followed her.

"The house looks fantastic. You and Cindy have done a great job of renovating it."

"Thank you. You should see the inside. It looks a lot different from when you were here last."

"I don't know where you guys find the time," Thomas remarked. "Where's Cindy?"

"She's inside making a salad and should be out in a few minutes. What have you been up to?" Patrick asked.

"I spent a few hours on the Internet this morning learning about the financial services industry. It's incredible how much information there is."

"Isn't it? It took me a few days of heavy reading to learn everything that I know. Once I understood the basics, though, the rest was easy," Patrick admitted.

Cindy came through the screen door holding a salad.

"Hi, Thomas. How are you?" she asked, kissing him on the cheek.

"I'm well. How about you?" he asked back.

"I can't complain. We've been very lazy today and haven't really accomplished much, which is nice for a change. One of the summer students we recently hired is minding the store. I thought it would be nice if both of us were home with the kids this afternoon. Besides, it's such a beautiful day that I don't think the store will be that busy. Are you staying for the afternoon?" Cindy asked Thomas. "When I spoke with Rachel she said that one of you would be dropping the kids off. There's plenty of food," she said, motioning to the pile of hamburgers beside the barbecue.

Thomas looked over at the hamburgers and then at the potato salad Cindy was holding. He didn't hesitate a moment.

"Maybe I will stay," he said. "We wouldn't want all that great food to go to waste.

"Of course not," Patrick answered. "We wouldn't want that, would we? Can I get you a beer?" he offered.

Patrick stepped over to the cooler on the patio, reached in and pulled out an ice-cold bottle. He opened it and handed it to his friend.

"Before I forget, Rachel wanted to know if you and the kids would like to come up to the cottage next weekend?"

"We'd love to!" Cindy responded.

"I'll let you sort out the details with her. Did she tell you what I did this morning?" Thomas asked.

"Actually, she did. Did you find anything good?" she asked.

"I found quite a bit. I spent most of my time learning about the financial services industry. To be honest, I had no idea how massive it was. As far as I understand, the industry is divided into several distinct sectors, which include banks, trust companies, investment dealers and wealth management firms, insurance companies and finance companies," Thomas said.

"That's right," Cindy answered. "But, do you know who does what?"

"That's where I am a little confused. It seems as though most of the institutions offer similar services. Over the last few years, it seems as though there has been a significant level of product convergence occurring in both the Canadian financial services industry and in the global financial services industry."

"You're right," Patrick said. "Many years ago there were very distinct lines separating the various sectors within the financial services industry. If you wanted to deposit money you had to go to a bank. On the other hand, if you wanted to buy a life insurance policy you had to go to a life insurance company. Nowadays, you can get almost any service or product from one institution. It's incredible."

"Is this a good thing or bad thing?" Thomas asked.

"Actually, I don't think it's either good or bad," Cindy commented. "It's simply how the industry has evolved. And you're right in saying that it's a global phenomenon rather than just a Canadian one. If you look at the major financial institutions around the world, they are best described as 'financial groups' rather than simply banks, brokerages or insurance companies. Recently, a few firms have emerged that focus specifically on one or two business lines again. This has been most common in the wealth management sector. Only time will tell if these small companies can compete against the mammoth financial groups."

"Are you saying that I could walk into almost any major institution and deposit money, take out a mortgage, build a portfolio and buy a life insurance policy?" Thomas asked.

"In many cases you could," Cindy replied. "Take the Canadian banks, for example. There used to be a time when most people thought of a bank in terms of savings accounts, loans and mortgages. Nowadays, the banks have so many subsidiaries that they offer securities clearing, discount and full-service brokerage services, fee-based portfolio management, car insurance, life insurance, tax planning, estate planning and offshore banking. In most cases, they will refer you to one of their subsidiaries. Sometimes consumers don't even know they're dealing with a bank subsidiary because these companies have their own distinct name, logo and corporate branding."

"Doesn't this give the banks too much power?" Thomas asked, showing some concern.

"In some ways it does, but it's not necessarily a bad thing," Cindy answered. "Most of the financial groups offer similar services, so they all have to be somewhat competitive in terms of pricing. The banks are also heavily regulated by the federal government, and as far as heavy government regulation goes, the jury is still out on whether it is good or bad for Canadian consumers."

"I read about this on the Internet. The office through which the federal government oversees federally incorporated financial institutions is called the Office of the Superintendent of Financial Institutions (OSFI)," Thomas said.

"You did your homework," Cindy laughed.

"I actually learned a little about all of the various regulatory bodies this morning. Although it wasn't a very interesting subject to read about, it was comforting to learn that the industry is properly regulated. It gave me some peace of mind."

"Thomas, we know how skeptical you can be, so it's good that you learned about the regulatory bodies. They are there to ensure that there are no bad apples in the financial industry and that the Canadian consumers' best interests are always a priority."

"It does put me at ease, which is important. As I mentioned to Patrick, my biggest hurdle is learning to trust a complete stranger with our finances. This individual will have to know everything about our specific situation in order to be effective," Thomas said.

"Don't even worry about that yet. It sounds as though you know your stuff in regards to the various financial institutions. The next step will be to teach you about the various investment professionals who work for these institutions. This is a little more daunting because there are so many different positions in the industry. Some of these include mutual fund salespeople, insurance salespeople, financial planners, investment advisors, investment counsellors and portfolio managers. Despite what you may think, many of these professional titles are used haphazardly in the investment industry, too. You'll have to learn which services each of these professionals offer," Patrick said.

"More important, you'll have to decide which services you're interested in," Cindy added.

"Your needs will likely be completely different from ours. This means that you will be working with different people."

"I did learn a little bit about financial planners over breakfast," Thomas told her. "I know that a financial planner will help you in terms of saving, budgeting and retirement planning, but that's about it. I didn't have the opportunity to get into the specifics. I guess that will be the next step."

"Probably the next task for you and Rachel is interviewing the people that you are thinking of hiring," Patrick said.

"This is the most rewarding step in the entire process because you'll really learn to appreciate the amount of work it takes to prepare a financial plan, present an Investment Policy Statement and implement an investment strategy. Most people don't realize the amount of work this actually entails," he warned.

At that moment Marc walked over to the adults to let them know that all the children were hungry. That was Patrick's cue to start cooking the hamburgers.

While Patrick cooked, Cindy and Thomas continued their discussion. Thomas wanted help understanding what the various people he and Rachel would encounter in their research actually did.

"They are all very different," Cindy explained. "When we first met with our financial planner we didn't know that her skills and area of expertise were different from those of an investment advisor or portfolio manager, for example. We always assumed that everyone offered similar services, but this isn't the case," she pointed out.

"I guess that's why it's so important to figure out exactly what services we need," Thomas observed. "If we don't know what we're looking for we then won't know who to interview and hire. So, what do financial advisors do?"

"It's interesting that you started by asking us about financial advisors because that term is used very loosely in the financial services industry. Properly, the term 'financial advisor' means someone who gives financial advice in either professional or non-professional capacity. This means that it can be used to describe an insurance agent, a financial planner, an accountant, a close friend or family member. What's important to know is that the term 'financial advisor' does not necessarily identify someone who is qualified or licensed to offer financial advice. You really have to be careful," Patrick warned from behind the grill.

"Okay. Now, what about insurance professionals?" Thomas asked.

"An insurance professional generally specializes in life insurance and annuities. If you're looking for advice on any type of life insurance product you should meet with an insurance professional. In addition to selling insurance products, they are sometimes also licensed to sell mutual funds or securities even though this isn't their primary area of expertise. More experienced insurance agents and brokers may also offer services similar to that of a financial planner, such as estate planning. Typically, these people work for insurance companies, insurance agencies, banks and trust companies. Generally, they are paid a commission on the products they sell. In order to earn commissions, an individual has to be licensed to sell insurance. They have to earn continuing education credits in order to keep their licence up-to-date."

"What about financial planners?" Thomas asked.

"A financial planner will advise you on a wide spectrum of issues," said Cindy. "This can include saving and budgeting, retirement planning, estate planning and tax planning. Financial planners are often licensed to sell mutual funds and securities, too. Typically they work for independent financial planning firms, banks, trust companies, mutual fund dealers and full-service brokerages. They can be paid an hourly fee, commissions from the products they sell or a combination of both. Some financial planners are restricted to selling only the products of their firm. If this is a concern, you should work with an independent financial planner who may have access to a wider range of products. Some financial planners will focus solely on financial planning rather than selling mutual funds and securities. They will refer their clients to a reputable investment advisor, investment counsellor or portfolio manager who then manages the portfolio in accordance with the financial plan. This is a really good way to do it, because you can benefit from the expertise of two different professionals who are each highly experienced in one specific discipline."

"That makes a lot of sense. Are you required to be licensed to act as a financial planner?" Thomas asked.

"No, financial planners aren't required to be licensed to offer their services. 'Financial planner' is another term that is used loosely in the financial industry, so you have to be careful. A highly skilled and experienced financial planner is easily identified by one of several financial planning designations in the industry," Patrick said.

"Is an investment advisor different from a financial planner?" Thomas asked.

"Yes. An investment advisor typically helps you develop an investment plan and implements an investment strategy based on this plan. In the last several years, many investment advisors have been branching out into areas including selling insurance products and financial planning. Most investment advisors are paid a commission on the products that they sell, but some charge a management fee as a percentage of the assets under administration. These professionals work for full-service brokerage firms that are either independent or subsidiaries of the chartered banks. They have to be licensed by the provincial securities commission in any province in which they conduct business. In order to maintain their securities licence, they also have to earn continuing education credits."

"What about investment counsellors and portfolio managers?" Thomas asked.

"They provide investment planning and portfolio management services. They are money managers in every sense of the word. Before they begin to work with you, they will provide you with an Investment Policy Statement that outlines your investment objectives, risk tolerances, liquidity requirements, tax issues, target asset allocation, time horizon, their duties and a communication plan. Some portfolio managers manage billions of dollars on behalf of thousands of investors, while others work directly for high–net worth families and corporations. Many very wealthy families hire their own in-house portfolio manager to work for them on an exclusive basis. Portfolio managers and investment counsellors work for wealth management companies, chartered banks, trust companies, pension funds, mutual fund companies and full-service brokerage firms. They usually charge a management fee based on a percentage of the market value of the assets under management," Patrick said. "In terms of their own compensation, they may earn a salary and bonus or a percentage of the management fee."

"And these investment counsellors and portfolio mangers have to be licensed to manage money," Thomas said.

"Absolutely. They have to be licensed by the appropriate provincial securities commission. They also have to meet very strict educational requirements to earn their title," Patrick said.

"How do I know if someone's designation is legitimate? More important, how do I learn what it means? To be honest, they all sound they same to me," Thomas admitted.

"I suggest that you contact the various associations and ask them to mail you information on the requirements needed to be designated a financial planner. You can start by contacting the Financial Planners Standards Council (FPSC). The FPSC was created by several large organizations that wanted to collectively promote an internationally recognized designation.

"Who else should I contact?" Thomas asked.

"You should also contact the Institute of Canadian Bankers (ICB) and the Institute of Advanced Financial Planners (IAFP). Both of these associations administer financial planning designations different from the one administered by the FPSC. You should learn the difference between the designations so that you are well informed when you eventually encounter people who have earned one or more of these designations," Cindy recommended.

"What about insurance professionals? Do they belong to another association?"

"Yes, they do. A good place to start is with Advocis, which is the brand name of the Financial Advisors Association of Canada. In September 2002, members of the Canadian Association of Insurance and Financial Advisors (CAIFA) and the Canadian Association of Financial Planners (CAFP) decided to merge to create Canada's largest association of professional financial advisors. Before the merger, the CAIFA administered the educational requirements of insurance professionals and the CAFP administered the educational requirements of several financial planning designations. Now they are both under the same roof."

"What about investment advisors, investment counsellors and portfolio managers. I read that the Canadian Securities Institute (CSI) is responsible for educating most of the individuals in the Canadian securities industry. Is that correct?"

"Now I'm impressed. Who are you and what did you do with Thomas?" Cindy joked. "Seriously though, you're absolutely right. Individuals who want to work in the Canadian securities industry have to successfully complete one or more of the courses offered by the CSI in order to be licensed to sell securities. The various provincial securities commissions are then responsible for licensing these individuals."

"I appreciate your help. I'll contact each organization and ask them to send me some information. I'm actually looking forward to learning more."

"I strongly encourage you to be thorough when you learn about the various professional designations. One reason is that there is an ongoing debate as to what actually constitutes financial planning. As I mentioned, the term 'financial planner' is still used very loosely in the financial services industry. You don't want to end up working with a salesperson, thinking that they are going to provide you with a financial plan when they're actually only experienced in selling investment products."

"Do you have any suggestions on how I can be certain that the individuals that I will eventually be dealing with are actually qualified to offer financial advice?" Thomas asked.

"The best advice I can give you is to learn the difference between the various designations and gain a clear understanding of what each one represents. There are dozens of designations in the financial industry and the educational requirements are different for each of them. Some of the designations require course work, some of them require that the candidate pass a rigorous exam and some require course work and an exam. You'll also want to learn about what an investment professional needs to do in order to maintain his or her designations," Cindy added.

"In most cases they have to earn continuing education credits in order to keep the designation or licence valid. This is good because it ensures that financial professionals are up-to-date in their particular area of expertise," Patrick said.

"That's reassuring. Can you give me some examples of the designations I should look out for?" Thomas asked.

"In terms of insurance professionals there is the Chartered Life Underwriter (CLU), the Chartered Financial Consultant (ChFC) and the Registered Health Underwriter (RHU)," Cindy said.

"What about financial planners?" Thomas asked.

"In terms of financial planning, there are the Personal Financial Planner (PFP), Registered Financial Planner (RFP) and Certified Financial Planner (CFP) designations," Cindy said.

"And investment advisors?" Thomas asked.

"In terms of investment advice, an individual can earn her Financial Management Advisor (FMA) designation or Derivatives Market Specialist (DMS) designation. The DMS is a highly specialized designation that identifies a professional who specializes in advising investors on derivatives markets," Patrick said. "The CSI also recently introduced a new charter called the Chartered Professional (Ch.P.) Strategic Wealth. This is an extremely demanding course and anyone who has earned this designation is highly qualified."

"And what about getting registered as an investment counsellor or portfolio manager?"

"As far as investment counsellors or portfolio managers go, an individual can earn either their Canadian Investment Manager (CIM) or Chartered Financial Analyst (CFA) designation. Professionals can then be licensed to manage money on a discretionary basis. Many of these people will also earn their Fellow of the Canadian Securities Institute (FCSI) designation, which is the highest honour earned in the Canadian securities industry."

"Those sure are a lot of acronyms to learn, but I really appreciate the advice. Again, you guys have been great. Rachel and I wouldn't know what to do without you," Thomas said.

"It's our pleasure. You can make it up to us by making us your famous beef tenderloin at the cottage next weekend. Just remind me to bring my saw and chisel," Patrick teased.

"With that type of attitude, you won't get any of the Black Forest cake that Rachel made," Thomas threatened lightheartedly.

"Why didn't you say Rachel made it? In that case, I'll be on my best behaviour," Patrick laughed.

As he enjoyed the beautiful afternoon with his friends, Thomas decided that his goal over the next few days should be to learn more about the various professional designations. If he could learn as much about this subject as he had about the industry itself, he and Rachel would be well prepared to continue the search for a financial advisor together. The next step would be to establish which services they needed. Did they need a financial plan? Who would manage their portfolios? What skills were they supposed to look for in a financial advisor? What questions were they supposed to ask during the initial interview? All of these questions had to be answered.

Key Point

Learn as much as you can about the professionals and services you will encounter at the various financial institutions. Then, think about what specific services you need. If you know what the various designations and titles actually mean, you will be able to judge which professional is best suited to provide you with financial advice.

| 11 |
Almost There

Back home, with his three tired daughters asleep in bed, Thomas flipped through the morning's paper until he found the article titled, "Financial Advice and The Fees You Pay." He cut it out.

"What are you doing, honey?" Rachel asked.

"I'm going to start a scrapbook. This is my first addition," he said, holding up the article. "I thought that it would be a good idea to collect cuttings about personal finance. These could come in handy when we eventually interview the financial advisors on our short list."

"That saying about great minds thinking alike must be true then," Rachel responded, as she got up and walked over to the desk in the next room.

"What do you mean?" Thomas asked after she came back into the kitchen.

"Look!" she said, holding up a thick folder full of clippings from newspapers and magazines. "This is my scrapbook. It looks as though I've got a little head start on you," she said proudly.

"That's incredible! If you already have a scrapbook, it doesn't make much sense for me to start my own. How about if I just add clippings to yours? What do you have in there, anyway?" he asked.

Rachel sat down in the chair beside him and opened her folder. She spread the clippings across the table. There were dozens of them. The articles ranged from simple things like opening a savings account for kids to more sophisticated strategies such as using a universal life insurance policy to pay for the capital gains tax levied on an individual's estate.

"I can't believe you've been cutting out all of these articles. How long have you been doing this?" he asked.

"Almost a year now. It was actually Megan's idea. So far, this is what I've collected."

Thomas looked through the articles and picked one that caught his attention. The caption read, "The Coming Retirement Crisis." After quickly skimming over the article, he realized why it looked familiar.

"Isn't this the article that woke you up in the middle of the night?" he asked. "And also the reason why I've been trying to read everything under the sun about the financial services industry?"

"Yes it is. I'm surprised you remembered. I didn't think that you would."

"Of course I noticed. To be honest, I just didn't want to think about it. I think I was hesitant to talk about our finances because I didn't want to acknowledge that we were disorganized. I've realized now that the longer we wait, the worse it could get."

"You have no idea how glad I am that you said that. It sounds like we're finally on the same page," Rachel said.

"Well, we are and we aren't."

"What do you mean?" Rachel asked.

"Compared to you, I still have a lot to learn. I've been told that before we actually interview prospective financial advisors, we should both have an equal understanding of the overall process, so that we can both make an informed decision together."

"Well, what have you learned so far?" Rachel asked.

"The first thing that I learned was how the financial services industry is structured. I think I have a good understanding of the different types of institutions and what services they provide. It seems as though most of the large financial groups offer almost every type of service under the sun."

"That's a good start," Rachel said approvingly. "What else have you learned?"

"I also learned about the various regulatory bodies in the industry. Although this material was a little dry, it was reassuring to learn that the financial industry isn't like the Wild West. It seems to be very well regulated, which is good to know."

"Excellent. Anything else?"

"This afternoon I learned a little about the various designations that investment professionals can earn. Patrick and Cindy suggested that I call the various associations and institutes and ask them to send me some information on the educational requirements needed to earn the various designations that they oversee. It would be nice to know how much work it takes in order to earn the letters behind your name. It would also be nice to learn what those letters actually mean."

"Today is your lucky day," Rachel said. "I already called all of the associations and had them send me the information that you're talking about," she said, pulling the brochures from her folder. "I've had them for months," she added.

"That's good news because it will save me some time," Thomas said. "Why don't we go through the information tonight, since it's right in front of us?"

"That's a good idea. It's better than sitting in front of the television. It'll also be fun to see how much more you know," Rachel said.

"I think you'll be quite impressed," Thomas answered. "This afternoon, Patrick and Cindy and I talked about what services the various professionals offer. We discussed insurance professionals, financial planners, investment advisors and investment counsellors and portfolio managers. We also went over some of the associations to which each of these professionals may belong. Some may belong to more than one because they do more than one thing."

"Did you discuss accountants and estate lawyers, by any chance?" Rachel asked.

"No, we didn't. I have a pretty good understanding of what services accountants and lawyers provide. I didn't realize that they are an important part of the financial planning process, though."

"Yes, they will often help reduce taxes and make sure that your will is up-to-date. Most people think that financial planning ends when they die. This isn't the case, though, because what happens after you die is just as important as what happens during your lifetime. We'll talk a little bit about this later. Why don't we start with insurance professionals? What did you learn about the insurance industry?" Rachel asked.

"I learned that people who work there sell insurance products and advise on insurance needs. I also learned that some insurance professionals provide financial planning services and may even sell securities. In terms of designations, I think they can earn their Chartered Life Underwriter (CLU), Chartered Financial Consultant (ChFC) or the Registered Health Underwriter (RHU) designation and that these designations are administered by Advocis."

"That's pretty good. But, do you know the difference between the three?" Rachel asked.

"To be honest, I'm not really sure," he answered.

"The Chartered Life Underwriter (CLU) indicates that the individual is a qualified life insurance agent. In order to earn the CLU designation, an individual has to complete six courses, which takes between two and three years. Once an individual has successfully completed the courses and earned the designation, they then have to complete sixty hours of continuing education credits every two years."

"That seems as though it's well earned. What about the Chartered Financial Consultant (ChFC) designation?" he asked.

"The ChFC indicates that an individual is a financial advisor who is knowledgeable about wealth accumulation and retirement planning, in addition to being able to advise on insurance needs. This designation also requires the completion of six courses. In terms of continuing education, a ChFC also has to complete sixty hours of credits every two years."

"And the Registered Health Underwriter (RHU)?" Thomas pressed.

"The RHU is an insurance advisor with advanced knowledge of disability insurance and health benefits. There are two courses required to receive the RHU designation and students can earn the RHU designation over two semesters, if they meet the prerequisites set by Advocis. An advisor with an RHU has acquired the knowledge to offer advice on individual disability income insurance needs," Rachel answered.

"You certainly know your stuff," Thomas admitted. "Just to be certain, each of these designations identifies a professional who is primarily knowledgeable about insurance, right? The ChFC, however, identifies someone who is knowledgeable in insurance, wealth accumulation and retirement planning," he said.

"That's right," Rachel answered. "What about financial planners? Do you know which designations identify a financial planner?"

"As far as I know, there are three distinct acronyms that identify a financial planner. They are the Personal Financial Planner (PFP), Registered Financial Planner (RFP) and Certified Financial Planner (CFP). Am I right?"

"Very good. The PFP is awarded by the Canadian Institute of Bankers. It's typically reserved for individuals who work for the chartered banks. It requires the completion of five courses or five exams, which require approximately three hundred hours of study time. The candidate must also have six months of work experience. Most personal financial planners are found in the retail branches of the major banks."

"Who awards the RFP designation?" Thomas asked.

"This designation is awarded by the Institute of Advanced Financial Planners (IAFP). The IAFP controls and licenses the RFP designation. It is considered to be the most advanced designation due to the additional educational requirements that are needed to earn it," Rachel said.

"What about the CFP?" Thomas asked. "And what's the difference?"

"The Certified Financial Planner (CFP) is an internationally recognized financial planning designation that is becoming widely regarded as the world standard for financial planning accreditation. The Financial Planners Standards Council (FPSC) administers the CFP. Licensees must meet the Council's standards in education, experience, examination and ethical procedures. A CFP licensee must also have thirty hours of continuing education every year to sustain their designation. Certified Financial Planners can be found in a wide array of financial services firms."

"It certainly seems as though it takes a great deal of work to complete these designations," Thomas said, somewhat impressed. "I had no idea. Patrick also mentioned the Financial Management Advisor (FMA), Derivatives Market Specialist (DMS) and the

Chartered Professional (Ch.P.) Strategic Wealth designations. Do you have any information on these?" Thomas asked.

"These designations are administered by the Canadian Securities Institute and are typically earned by individuals who work in the Canadian securities industry. They are most widely held by investment advisors who work for investment dealers that are members of the Investment Industry Regulatory Organization of Canada (IIROC). Financial Management Advisor (FMA) designates that an individual specializes in counselling clients on complex wealth management issues beyond the scope of basic financial planning. In order to earn this designation, a candidate has to successfully complete the Canadian Securities Course, Professional Financial Planning Course and Wealth Management Techniques Course, all of which are extensive on a stand-alone basis."

"Is it just as difficult to become a Derivatives Market Specialist (DMS)?" Thomas asked.

"Although it isn't quite as demanding, it requires a great deal of work nevertheless. In order to earn the DMS designation, a candidate has to complete the Derivatives Fundamentals Course and four other elective courses," Rachel said.

"What about the Ch.P. Strategic Wealth? I heard that this designation takes at least eighteen months to complete. Is that right?"

"Earning this designation is extremely demanding. Before someone can even enrol in this program he or she must already hold a recognized financial planning designation or have completed the CSI's Canadian Securities Course (CSC) and Professional Financial Planning Course (PFPC), or the CSI's Canadian Securities Course (CSC) and Wealth Management Essentials (WME) course. In terms of the program itself, an individual must complete four core courses, two elective courses, prepare a wealth plan based on a complex case study and, finally, present the wealth plan to an expert advisory panel."

"I'm assuming that the designations earned by investment counsellors and portfolio managers are even more rigorous," Thomas suggested.

"In order to work in the Canadian securities industry, investment counsellors and portfolio managers are required to earn either the

Canadian Investment Manager (CIM) or Chartered Financial Analyst (CFA) designation in order to be licensed as a discretionary portfolio manager. Without one of these two designations, professionals aren't able to manage money on a discretionary basis," Rachel said.

"Isn't the CIM also administered by the Canadian Securities Institute?" Thomas asked.

"Yes, it is. The CIM is specifically designed to meet the educational requirements for IIROC registration as an associate or full portfolio manager.

"What about the CFA?" he added.

"The CFA is administered by the CFA Institute, which is an international, non-profit organization of more than fifty thousand investment practitioners and educators in over one hundred countries. The CFA designation requires that a candidate successfully pass the Level I, Level II and Level III exams. This designation is internationally recognized and is typically earned by securities analysts, investment counsellors, portfolio managers or individuals in any high-level finance position. It is one of the most highly respected, internationally known designations that a professional can earn."

"Is it safe to say if an individual has either of these designations, he or she is adequately qualified to manage our portfolio?"

"Yes, but experience and integrity are just as important. We'll want to find someone who has at least ten years' experience and can provide us with references. We'll talk about this when we're at the cottage next weekend. Did you remember to ask Cindy and Patrick if they wanted to come up?" Rachel asked.

"They said that they'd love to visit for the weekend. I warned them that we wanted to set aside a few hours to take our discussion further and they said that they would be glad to help us."

"That's great. I'm really looking forward to it. Now, in terms of the various positions and designations in the investment industry, do you feel that you have a good understanding of what each means?" Rachel asked.

"Yes, I do," Thomas answered. "It will take me a little while to memorize all of the acronyms, but I now have a good idea what each one means. What's important is that I now know what services the various professionals offer. I now also know that it takes a great deal of work in order to earn these designations. Individuals with any of these letters behind their names are probably fairly dedicated to their profession."

"If you ever need to brush up on what you learned, just look through the scrapbook. All of the information will be in here. We'll keep adding to it as we go along. That way we can always come back to it if we need to."

"What will we talk about next weekend?" he asked.

"I think we're finally ready to start talking about what services we need. As it currently stands, I feel that we need a healthy dose of everything, but I know this isn't really the case. What we'll need to do is talk about what specific areas of our financial situation need to be focused on. Although I have some idea of what we need, I think it will be beneficial if we talk to Megan, Cindy and Patrick before we start the interview process. We should also discuss the interview process itself. I'm hoping that everyone can help prepare us in terms of what we should ask the various candidates, what to look for and what to bring to the interview. I think our chances of finding a top-calibre financial advisor will increase if we're thorough during the interview process."

"That makes a lot of sense. We'll have to be well prepared with a list of questions," Thomas added. "It would be nice if the interview process went smoothly."

"I agree. I think next weekend will be very productive. I'm glad our friends are so willing to help us. I'm looking forward to it," Rachel admitted.

"So am I," Thomas agreed.

For the rest of the evening, Rachel and Thomas discussed the details of the following weekend. They were both looking forward to spending time at the cottage. It was now obvious to Rachel that Thomas was fully committed to taking the next step. In fact, he actually seemed excited about it.

Key Point

In today's complex financial environment, it is important for financial professionals to hold at least one professional designation. In addition, you should only consider working with an investment professional if he or she is licensed with a regulatory body.

| 12 |

Hemlocks, Granite and Marshmallows

By the time Thursday evening arrived, Rachel and Thomas were ready for their weekend at the cottage. It wasn't often that the entire family was able to leave for the cottage on a Thursday. It didn't take much time to get everyone ready, and by the time they were well into their drive all three girls were sleeping soundly.

"How was your week?" Thomas asked.

"Busy. I feel a little guilty for leaving Megan with all the work tomorrow. She's going to have her hands full."

"I wouldn't worry about it. Megan can take care of herself. Besides, she wouldn't have encouraged you to go if she didn't think she could handle it."

"You're right. I'll call her tomorrow to see how she's doing. She'll appreciate that," Rachel said, feeling better. "How was your week?"

"It was long, to say the least. We helped one of our biggest clients upgrade their network. We had a lot of bugs to iron out, and I thought we'd never get everything up and running, but we finally got things right."

"Did you have a chance to go through any more financial information over the last few days?" Rachel asked.

"I didn't look at any new information, but I did go through the scrapbook again. I wanted to have a list of questions prepared for this weekend. After reading all the articles, I realized that there are still so many things I need to learn. For instance, I'd like to have a much better understanding of how financial professionals are compensated, what their services cost, whether they have to sell proprietary products and what recourse we have if we are unhappy with their service. All of these questions seem pretty important."

"Yes, they are very important. We'll use this weekend to answer all of our questions. By Sunday it would be nice if we were ready to meet with several candidates, conduct productive interviews and have the confidence to choose the right advisor based on the information we've gathered. Megan has a pretty good idea of what we still need to know and she'll guide us in the right direction. She'll make sure that we're well prepared and that we're comfortable with the whole process."

"That's good to know. Although I'm anxious about our first interview, I'm looking forward to it. It's similar to anticipating your first day on a new job—it's exciting because you don't know what to expect."

"I know exactly what you mean," Rachel agreed. With that she closed her eyes so she could fall asleep.

Other than the soft hum of the engine, the car was completely quiet. Thomas didn't mind that everyone was sleeping because it gave him a chance to collect his thoughts. As they continued further north, the farmer's fields slowly changed into stately pines, granite rock and crystal clear lakes. This was his favourite part of the drive because he enjoyed watching the landscape transform as they approached the Canadian Shield.

When they were within twenty minutes of the cottage, Thomas decided that it was time to wake his family. In order to do this as gently as possible, he turned on the radio, tuned it to a classical station and turned up the volume a little. Although his method was subtle it was always effective, and within a few minutes he heard the girls stirring in the back seat. Once they were awake, Rachel usually followed.

By the time they arrived at the cottage, the kids were close to bursting with excitement. As they proceeded down their long, winding driveway, Rachel pointed out the interesting shadows that were being cast on the ground by the huge hemlocks that lined both sides of the lane. The density of the trees made their property very private, which was one of the reasons why they had chosen it.

The property was almost four acres in size and rather than landscape, Rachel and Thomas had chosen to keep it in its natural state. Other than the trees that were cleared to install the driveway and construct the cottage, the land looked the same as when they had originally bought it. The waterfront consisted of large platforms of granite rock sloping gently towards the clear, rocky and deep lake. The water was excellent for trout fishing and Thomas spent a lot of time in pursuit of a trophy laker.

Once all the groceries were put away, the family relaxed on the deck with lemonade and pretzels. It was a warm evening and the girls asked if they could go swimming.

In terms of swimming, the rules were quite simple. The girls weren't allowed to be in the water after the sun slipped low enough behind the hills that it was no longer visible. This let them know that once the sun started to drop out of sight they only had a short while left. Although it was a simple rule, it worked quite well because it kept the girls out of the lake after dusk. Judging from the sun's position, the girls had about forty-five minutes left before it dropped from sight.

"Do you know what I just realized?" Thomas said as he and Rachel watched the children playing in the water. "We forgot to bring our scrapbook with us. All of our information is in there."

"You may have forgotten your scrapbook, but I brought mine," Rachel said coyly.

"You did? That's good. I should have known that you would remember to bring it along. Do you think we should have brought anything else?"

"Just to be sure, I brought our portfolio statements, bank account statements, last year's tax information and a few other things that I've collected over the last few months. I thought it would be better to be safe than sorry. This way we'll have everything at our fingertips in case we need it."

"That makes sense to me. Now if I could just be as helpful as you have been," Thomas said.

"You are being helpful just by taking this process seriously. Just keep doing what you're doing," Rachel encouraged.

"I will. I'm very curious to find out what we need to do to improve our overall financial picture. When I said that I was looking forward to the next step, I really meant it."

"I know you did," Rachel said, not needing any convincing.

After the sun fell behind the hills, the girls came out of the lake without having to be reminded. While Rachel dried them off, Thomas built a campfire so the family could roast some marshmallows. As always, Dexter patrolled the perimeter of the fire in case someone accidentally dropped one. Tonight was his lucky night because he ended up with four. When the girls started to look drowsy everyone went inside to get ready for bed. Once the girls were changed they all hopped into their respective bunk beds so Thomas could read them a story. Within a few minutes all three were fast asleep. Seeing them cuddled up in their beds made Thomas want to do the same.

Key Point

Have all your financial information readily available so that you can refer to it as often as needed. This information may include your bank and portfolio statements, RRSP contribution slips, confirmation slips, Notice of Assessment and pension statements.

| 13 |

The Guests Arrive

The children slept in later than usual the following morning, probably due to all the fresh air. Rachel made pancakes, looking forward to eating on the deck with a view of the lake. The still morning water was one of her favourite sights.

Unfortunately, as the family was sitting down to breakfast, the peace and quiet was broken by the all-too-familiar sound of Dexter barking. Thomas got up from the table to see what the commotion was about. As he walked inside he heard someone knocking at the front door. It was their neighbor, Jacob.

"Hope I'm not disturbing you," Jacob said. "I saw your lights were on last night. You're usually not up until Friday so I thought I'd check in to see if everything was okay."

"We were lucky and had the chance to get out of town a day early this week," Thomas explained. "Come on in and have a cup of coffee."

Jacob and his wife, Isabel were in their early sixties and had been cottaging on the lake for a little over thirty years. Their property had been in Isabel's family for two generations when her parents gave it to them as a wedding present. Initially, they built a cabin, which they enjoyed only during the summer, but after they retired they decided to live on the lake permanently and replaced the small cabin with a beautiful winterized house. Because they lived on the lake year-round, they kept an eye on everyone else's property.

"I just saw her parents a few weeks ago. We all had dinner together when we were in the city," Jacob said when Thomas told him Megan was coming up for the weekend.

Jacob and Isabel had been friends with Megan's parents ever since Jacob and Megan's father began working together at the same company. After Jacob retired as the company's CEO, Megan's father was appointed as his successor. It was through him that Thomas and Rachel had bought their own land on the lake.

"How is Isabel doing?" Rachel asked.

"She's doing fine, busy with her woodworking and the garden. She'll be happy to see you. Last weekend was so quiet. When is everyone else coming?"

"They should be here by early afternoon. Megan and Cindy and Patrick are helping us find a financial advisor. We thought we would have everyone up this weekend so that we could learn what we need to know in order to begin interviewing people."

"If you have any questions, ask me," Jacob offered. "We've been working with the same group of investment professionals for years, and we've been very happy with their service. The best advice that I can give you is to hire someone as soon as possible. I wouldn't have told you this, but a long time ago I took care of our financial affairs by myself. As the CEO of a large company I was confident that I had the skills to manage my own money—and I use the term 'manage' very loosely. What I didn't realize was that managing our financial affairs and managing them properly were two entirely different things. After a few years, our portfolio looked like a disaster zone. It consisted of speculative stocks from just two or three different sectors. To make matters worse, I only had a small percentage of our assets invested in treasury bills and bonds, which was a bad decision because interest rates were dropping from their all-time highs. At work, I consistently delivered a compounded annual growth rate in the low teens, eliminated almost all of the company's long-term debt and increased our annual dividend five times, but at home, I couldn't seem to do this with my own investments."

"What made you finally seek professional advice?" Thomas asked curiously.

"I finally made the decision to get a second opinion after realizing that running a company on behalf of shareholders was different from investing in a company on behalf of myself. Looking back, you'd assume that my portfolio would have consisted of companies that had similar fundamentals to the one that I was running so effectively. That wasn't the case though. What finally pushed me over the edge was when I realized that our portfolio's average annual rate of return was consistently below those of the major indexes such as the Toronto Stock Exchange (TSX) and Dow Jones Industrial Average (DJIA). The difference between the indexes and our returns was surprising. When I finally saw that, I decided to meet with a professional money manager."

"That makes me even more concerned now because we've never really monitored our performance. To be honest I don't have the slightest clue how our investments have been doing," Rachel said, looking worried.

"It's good that you're in the process of finding out. If you're well diversified I'm sure it hasn't been too bad," said Jacob, trying to reassure her. "The money management game can be tricky because most investors have a tough time making good decisions when it comes to their own money. It's actually quite difficult to be objective—which is why an outside opinion is so important."

"This is making more and more sense," Thomas said.

"You'd be surprised how many people still manage their own financial affairs—many of them unsuccessfully. The cost of using a top professional is so reasonable nowadays that it simply doesn't make sense to do it on your own," Jacob said.

"The hurdle we're facing isn't deciding to use a financial advisor, it's finding someone with a high level of integrity who is knowledgeable in their field. We're worried that we're going to have a bad experience, which is why Megan is helping us," Rachel admitted.

"The best thing that you can do is be well prepared before you start interviewing candidates," Jacob pointed out. "Despite what you may think, most top financial advisors prefer working with clients who have at least a basic understanding of the investment process because these clients tend to have realistic expectations, thereby laying the foundation for a sound, long-term professional relationship. In most cases, unrealistic expectations stem from being misinformed, so it's important to at least learn the basics. It's also important that you are able to clearly identify what you're expecting in terms of service. You are much less likely to have a bad experience if you clearly establish your expectations before you enter into the working relationship. Figure those out and you'll be ready to start the interview process by Monday," Jacob said.

"That makes a lot of sense. If you're not busy, how would you and Isabel like to come over for lunch tomorrow? That way you can see Megan while helping us out at the same time. We'd really appreciate it," Thomas said.

"We'd like that. What time would you like us to be here?" Jacob asked.

"How about at around one o'clock?" Rachel said.

"Perfect. We'll bring some appetizers and a salad," Jacob offered. "I'd better be off now though, because Isabel will wonder what happened to me. I don't want her calling out a search party."

"Give her my best. We'll see you tomorrow," Rachel said.

For the rest of the morning, Thomas and the children played by the lake while Rachel got everything ready for their guests. When lunchtime eventually rolled around he decided to take them to the snack bar at the marina for a bite to eat.

Despite being just shy of its tenth birthday, Thomas' Boston Whaler was still in great shape. As the boat pulled out of the bay, Thomas leaned on the throttle. Within seconds the boat was gliding across the sparkling water.

In about fifteen minutes they reached the marina. As they approached the dock Ashley stood up and helped Thomas verbally guide the vessel into place. Although he didn't need her assistance, he appreciated the fact that she tried to help get the boat into its mooring spot. After they tied the boat to the dock they took off their life jackets, threw them in the boat and walked up the ramp to the restaurant.

"Do you guys want to eat inside or outside?" he asked.

"Outside!" they all shouted.

"Are you sure? It's pretty hot out here," he said. They all nodded.

They chose to sit at the picnic table closest to the water so they could enjoy the view. Shortly after they sat down the waitress came outside and gave them each a menu. For lunch the kids always ordered the same thing—Ashley ordered the hamburger and fries, Hilary ordered the hot dog and fries and Anna ordered just fries.

Back at the cottage after another swim, the children lay down for a rare afternoon nap and Thomas wandered into the kitchen to see what Rachel was doing. He found her finishing making that night's dinner.

"It smells incredible," he told her. "What are we having?"

"Roasted tomato soup to start, and then I'm throwing a lamb roast in the oven with apples and vegetables," she said. "I also made a fruit salad for dessert."

"That sounds great. Are you sure I can't help you with anything?"

"How about keeping me company down by the lake after I've finished? Why don't you pour us two glasses of wine and go and get comfortable? I'll be down in a few minutes."

Thomas went to the cupboard, pulled out the ice bucket and filled it with ice. After grabbing two goblets he opened a bottle of white wine and placed it in the bucket. He then went down to the lake and settled in a Muskoka chair on the dock. A few minutes later, Rachel joined him carrying her new camera.

"What a beautiful afternoon," she said. "There isn't a cloud in the sky."

"It's supposed to be like this all weekend," Thomas added. "I really love this place."

"Do you think we need to make any plans or should we just play everything by ear for the entire weekend?" Rachel asked.

"I thought that we would discuss financial matters during lunch on the deck tomorrow. That way, if we need more time, we can continue our conversation through to dinner."

"That's a good idea. I'll make lunch for the kids about an hour before we sit down to eat so that we'll have some time to ourselves while the kids play together."

"That sounds good to me. I'm going to make my beef tenderloin for dinner tomorrow night. That way you don't have to worry about cooking."

"That's sweet of you," Rachel said. "Thanks, honey."

For the next hour Thomas and Rachel hung out on the deck, chatting and taking photographs. The wind had died down and the water was as smooth as glass. Off in the distance, two loons were taking turns diving deep into the lake in search of their next meal. It amazed Thomas how long the birds could remain under water. When the children woke up, they all enjoyed watching the birds. Eventually they heard two quick bursts of a car horn—their guests had arrived. The family went up to the driveway to greet their friends.

"Hi guys!" Cindy said, as everyone climbed out of the car. "We made it."

"I'm glad you came up early. It's such a beautiful day," Rachel said.

Once everything was unpacked, the children rushed to get back in the lake while their parents relaxed on the dock discussing their plans for the working lunch the next day.

"The first thing that we're going to do is look at your overall financial picture and decide what kind of help you need to get your affairs in order," Cindy said. "I have a feeling that your situation is similar to ours so you'll probably need some insurance, financial and estate planning. As far as investment management goes, I think that you're in a position to hire a portfolio manager. We'll go through all your statements tomorrow to help us decide. Did you remember to bring them with you?" Cindy asked.

"Yes, I brought almost everything. It's in a folder in the cottage. Do you want me to go grab it?" Rachel asked.

"No, it's okay. We won't need it until tomorrow. Once we know what kind of help you need, we can prepare you for the interviews themselves. The interview process is very important because it helps you to establish whether you and the investment professional are compatible. Thomas says that trust is a really big issue for him. The initial interview should allow you to decide whether or not you think that you could grow to trust the individual with your personal information," Cindy said.

"The most important thing to remember is that the interview is designed to evaluate the individual as a potential candidate. As the clients, you are the ones doing the hiring—it's not the other way around. During the interview, no stone should be left unturned, including the candidate's educational background, experience, how he is compensated and so forth. If you leave the interview feeling that you know almost everything about the person then you've done a good job," Patrick added.

"You make it sound like a job interview," Thomas said.

"That's the point we're trying to make—it is a job interview! You are hiring and paying a professional to manage your financial affairs. The biggest mistake people make is that they don't take the interview process seriously. In many instances they hire the first person they meet, whether or not the candidate is suitable."

"It sounds like we have our work cut out for us tomorrow. I thought we were so close to sorting everything out," Thomas said.

"You're actually closer than you think. After tomorrow, it will all be up to you," Cindy said.

Key Point

No matter how successful you are in business, you will likely benefit from a second opinion when it comes to your personal finances. When hiring an investment professional, remember that during the interview process you are choosing someone to employ; he or she is not choosing you as a client.

|14|

The Financial Needs Pyramid

At lunchtime the next day, the two couples, Megan and Jacob and Isabel gathered around the table enjoying Rachel's special barbecued salmon with a salad from Isabel's garden. As promised, the conversation concentrated on Thomas and Rachel's financial planning project.

"We're pretty up-to-date as far as our knowledge of the financial services industry is concerned," Thomas said, taking a bite of salad. "We have a good grasp of the differences between the various financial institutions, investment professionals and professional designations that we'll likely encounter."

"That's good," said Jacob. "It sounds like you've already covered quite a bit. Where are you in terms of deciding on what services you're looking for?"

"We're at that point now. We haven't really discussed what services we're looking for, so we'd like to figure that out today. If we have time, we'd also like to discuss the interview process itself so we know what to expect," Rachel said.

"We will try our best. That's a lot of information to cover at once. As far as deciding on what you need in terms of financial advice, the best thing to do is start at the bottom."

"At the bottom? Don't you mean at the beginning?" Rachel asked.

"No, at the bottom. Let me explain," Jacob offered.

"The best means of assessing your financial needs is to establish where you fit into the Financial Needs Pyramid. Depending on your age, earning power and net worth, you will fall into one of the five levels of the pyramid. As your financial situation evolves during your life, you will eventually pass through each level of the pyramid. Some people will stay at the first level for their entire lives, while others will move to the top of the pyramid fairly quickly."

"What are the five different levels of the pyramid?" Rachel asked.

"The first level, or base, of the pyramid is called the Cash Management Stage (Level I). The base consists primarily of individuals who have entered the work force for the first time in their lives. As a result, they are learning to balance their chequebooks, pay their monthly bills and manage their cash flow. They have virtually no savings whatsoever."

"It's as though you're describing our situation after we graduated from university and started working," Rachel said.

"At one point or another, most individuals find themselves entering the base of the pyramid. For some people, it happens sooner, and for others, it happens later. Once an individual grows comfortable with earning a regular income and paying their bills, the transition to the second level of the pyramid comes naturally," Jacob said.

"The second stage is called the Savings & Loans Stage (Level II). After having been in the workforce for several years, most people are comfortable with managing their cash flow and are ready to purchase their first big ticket item, which can include a car, a house or condo or even a recreational property. In order to do this they usually have to rely on financing from a bank, trust company or credit union. This can be in the form of a loan, personal line of credit (PLC) or mortgage. Throughout this stage, individuals learn the importance of their net worth statement, credit rating and debt management skills. In most cases, individuals at this level of the pyramid rely heavily on the advice from the financial services manager or loan officer at their local bank, which is why a good relationship with one of these people is extremely important."

"I don't think we fall into this category. Although we still have a mortgage on our house, we have very little in terms of debt. All of our credit cards, personal lines of credit and car loans are practically paid off. We also have a great relationship with the branch manager of our bank. He has been an excellent source of information," Thomas said.

"That's why we're ready to discuss the third level of the pyramid which is the Financial Planning Stage (Level III)," said Cindy, who knew all about the pyramid.

"When you enter the Financial Planning Stage you're really getting to the heart of the matter," Megan chipped in. "This stage is arguably the most important level of the pyramid because the decisions that you make during this stage will affect your financial well-being for the rest of your life. Quite often, individuals pass through this stage very quickly because they lack the discipline or patience to get all of their financial ducks in a row."

"Is it possible that we've already addressed many of the needs of this stage?" Thomas asked.

"It's possible, but highly unlikely. If you were confident that you'd already addressed these needs, we probably wouldn't be sitting here today. As I said before, the Financial Planning Stage is the heart of the pyramid. It includes retirement planning, insurance needs planning, tax planning, business planning and estate planning—all which fall under the umbrella of financial planning. It is possible that you have already addressed one or two of these needs at some point in the past, but in order to move to the next level you have to ensure that you have a sound financial plan in place. In order to do this properly you'll have to rely one or more of the financial services professionals that we talked about earlier," Megan said.

"It sounds like we're at this level of the pyramid. Why don't we take a few minutes to figure out which of our needs have to be addressed," Rachel suggested.

"The first thing we need to do is discuss each of the five needs of this level of the pyramid in some detail. A financial planner will usually do this by asking you specific questions or having you complete a financial planning needs questionnaire. We'll quickly go through everything so we know where you stand. Why don't we start with retirement planning? Do you know at what age you'd like to retire? Also, do you know how much you need to retire?" Megan asked.

"To be honest, we don't really know how much money we need to retire comfortably. I've read that a general rule of thumb is that you need to earn seventy per cent of your current income to maintain a similar standard of living during your retirement, but I don't know if this is accurate. Although we've been maximizing our annual RRSP contributions the jury is still out on whether or not we'll have enough to live on when we eventually stop working," Rachel said.

"Enough said—you need retirement planning. Although it seems as though you guys are doing a good job of saving money, you should have a fairly good idea of how much money you should be putting away. A good financial planner will prepare a report for you that will outline the steps you need to take in order to meet your retirement goals. Also, have either of you looked into a spousal RRSP? If one of you decides to retire earlier than the other, you would be able to take advantage of income splitting. This is something that needs to be considered as well," Megan suggested.

"To be honest, we haven't even thought of that. We thought simply saving for retirement was enough," Rachel admitted.

"What about insurance?" Jacob asked. "Do you have enough coverage in place?"

"Again, I'm not really sure," Rachel answered. "Maybe it's time for me to get the folder with all of our financial statements."

"Okay," said Jacob when Rachel returned with her folder. "Where are your life insurance statements? We need to find out whether or not the policies will meet your financial needs if either of you were to die unexpectedly."

Rachel flipped through the stack of statements until she found the ones that she was looking for and passed them over to Jacob.

"If you had to guess, how much insurance coverage would you say each of you have?" Jacob asked.

"I think we each have about two hundred and fifty thousand dollars in coverage. I'm not sure of the exact amount," Thomas answered.

"Do you know how much coverage you actually need?" Jacob asked.

"I don't have the slightest clue," Thomas admitted.

"Neither do I," Rachel added.

"Let me ask you something," Jacob said.

"Oh, no. Here come the questions!" Megan warned with a smile.

"If you were to receive an enormous inheritance tomorrow, would you need to increase or decrease your insurance coverage?" Jacob asked.

"I think we would need more insurance because our net worth would be much higher," Thomas answered.

"Megan, what do you think?" Jacob asked.

"Less insurance," she answered confidently.

"That's right. A common misconception is that the more money you have the more insurance you need. In most cases, the opposite is true. It all depends on your specific cash flow needs," Jacob said.

"Can you explain this? I don't know what you mean," Thomas asked.

"The purpose of life insurance in its traditional sense is to replace lost income. To give you an example, let's assume that you each earn one hundred thousand dollars per year, which is needed to cover all of your annual household expenses. This includes things like groceries, utilities, automobile costs and mortgage payments. If one of you were to suddenly die then the total household income would drop from two hundred thousand per year to one hundred thousand per year. The annual household expenses, however, would remain roughly the same. Where will the extra money come from to continue to pay these expenses?"

"It should come from the insurance policy," Rachel said.

"That's right. In order to earn the equivalent of one hundred thousand dollars per year you would need a nest egg of at least one million five hundred thousand dollars assuming that you do not want to touch the principal."

"One million five hundred thousand dollars! That can't be right," Thomas said, shocked at the amount.

"It's hard to believe but I can assure you that it's right. If you took out the appropriate amount of life insurance you would receive one million five hundred thousand dollars tax free from the insurance company upon your death. Once you received the money, it would then have to be invested so that the surviving spouse could use the investment income to supplement the lost employment income. At an annual average rate of return of seven per cent, you would earn a little over one hundred thousand dollars a year in investment income. If the insurance policy were inadequate, the surviving spouse would have to drastically reduce his or her living expenses. With three young children, this would be extremely difficult to do."

"So do we have enough?" Rachel asked eagerly.

"It's not as easy as just looking at the policies and deciding whether you have enough. The example I gave you is very simple because I am only looking at what you need to replace your income without taking any other factors into consideration. In order to give you an accurate amount, you would need to have an insurance specialist evaluate your insurance needs just to be safe."

"I agree completely. Coming back to something you mentioned earlier, you said that in its traditional sense life insurance is designed to replace lost income. Does this mean that life insurance can be used in another way?" Thomas asked.

"A lot of people don't know this but life insurance is also an effective estate planning tool. It can be used to supplement your retirement income by signing the policy over to a bank as collateral for a retirement loan. It can also be used to pay any capital gains tax that your estate may be liable for upon your death, including taxes on your registered and non-registered plans, sale of a cottage or other investment properties."

"I didn't know that. We'll definitely have an insurance specialist look at our situation. If we could take out a policy to pay the capital gains tax on this place, the kids would receive a much larger inheritance because the taxes payable would be covered. What's next?" Rachel asked.

"The next step is ensuring that you are minimizing your taxes," Cindy said. "Because we're running our own business we pay particularly close attention to our tax planning needs. We didn't want to pay higher taxes than necessary because that means that at the end of the year there is less money in our pockets."

"We have always filed our own returns. To be honest, I don't know if we've been minimizing our taxes. I'm embarrassed to admit that we usually always end up filing at very the last minute," Rachel said.

"A tax specialist is very important. As the federal and provincial budgets are released each year there are sometimes some significant changes in the tax laws. It's very important to be up-to-date on all the changes in tax legislation or else you may be paying more tax than you should," Patrick said.

"We'll add a tax specialist to our list of professionals," Thomas said.

"This brings us to estate planning, one of the most neglected needs in the Financial Planning Stage," Jacob said. "Do each of you have updated wills?"

"No, the only wills we have are the ones that Thomas prepared with one of those do-it-yourself will kits that are advertised on television," Rachel said reluctantly. "We did them when Ashley was born."

"I completely forgot that we have a diehard do-it-yourselfer in our midst!" Jacob announced.

"A reformed do-it-yourselfer," Thomas rebutted. "I've finally seen the light."

"Don't be embarrassed, Thomas," Isabel said gently. "Jacob used to be the same way until he came to his senses."

"It's reassuring to hear that you have a will—whether or not it's up-to-date. One of the most common mistakes that people make is that they forget to include details like appointing a legal guardian for any children that are under the age of majority or laying out guidelines in the event that one or both parents are incapacitated in one way or another. The best advice that I can give you is to get your wills updated by an estate planning lawyer. Not only will he ensure that all your bases are covered, he will also periodically review and update your wills as needed."

"We'll have our wills prepared by an estate lawyer," Rachel said.

"As far as the Financial Planning Stage is concerned I think we've covered all the bases. Based on what we've talked about, it's obvious that you would benefit from a well-rounded financial plan that covers all of your financial planning needs. A good financial planner will help you with this," Jacob said.

"What's the next level in the pyramid?" Rachel asked curiously.

"The fourth level is the Wealth Accumulation Stage (Level IV). Once you've addressed your financial planning needs, you will then be in a position to focus on building on what you've accumulated. At this level of the pyramid, individuals have usually been in the workforce for at least twenty years. In most cases they have paid down a majority of their debt and are starting to save a good portion of their income," Megan said.

"Aren't we at this level even though we've only been working for a little over fifteen years?" Thomas asked.

"Yes, you are. You've gotten to this stage a little earlier because both of you earn above-average incomes," Megan explained.

"Once we have a sound financial plan in place, what should we expect during the Wealth Accumulation Stage?" Thomas asked.

"During this stage you should be focused on increasing your net worth through savings and capital appreciation. In order to do this, you need to implement an investment strategy. A qualified investment advisor or portfolio manager should help you with this," Jacob said.

"Until now we've always just invested in mutual funds and forgotten about them. Isn't this a good idea?" Thomas asked.

"The problem with just forgetting about your portfolio is that the investment climate is constantly changing. If you're not on top of everything at any given time then your portfolio's performance may be compromised. A qualified investment advisor will develop and implement an investment plan based on your specific investment objectives. If you are serious about getting your financial house in order then you really want a professional at the helm of any long-term investment plan. There is no nobility in developing and implementing your own investment plan unless you're going to devote a great deal of time and energy to the process," Jacob warned.

"Do we have enough money to work with an investment manager? I was under the impression that we needed a sizable portfolio before an investment advisor or portfolio manager would even look at us," Rachel asked.

"It actually depends on the individual investment advisor. There are many advisors that have no restrictions in regards to account size, while others may set their minimum account size at several hundred thousand dollars or higher."

"What can we expect in terms of our relationship with an investment advisor? Do we just hand our money over and let him do his thing?" Thomas asked.

"The first thing I should mention is that the role of an investment advisor is advisory in nature. Very few investment advisors are licensed to manage money on a discretionary basis. This means that before any changes are made to your portfolio the advisor should discuss them with you," Jacob said.

"Doesn't that mean that we're making the investment decisions?" Rachel asked.

"Absolutely not. In order for your investment advisor to be effective, all of the investment decisions should be left up to him or her. Your role is simply to confirm that each recommendation is in line with your specific investment objectives," Jacob said.

"What about putting the portfolio together?" Rachel asked.

"The first step in the investment management process is to evaluate your investment objectives and risk tolerance. This will dictate what percentage of your portfolio is allocated to each of the three major asset classes—cash, fixed-income and stocks. Once the investment advisor has decided on the appropriate asset mix, he will then recommend the appropriate securities to reflect this asset mix. From that point forward, the investment advisor will monitor the portfolio and contact you if any changes need to be made," Megan said.

"This sounds like something that we might be interested in. What about monitoring our rate of return? Right now, we have no idea how our investments are performing."

"You should review your portfolio's performance annually. This can be in a face-to-face meeting or a conference call where everyone is on the line," Megan suggested. "After a few years, you'll know whether or not the relationship is going well. If the contact, trust and performance are there, then you'll probably be working with your investment advisor for many years."

"That sounds good. What's the next level of the pyramid?" Thomas asked.

"The top and final level of the pyramid is called the Capital Preservation Stage (Level V). Typically, individuals only enter the top of the pyramid after they have built up a significant amount of wealth. Their primary focus is on capital preservation because they want to ensure that the assets that they have built up are eventually passed on to their kids. These individuals usually rely on several highly skilled professionals to manage their financial affairs. In addition to the professionals we discussed, they may also use the services of private bankers, trust officers, investment counsellors and portfolio managers," Jacob said.

"Jacob, what's the difference between these professionals and the ones we've talked about?" Rachel asked.

"It essentially comes down to your net worth. As your net worth increases, your situation often becomes more complex and requires specialized solutions. A private banker, for example, provides banking solutions with an international scope as opposed to just a domestic one. You usually need at least one million dollars to make the services of a private banker worth your while."

"What about investment counsellors and portfolio managers? Do they also require clients to have minimum account sizes?" Thomas asked.

"Yes. They typically require you to have at least five hundred thousand dollars in investable family assets; many require more. In certain situations, they will accommodate families that have less than this amount. You simply have to ask if they will work with you."

"If these professionals have higher minimum requirements in terms of assets, does this mean that they offer a higher level of service than most of the other professionals?" Rachel asked.

"It's not necessarily that these professionals offer a higher level of service, it's simply that they offer a specialized service. Private bankers, trust officers, investment counsellors and portfolio managers are specialists as opposed to generalists. As a result of their experience, education and specialized skills they are able to set minimum asset requirements. In many cases, these are the most sought after professionals in the financial industry," Megan explained.

"Does anyone mind discussing who they currently work with and why they chose to work with them? I think it will give us a better idea in terms of which professionals to consider for our specific financial situation?" Rachel asked.

"Of course we don't mind. Why don't I start?" Patrick offered. "After I lost my job, we weren't sure if we were in a financial position to start our own business, so we decided to get a professional opinion. Before we started looking for the right person we knew that we needed to address our cash flow needs, insurance needs and estate planning needs, all with an emphasis on business planning. When we talked to Megan, she suggested that we interview financial planners who specialize in advising small-business owners."

"So how many financial planners did you interview?" Rachel asked.

"We interviewed three in total. The first one worked at our local bank branch. He had his PFP designation and was licensed to sell mutual funds. The second financial planner worked for a major insurance company. She had her ChFC designation and was licensed to sell life insurance and mutual funds. The third person worked for a small independent fee-for-service financial planning firm and she had her RFP designation."

"I'm surprised that three financial planners can work for such completely different financial institutions," Thomas said, "and sell such different products on top of that."

"This is fairly common in the financial planning industry, which is why it's important to interview a diverse group of professionals at different financial institutions," Megan suggested.

"How did the each of the interviews go?" Thomas asked curiously.

"They all went extremely well. What surprised us most was that each financial planner put a different spin on the services he or she offered."

"Who did you eventually choose?" Isabel asked curiously.

"Although all three candidates were equally impressive, we decided to hire the fee-for-service financial planner because she specialized in financial planning for small business owners. As new business owners this was very important to us."

"So you hired her?"

"We did hire her, but we also ended up working closely with the other ones as well," Cindy said.

"What do you mean?" Rachel asked.

"After we signed a contract with the fee-for-service financial planner, she took a few weeks to gather all of our personal information. Once she had what she needed, she analyzed the data and presented us with a final draft of the financial plan. As soon as we saw the document we were blown away. The plan outlined the exact steps we needed to take in order to achieve our financial goals—nothing was left uncovered. As a fee-for-service financial planner, however, her service was strictly limited to preparing financial plans. Whenever specific investment products were needed to implement any parts of the financial plan, she relied on outside professionals to recommend those products," Patrick said.

"Wouldn't it have been easier to work with someone who could prepare a financial plan and recommend the products needed to implement it?" Thomas asked.

"It would have been a lot more convenient, but we appreciated the fact that our planner focused entirely on gathering information and preparing the financial plan. By using outside sources to recommend specific financial products we benefited from the expertise of several professionals," Cindy said.

"So you hired the other two financial planners specifically for product selection?" Isabel asked.

"That's right. After reviewing the financial plan, our first priority was to buy some life insurance. Although our planner had someone that she could have referred us to, we wanted to go back to the woman we interviewed at the life insurance company because she had a lot of insurance experience and was very professional. We knew we made the right decision because she ended up doing a wonderful job."

"What about the financial planner at the bank?" Isabel asked.

"After we addressed our insurance needs we turned our attention to our retirement needs. In order to achieve our retirement goals we needed to invest in a balanced portfolio. Due to our account size, our financial planner suggested that we invest in mutual funds because they provided us with the diversification that we needed. Without a moment's hesitation we went back to see the financial planner at our branch because we knew he was knowledgeable in regards to recommending mutual funds."

"It sounds like it all worked out for the best. And you didn't offend any of the financial planners because you hired all of them," Rachel said, sounding relieved.

"It's funny that you say that, Rachel," Jacob said. "One of the most common mistakes a consumer can make is to enter into a professional relationship simply because they don't want to offend the person that they interviewed. Most financial professionals know that they're not always going to be a perfect fit. This goes with the territory. If you don't think the potential for a good relationship exists after the initial interview, meet with someone else."

"That's reassuring. I sometimes find it hard to say no."

"What about you, Megan? Where do you get your financial advice?" Thomas asked.

"I have three individuals that advise me on my financial affairs—a private banker, a chartered accountant and an investment advisor.

"In terms of banking, I need the specialized services of a private banker because I have some assets invested outside of the country. As far as my taxes are concerned, I needed someone who specialized in tax planning for small business owners, specifically those who own restaurants."

"Is this the same accountant that you referred to Cindy and Patrick?" Thomas asked.

"Yes, it is. I have been working with him for as long as I can remember. He has always done a great job so I knew that he would be able to help them with their taxes."

"What about your investments?"

"In terms of my investments, I work with an investment advisor at a large bank-owned investment dealer. We've been working together for many years and we have an excellent relationship."

"I'm a little surprised. I would have assumed that because of your busy schedule, you'd prefer leaving the day-to-day management of your portfolio up to a discretionary portfolio manager." Isabel said.

"Actually, I've been working with the same investment advisor since just after my twenty-first birthday. That was when I received the proceeds from the trust that my grandparents had established for me."

"That's a long time. Good for you," Isabel said.

"What I appreciate most about our working relationship is that we are both involved in the investment decisions. As you know, I have a fairly good understanding of the financial markets and I enjoy following them. This type of relationship allows me to keep a watch on what's happening in the economy."

"You're just like your father, dear," Isabel said smiling.

"How about you?" Rachel asked Jacob and Isabel.

"We also work with a private banker who takes care of our banking needs. Our accounting needs are fairly complicated so we rely on the services of a team of accountants at one of the major accounting firms," Jacob said.

"What about your investment management needs? Yesterday you mentioned that you made the decision years ago to have your money managed by a professional," Thomas asked.

"That's right. Our money is managed by a small team of portfolio managers who manage money on behalf of high–net worth families, foundations and institutions," Jacob said.

"Do they manage your money on a discretionary basis?" Rachel asked.

"Yes, it's money management in its purest form. Once we signed the discretionary management forms, we handed the management of our portfolio over to the portfolio manager and his team. And they have been taking care of it ever since."

"What about performance? Who monitors how well your investments have been doing?" Thomas asked.

"Performance is reviewed on an annual basis. It's important to mention, however, that a portfolio manager's definition of performance is different from your definition of performance."

"What do you mean?" Rachel asked curiously.

"If you ask someone what they expect in terms of a rate of return, the most common answer, regardless of that person's investment objectives, is usually ten per cent."

"That's the answer I would give," Thomas admitted.

"The problem with this type of thinking is that you're disregarding several important factors such as your investment objectives, risk tolerance and the investment climate. If you are a conservative investor who only invests in GICs, for example, how are you going to earn ten per cent if GIC rates are only five per cent?"

"That's a good point," Rachel said.

"The same example applies to the stock market. If, for instance, global stock markets have three years of negative returns, it is unrealistic for investors to expect to earn ten per cent per year during this same period. Unfortunately, many investors don't see it that way and simply assume that their investment advisor or portfolio manager is doing a poor job."

"How does a portfolio manager measure performance?" Thomas asked.

"A portfolio manager focuses on relative performance in addition to absolute returns. He does this by comparing the portfolio's rate of return to an appropriate benchmark," Jacob answered.

"Can you explain this benchmark?" Thomas asked.

"Let's assume that your investment objectives are growth. If this were the case, your portfolio would consist of some cash, bonds and stocks. With this type of asset mix, it would be meaningless to compare your portfolio's performance to a short-term bond index, because your portfolio also holds stocks. This would be like comparing apples to oranges."

"What would you measure it against then? I always assumed that the purpose of the major indexes was to gauge the performance of their respective markets," Thomas asked.

"You hit the nail right on the head—the key word is 'respective'. In order to measure your portfolio's performance properly, you should compare it to a benchmark that includes the indexes that accurately reflect the asset allocation of your portfolio. For example, if fifteen per cent of your holdings are in Canadian equities then a similar percentage of the benchmark should consist of the S&P/TSX Composite Index to reflect this, because this is what's used to gauge the performance of blue-chip Canadian companies."

"What other indexes might be included? When I watch the financial news it seems as though there are dozens of different stock indexes that are used to measure markets from around the world."

"In most Canadian growth portfolios, the benchmark would likely include the S&P/TSX, S&P 500, which represents US equities, Morgan Stanley Capital Inc. (MSCI) EAFE, which represents international equities, SCM Universe Bond Index, which represents bonds, and SCM 91 Day T-Bill Index, which represents cash. All of these indexes would then be proportionately reflected in a benchmark that would serve as a measuring stick for performance purposes. As long as your investment objectives remained the same, this benchmark would be meaningful."

"Just to make sure that I understand this correctly, if my investment objectives change from growth to income, the portfolio manager would use a new benchmark that more accurately reflects a fixed-income portfolio?" Thomas asked.

"You've got it. This will allow you to measure how the portfolio manager is performing relative to the fixed-income markets," Jacob said.

"How often should we review our portfolio's performance?"

"You should review the portfolio once a year to make sure that you are on track. It's also important to evaluate whether your investment objectives have changed during the year because this will dictate whether or not the asset allocation of your portfolio needs to be modified."

"What about evaluating the performance of our portfolio manager?" Rachel asked.

"You should give your portfolio manager three years at the very least to demonstrate that he is capable of doing a good job. If you try to gauge his performance over a period shorter than this, you probably won't have the chance to evaluate the portfolio manager during varying market conditions."

"Are there any sort of guidelines that we should use in deciding whether the performance of our portfolio is adequate?" Thomas asked.

"There aren't really any strict guidelines. In a perfect world, the portfolio manager would outperform the benchmark on an ongoing basis. This is fairly difficult to achieve, so if long-term performance of your portfolio is within one or two percentage points of the benchmark, this should be reasonable for most investors. As with other professional relationships, some emphasis should be placed on the integrity and professionalism of the portfolio manager. If you've been working with someone who you trust implicitly, it shouldn't matter if he delivers a few periods of poor performance. This type of relationship is too hard to find and isn't worth ending it because of a few bad years," Jacob said.

"It's nice to hear you say that. We're more interested in working with individuals we can trust. As long as the advice and recommendations are made with our best interests in mind and the performance is competitive, we imagine that we'll work with our financial advisor for many years," Rachel said.

"Before we get ahead of ourselves, we still have to decide what type of investment professional should help you with the administration of your portfolio. After everything you've heard so far, do you think that you'd prefer one over the other?" Jacob asked.

"I'm not sure. Should we look at our portfolio statements?" Rachel asked, holding them out.

"That would be a good start. As you know, there are several factors that will dictate which type of investment manager is right for you," Jacob said, taking the statements from Rachel.

After quickly flipping through their statements, he immediately realized that they would benefit from the help of an investment manager.

"The first thing that I notice is that you have far too many mutual funds in your portfolio. This has probably hindered your performance in the long run. The second thing I notice is that you are almost entirely concentrated in just a few sectors. This suggests that you were probably chasing returns when these sectors were performing well," Jacob said.

"Tell me about it. I moved most of our money into these sectors at the worst possible time because they've dropped steadily since. I've had many sleepless nights after making that decision," Rachel admitted reluctantly.

"Chasing the flavour of the month is one of the most common mistakes a novice investor can make. Don't let it bother you too much. In terms of your account size, I think many portfolio managers would consider taking you on as a client. You should inquire about this before you schedule any interviews, however."

"What if we don't meet the minimum account size? Do we have any other options?" Thomas asked.

"The other option is to work with an experienced investment advisor. By experienced I'm talking about someone who has been advising clients for at least ten years."

"How will we know whether to use an investment advisor or a portfolio manager? What should we base our decision on?" Thomas asked.

"The decision will come down to what type of relationship you're more comfortable with. A few of the things that will influence your decision are your desired level of involvement in the investment decisions, how you'd prefer to compensate your investment manager and how accountable you'd like him to be in terms of your portfolio's performance."

"At this point, we're not sure of any of those things. Do we have to decide now?" Rachel asked.

"Of course not. What you should do is interview each of these professionals so that you gain a better understanding of the nature of their roles. They are different so it's important that you understand the pros and cons of working with either of these professionals."

"We'll do that. Speaking of the interview, does anyone mind if we talk a little bit about what to expect? I think the biggest hurdle for us is to know what questions to ask during this process. I don't even know where to begin," Rachel said.

"What's to mind?" Isabel asked. "We have nothing else to do this afternoon."

"Thank you. We appreciate it. Why don't I quickly clear the table and go get the dessert?"

While Rachel was inside, Patrick and Thomas went down to see how the kids were doing. He wanted to make sure they knew that the adults were keeping an eye on them in order to discourage them from getting into mischief.

After seeing that the kids were doing fine playing on their own, Patrick and Thomas headed back to the deck. As they sat down in their chairs, Rachel walked through the screen door holding her homemade chocolate soufflé in one hand and a container of French vanilla ice cream in the other.

"So where were we?" she asked, as she served dessert to her guests.

Key Point

The Financial Needs Pyramid consists of five levels:

I.   **Cash Management Stage**
II. **Savings & Loans Stage**
III. **Financial Planning Stage**
IV. **Wealth Accumulation Stage**
V. **Capital Preservation Stage**

|15|

Interviewing Financial Advisors

"Rachel, this soufflé is excellent," Patrick said, taking another bite.

"So what's next?" Thomas asked, eager to get back to the topic at hand.

"So far we've identified that you need to update your wills, take a close look at the taxes that you pay, develop a financial plan and implement a long-term investment strategy. This means that you'll have to hire an accountant, an estate lawyer, a financial planner, an investment advisor or an investment counsellor or portfolio manager. If you are interested in finding and working with the top professionals in each of these fields you'll have to interview several candidates for each position," Jacob said.

"That's a lot of interviews," Rachel sighed, "which is why we want to be well prepared before we meet with anyone."

"That's the right attitude to have," Megan said. "If you don't take this part of the process seriously, you can't expect to find someone to work with for the long term."

"Megan's right," Jacob agreed. "The fact that you want to be well prepared tells me that you are serious about finding the right professional. All we need to do now is take you through the interview process itself so that you'll know what to expect. Before we do this, we should talk about where you should start looking for suitable candidates to interview."

"That was my very next question," Thomas said. "Where do we find these people? Is it as easy as simply looking in the phone book?"

"That's one place to start looking, but probably not the best place to start. The first thing that you should decide is what type of financial institution you'd prefer to deal with. As you've now learned, financial companies can vary greatly in terms of size, reputation and the services they offer. Some people prefer working with companies that specialize in one area, while others prefer the convenience of one-stop shopping and the security of the largest banks."

"Is there a right or wrong answer?" Rachel asked.

"No, there isn't. It's really a matter of personal preference. There are a couple of things that you should look for before you hand over your money to any financial institution, however. The first is that the financial institution should offer some sort of investor account protection or deposit insurance. This type of protection is extremely important, because if the institution were to become insolvent, your assets would be protected up to the firm's stated limit," Jacob answered.

"Is the Canadian Investor Protection Fund (CIPF) an example of this type of protection?" Thomas asked.

"Yes. The coverage offered by the CIPF is limited to one million dollars per group of accounts and typically protects those investments held at investment dealers and wealth management firms."

"What if an investor has more than one million dollars?" Thomas asked. "Will they lose the rest?"

"It's highly unlikely because the limit applies to the shortfall in your account after a trustee in bankruptcy has returned all the customer assets that are available to be returned. In most cases the shortfall, if any, will be substantially less than the value of your account."

"And don't forget about the Canada Deposit Insurance Corporation (CDIC). The CDIC insures eligible deposits at member institutions, which includes most trust companies and banks, up to one hundred thousand dollars per depositor," Megan added.

"If a company doesn't have insurance, should we still consider investing our assets with that company?" Rachel asked.

"In my opinion, only if it is a well know and reputable company. If, for one reason or another, a firm without account protection becomes insolvent, you could lose any assets held by that company," Jacob said firmly.

"What's the other thing that we should look for before depositing our money at an investment management firm?" Thomas asked.

"The second thing is that you should focus on companies that offer non-proprietary investment products in addition to their own in-house products. It doesn't make sense to deal with a company that only allows its employees to sell its own products. You are short-changing yourself if you don't have access to all of the products available in the marketplace. Plus, if a company is only able to offer products from its own product line, there may be a conflict of interest in terms of the investments that the financial advisor recommends to you."

"Now that we know what to look for in a financial institution, how do we go about choosing one?" Thomas asked. "Does anyone have any suggestions?"

"Why don't you do what we did? We started by compiling a list of companies that included subsidiaries of our bank, firms we recognized by name and referrals from friends. We then called each company and asked them to mail out some information on the services that they offer, their insurance coverage, corporate history and so forth," Cindy suggested.

"We found that this was a good way to start because we could review the information at our leisure," Patrick added.

"That sounds good to me. On Monday I'll contact a wide range of financial institutions and ask them to send me some information," Thomas said. "Once I do that, then what?"

"The next step is compiling a list of financial advisors that you'd like to interview. This is an important step in the overall process because your list will dictate the calibre of the professionals you interview. What you want to do is compile a list of the best and brightest professionals in the industry. This will improve the likelihood of finding a highly skilled financial advisor," Jacob said.

"So how do we go about doing this?" Rachel asked.

"The first thing you need to do is compile a list of characteristics you'd like the financial advisor to have," Jacob instructed.

"What about integrity?" Thomas asked.

"That's a good example. You will also want to consider years of experience, professional designations, types of products that he or she can recommend and the individual's area of expertise," Jacob said, citing a few examples.

"As far as I'm concerned, all of those are very important to us. In regards to years of experience, is it unrealistic to only consider candidates who have at last ten years of experience under their belt?" Rachel asked.

"I don't think so. If a financial advisor has any less than this, it is unlikely that he has experienced a variety of market cycles. Focusing on those professionals that have at least ten years' experience is very reasonable. What about professional designations? Is it essential that the candidates have some sort of professional designation?" Jacob pressed.

"After learning about how much work it takes to earn the various designations, I think it says a lot about someone who has taken the time and energy to earn some letters behind his or her name. It's also reassuring because we know that the professional is required to earn continuing education credits to keep the designation. This will allow him to keep abreast of any changes or developments in the industry. This is important to us, so it should also be a requirement."

"What about the types of products the financial advisor can recommend? Don't forget what Jacob said earlier," Megan added.

"You said that it's important to deal with someone who is able to recommend non-proprietary products because this will help to avoid conflicts of interest. I think that we'd prefer dealing with someone who isn't pressured to sell his or her company's in-house products. I can see why this makes sense," Rachel said.

"What about area of expertise? Would you like to work with a generalist or a specialist?" Cindy asked.

"Although it would be much more convenient to work with one individual as opposed to a group of individuals, I think we'd prefer to work with several specialists as opposed to one generalist. I think our needs will be more adequately met if we have one individual focus on our wills, another on our financial planning needs and someone else on our investment management needs," Rachel said.

"That makes sense," Jacob said. "Is there anything else that you can think of?"

"What about the financial advisor's investment personality or portfolio management style? Isn't this something we should consider before we meet with anyone?" Thomas asked.

"Absolutely. Most people overlook this because it's not something that they tend to think of before entering into a relationship. If, for instance, you're interested in conservative long-term growth and end up working with a financial advisor who focuses on high-risk, short-term gains, you'll be disappointed with the results. This is why it's important that you decide on the type of investment personality that suits you and then interview various candidates."

"As far as I'm concerned, I think our objective is conservative long-term growth and eventually capital preservation," Rachel said.

"If you already have a general idea of what your investment objectives are, you're moving in the right direction. A good investment professional will assess your objectives before making any recommendations. This will be one of the first steps that you will take during the interview process," Megan said.

"Just to confirm the type of individual you'd like to interview, you've decided that candidates must have at least ten years of experience, a professional designation relevant to their area of expertise, are able to recommend non-propriety investment products, are specialized in one or two particular areas and have a conservative investment personality. Does that sound about right?" Jacob asked.

"That sounds right, but when you put it like that, it sounds like we're looking for the Super Advisor!" Rachel said. "Do advisors like this actually exist?"

"Of course they do," Jacob answered. "And now that you know what type of financial advisor you're looking for, you're one step closer to finding the right person for you."

"So where do we start looking?" Thomas asked.

"There are many options available to you. One of the best ways to start compiling your list is to ask co-workers, friends and family members for referrals. If they are extremely satisfied with the relationship they have with their financial advisor and the person meets all of your criteria, you should add the candidate to your list. It's important to remember that even though the referral was provided by someone you trust, it doesn't mean that the financial advisor is right for you. Your friend's investment profile may be completely different from yours, so it might not be a good fit."

"All of you seem to have good relationships with your financial advisors. If they meet our criteria, is it okay if we add them to our list?" Thomas asked.

"Of course," Megan said. "My investment advisor is an excellent candidate and has done a great job, as both of you know."

"Absolutely," Cindy said. "We'd be more than happy to give you our financial planner's name and phone number. One thing to keep in mind is that she focuses primarily on advising small business owners. She may, therefore, not be the perfect fit for you."

"We'd be glad to help out," Isabel said. "Our team of investment managers has been a blessing. I'd hate to imagine what would have happened if we'd left our finances in Jacob's hands," she said with a grin, nudging him.

"Well, I guess that's a start," Thomas said. "Where else can we find some names to add to our list?"

"Another good option is to ask other professionals, such as your bank manager, lawyer and accountant. These individuals usually work quite closely with the advisors of their clients so they are well positioned to recommend good potential candidates to you."

"Good idea. Anything else?"

"You can also contact the various industry associations that you learned about and ask them for a list of suitable candidates. They would be more than happy to refer you to their members. Don't forget that most of these financial advisors needed to earn a professional designation in order to earn membership in the association. They are also required to earn continuing education credits to maintain their membership. The quality of the candidates is, therefore, likely to be high."

"A less traditional method is to collect the names of financial advisors who are quoted in newspapers, magazines and books. Most of these financial advisors have a great deal of experience, which is why they are in high demand as sources of information on the latest trends in the financial services industry," Megan suggested.

"I would never have thought of that. That's also a good suggestion," Thomas said. "I always assumed that those advisors would be too busy to talk to us."

"Actually, they'd be quite flattered to hear from you," Jacob assured.

"As far as compiling our list, it looks as though we'll have no problem finding high-quality candidates. The only question is how many candidates do we add to our list?" Rachel asked.

"In order to ensure that you hire the best people, you'll want to interview at least two or three professionals for each position. This means that you'll need a list of eight to ten candidates," Patrick recommended.

"Once we have our list, what do we do next?" Thomas asked.

"The next step is to prescreen each individual on the list in order to make sure that the financial advisors have the qualifications that you are looking for. You should start by calling them directly and introducing yourself. You should also ask if they're accepting new clients, whether they have minimum requirements in terms of account size and if they would be willing to provide you with references," Megan said.

"Assuming they are taking new clients and that they are willing to provide us with references, is it okay just to come out and ask them about their qualifications?" Rachel asked.

"Without question. This really is the first step of the interview process. Simply ask them how many years of experience they have, whether they have a professional designation, whether they are able to recommend non-propriety investment products and how they would describe their investment personality. If you find advisors you'd like to interview, tell them that you would like to meet with them because you need some professional advice. You should also ask them to mail you any information that they think may be of interest to you. It's as simple as that," Jacob said.

"Quick and painless," Patrick added.

"That sounds easy enough. After we've done this with each candidate and we've compiled our list of interviewees, are we ready to set up meetings?" Thomas asked.

"Yes, you're finally there!" Megan said with excitement. "And this is the best part."

"After prescreening each candidate on the telephone, won't we know everything we need to know about the financial advisor?" Thomas asked.

"The prescreening process is the early stage of a long process. It's during the actual face-to-face meeting that you'll decide whether or not you'd be comfortable working closely with this person," Jacob said.

"You're talking about the trust factor, aren't you?"

"That's right. On paper, the financial advisor may have qualifications that readily surpass all of your expectations. If you don't trust him, however, the relationship will be short lived. The purpose of the interview is to help you decide whether or not you feel comfortable trusting this individual with the intimate details of your financial affairs."

"So, what should we ask during the interview?"

"A lot of it comes down to using common sense. With this said, there are a handful of questions that you'll need answered before you are in a position to decide whether or not you will be able to work with this person," Jacob said.

"Can you give me an example?" Thomas asked.

"A good way to start the interview is to ask the financial advisor what he thinks his clients would say about him. This is a nice way to break the ice and gives him the opportunity to tell you some things about himself. You'll want him to tell you about both his strengths and weaknesses. If he is comfortable talking about this, it suggests that he is confident and well rounded. It takes a certain type of individual to openly talk about their shortcomings with a stranger. If the financial advisor does this comfortably, it's usually a good sign."

"That sounds like a good way to start the interview. Do you have any other suggestions?" Thomas asked.

"You should also ask him how long, on average, he has worked with the majority of his clients. If he has been working with most of his clients for many years it demonstrates that he is good at nurturing long-term relationships," Patrick said.

"Another question to ask is whether he is willing to work together with other professionals, such as your lawyer and accountant, when required. This will tell you if he will consider your overall financial situation," Cindy added.

"You should also find out if he only gives advice or if he'll also help you to implement your plan," Jacob said. "This will lead to other questions regarding what services he offers, something which should be discussed in detail."

"You should also discuss how quickly he will return your calls, how often he will review the financial plan or portfolio and what products he is licensed to sell," Cindy said. "These are always good to address ahead of time so everyone's expectations are clear."

"Although it seems like a very blunt question, ask him whether or not he has ever faced any disciplinary proceedings while working in the financial services industry. This is a fair question to ask because this information is a matter of public record so there isn't a reason for him to hide it. If he has, you'll want to have him discuss the details openly with you."

"What about how he is compensated?" Rachel asked. "Is that polite to ask?"

"Considering that you're the one paying him, I think it's a pretty fair question," Jacob said. "You'll want to ask how he is paid and what his services cost."

"When you put it that way, it does seem like a fair question," Rachel answered.

"You should also ask him to describe his typical client in terms of age, net worth and investment objectives. This will tell you whether or not you fit the general profile of most of the people he works with," Megan suggested.

"Anything else you can think of?" Thomas pushed.

"Finally, it's very important that he discusses how he'll assess your risk tolerance, develop the financial plan or implement the investment strategy. This will give you a good idea of what to expect in terms of service and what to expect if you choose to have a second meeting," Jacob said.

"That seems like a pretty extensive set of questions. Do most financial advisors expect to be interviewed so thoroughly?" Rachel asked.

"Most top financial advisors wouldn't expect anything less because they understand better than anyone how hard people work for their money," Jacob replied.

"Although I now know what to ask during the interview process, how will I know if we are making the right decision when the time comes to choose someone?" Thomas asked nervously.

"The honest answer is that you won't know if you've made the right choice until after the fact. You have to give the relationship an opportunity to grow before you know if it's going to work," Megan said.

"I think I've asked this before, but isn't that risky considering we're talking about our financial assets?" Thomas replied.

"Again, you shouldn't associate qualified financial advisors with the potential for financial loss. It's unreasonable for you to think that a top financial advisor could make your situation worse, rather than better. The risk of not being prepared for unforeseen financial disasters is much greater than the risk of starting a new relationship with a skilled financial advisor," Megan answered.

"That's a good point. I'm actually much more comfortable with the thought of meeting potential candidates than I was even this morning," Thomas admitted.

"Can any of you think of anything else that we should talk about?" Rachel asked.

"Actually, I think we've done a pretty good job covering the interview process. You've learned where to find some candidates for your list, which questions to ask them and that your decision will be heavily based on your personal comfort level with that individual. As I said before, you just have to use your common sense," Jacob said.

"I guess that means that the next step is to compile our list. We'll start early this week when we're back in the city," Rachel said.

"Good job! There's no turning back now. You've already come so far," Cindy said.

"We couldn't have done it without your help. Again, we really appreciate it. If there's anything we can do to return the favour, just ask," Thomas offered.

"There is one thing you can do," Patrick replied.

"What's that?" Thomas asked curiously.

"How about taking Jacob and me fishing tomorrow morning to try to catch one of those monster lake trout you've told me so much about?"

"Not me!" Jacob quickly answered. "Leaving my warm bed at the crack of dawn is not how I like to start my morning. You can tell me all about it when you get back."

"I'll tell you what," Thomas started. "If you are willing to crawl out of your warm bed at five-thirty in the morning while it's still dark outside, I'd be more than happy to take you."

"After all the fish stories I've heard, I'd like to find out for myself whether any of those monstrous lake trout actually exist," Patrick challenged.

"It will be my pleasure. For the record, I'll be impressed if you actually make it out of bed at that hour," Thomas answered.

"I think you might be pleasantly surprised," Patrick said, winking at Jacob.

Key Point

As a consumer looking for financial advice, do not hesitate to set standards in regards to the minimum qualifications of potential candidates. This may include years of experience, area of expertise and holding professional designations.

|16|

Where To Turn

Although it was still dark outside, the possibility of catching a giant lake trout was too tempting for Thomas and Patrick to resist. Trying not to disturb anyone, they quietly crept out of their beds, collected their fishing gear and walked down to the dock using a flashlight to find their way.

"I can't remember the last time I was up this early," Patrick mumbled as he put his gear in the boat. "What am I getting myself into?"

"You'll be fine. Once we're out on the lake we'll have some coffee and you'll be ready to go," Thomas encouraged.

After they climbed into the boat and pushed themselves far enough away from the dock Thomas started the motor, breaking the silence around them. With no other noises, the Boston Whaler sounded like an offshore powerboat.

"If we didn't wake everyone up when we fumbled around the cottage, we probably have now," Patrick said loudly over the sound of the motor as they headed out to the open water.

Once the men were in the middle of the lake, Thomas turned off the motor and let the boat drift. He then poured two cups of coffee from the oversized thermos that he brought with him and passed one to Patrick who was sitting across from him.

They set up their fishing gear and settled in to wait for a bite, drinking coffee and listening to the silence of the lake.

"Can I ask you something?" Thomas asked after a few minutes.

"Sure."

"What happens if we hire a financial advisor who has all of the characteristics that we are looking for—integrity, honesty and professionalism—only later to find that this advisor has acted in an unprofessional manner? Can we file a complaint? Is there the possibility for restitution? This is still bothering me."

"Even though the financial services industry is heavily regulated, one area of concern is that consumers find it extremely confusing and intimidating when it comes to filing an official complaint," Patrick replied. "In many cases, consumers are so overwhelmed by the process that they often decide to overlook the problem rather than address it. The best place to start if you have a problem is with the financial institution itself because the problem is often solved without having to rely on outside sources."

"Let's assume that I have a problem with my financial advisor. Who do I talk to first?" Thomas asked.

"The first logical step is to talk directly to your financial advisor because it is likely that the problem is the result of poor communication or is simply an honest mistake. In most cases the problem will be addressed immediately and both parties will acknowledge that mistakes can happen."

"What if the financial advisor and I aren't able to solve the problem or if it's more serious in nature. Who would I contact then?"

"The next step would be to call the financial advisor's direct supervisor because he or she will be able to address your concerns and offer impartial advice in terms of solving the problem."

"Wouldn't the financial advisor's supervisor take the side of his employee?"

"That's a big misconception. In the securities industry, for example, branch managers have to take the Branch Managers Course (BMC), which teaches them how to supervise employees and client's accounts, identify money laundering techniques and suspicious activities, and deal with questions and concerns from clients. As a result of their training, they are well equipped to deal with complaints. More important, the branch manager is accountable for each and every employee under his or her supervision. As a result, he or she will want to ensure that all problems are properly addressed. It wouldn't be in the manager's best interests to allow a complaint to go unaddressed or take sides with an employee who has violated the rules and regulations."

"That makes a lot of sense. What happens in the event that I feel that it would be prudent to seek advice outside of the firm? Are there any steps that I can take?"

"The best place to start is with the Financial Services OmbudsNetwork (FSON). This centre is the best place to contact if you have a problem with any type of financial institution. The staff are extremely helpful and they will advise you on your specific situation or refer you to the appropriate agency. They are also a great resource in terms of the complaint process in general. They will answer any questions that you may have."

"Do the various financial sectors each have their own Ombudsman?"

"Yes, they do. If you are having problems with a bank, investment dealer or mutual fund company, you should contact the Ombudsman for Banking Services and Investments (OBSI). If the ombudsman feels that you have a legitimate complaint, an investigation may be conducted. If the outcome is in your favour then a non-binding recommendation of settlement will be issued. The financial services firm is not obligated to abide by the terms of the settlement, but in most cases, however, they do. If you have a problem with an individual that works specifically for a brokerage firm that is a member of the Investment Industry Regulatory Organization of Canada (IIROC), you should contact them directly. As you already know, the IIROC is the national self-regulatory organization and representative of the Canadian securities industry.

"Are there any other agencies that could help me if I have a problem with a bank, investment dealer or mutual fund company?"

"If you feel that a bank has violated your rights under the law then you should call the Financial Consumers Agency of Canada (FCAC). This is a federal regulatory agency that is responsible for enforcing many of the federal laws that protect consumers in their dealings with financial institutions. They also have a mandate to educate consumers of their rights.

"What about the insurance industry? Is there any particular agency that I can contact that can help me with insurance-related problems?"

"The Canadian Life and Health Insurance OmbudService (CLHIO) will assist you in any insurance-related complaints, including problems with specific insurance products. The CLHIO can also make non-binding recommendations. There is also the General Insurance OmbudService (GIO). They will help you with any complaints involving car, home and business insurance."

"The fact that there are agencies to help consumers deal with complaints is very reassuring," said Thomas. "I was always under the impression that, in the event of a dispute, it was essentially the client versus the financial institution. The thought of David and Goliath comes to mind. This obviously isn't true, which is good to know."

"The most important thing to remember is that mistakes do happen," Patrick continued. "When they do, you should always address the problem by discussing it with your financial advisor first. If you don't have the type of relationship where you can be completely honest then you probably won't be working with that financial advisor for very long. In an optimal working relationship, the advisor and client should be comfortable giving and receiving positive criticism."

"How long does it usually take to get to that stage in a relationship?" Thomas asked.

"That's a pretty difficult question because everyone is different. Some individuals can grow to trust someone very quickly while others take years. The rule of thumb is that you should usually give the relationship at least three years to develop once you decide to hire someone. This isn't to say that in three years you will trust this individual unconditionally; it's just that after three years, you should have a good idea if your working relationship is moving in the right direction. If, after a few years, you feel that the advisor doesn't have your best interests in mind then it's probably not going to work out in the long term. If you feel that the advisor has your best interests in mind, and demonstrates a high level of integrity, then you should continue working with that individual because these characteristics serve as an excellent foundation to build on. If you get to this point after a few years, then it's likely that you'll be working with that person until you're old and gray."

"I'd like nothing more than to find someone that we can trust implicitly to manage our financial affairs. I'd like to be in a position where neither of us has to worry about staying on top of everything. I have absolutely no interest in keeping abreast of the economy, changes in tax laws, financial and estate planning and so on," Thomas said.

"That's exactly how we felt," Patrick replied. "And don't worry, you'll find someone. There are a lot of skilled and experienced financial advisors who would enjoy working with you. You just have to take the time to find them."

Almost immediately after Patrick finished his sentence, the tip of his fishing rod started bouncing up and down. Without a moment's hesitation, Patrick jumped out of his seat and grabbed his fishing rod. He gave it a hard tug and felt his line release from the clip. As soon as he felt his line release he knew he had hooked a fish because he could feel it swim away from the boat, taking dozens of feet of fishing line with it. The reel clicked quickly as the line was being pulled out.

Judging by the bend in Patrick's fishing rod, Thomas knew that his friend would be pleasantly surprised, as long as the fish didn't get away.

"My wrists are getting sore," Patrick admitted as he struggled with his fishing rod. "This isn't as easy as I'd thought."

"That's normal. You didn't actually think the fish would just roll over, did you?"

"No, I guess not," Patrick responded, laughing, as he continued to reel the line.

After several long minutes, the men saw something break the surface about thirty feet behind the boat. Although it was starting to get light, they had difficulty seeing the fish.

"Did you see that?" Patrick shouted. "There it is," he said, pointing at the fish.

"Keep both hands on the rod! It's not over yet," Thomas warned.

As if hearing what Thomas said, the fish headed for the depths below. As instructed, Patrick let the fish take out some line, making sure that it didn't go slack. Once the fish stopped running, Patrick started slowly reeling in the line.

"This is getting a little easier," Patrick admitted.

"That means the fish is getting tired. Try bringing it in slowly to the side of the boat and I'll use the net to get it into the boat."

After a few minutes Patrick was able to reel the fish in to within ten feet of the boat. Once they caught a glimpse of the fish in the faint light, they couldn't believe its size.

"Incredible!" Thomas said. "That's at least a ten pounder. Try to maneuver the fish as close to the side of the boat as possible."

Patrick did exactly as he was told. The last thing that he wanted was to lose his trophy trout just seconds before he landed it. Once the fish was within reach, Thomas scooped it into the net while Patrick held his rod steady. In order to get it into the boat, Thomas had to use both hands.

"Look at the size of that fish! It's huge!" Patrick shouted.

Thomas picked up his needle-nose pliers and removed the lure from the fish's mouth carefully, so as not to injure it. After he took out the hook, he picked the fish up with both hands so Patrick could get a good look at it. Patrick glowed as he stared at the long, silver creature in front of him.

"I brought my digital camera. Would you like me to take a picture before we let him go?" Thomas asked.

"Let him go! What do you mean? Aren't we keeping it?" Patrick asked with disappointment.

"Do you really want this nice looking fish to land on your dinner plate knowing that you could set it free?"

"If you put it like that, I guess not. You better take a few pictures then. If we don't have any proof, our wives will never believe our story."

Thomas passed the fish over to Patrick and showed him how to hold it without injuring it. He then took a few quick pictures, put his camera down and carefully took the fish from his friend.

"In order to make sure the fish will survive, you need to hold it in the water with both hands while moving it back and forth. As the water passes through the gill slits it oxygenates the gills. Once the fish begins to struggle you can then release it, making sure that it swims out of sight," Thomas said, while moving the fish back and forth through the water. Suddenly, with a flick of its tail the fish slipped though Thomas's hands and quickly headed back to the depths where it came from.

"Do you always release the fish you catch?"

"Yes. It takes a lake trout about seven years to reach maturity. I prefer letting them go because it gives someone else the opportunity to catch them. The one you just caught weighed between ten and twelve pounds, which means that it's probably older than Ashley. Anyway, with three small kids in the house, I've really gotten used to eating fish sticks anyway."

"I know what you mean," Patrick agreed. "I know exactly what you mean."

Key Point

If a dispute arises, you should first speak with your financial advisor directly. In most cases, the problem is the result of a simple minor misunderstanding and will quickly be resolved. If your concerns are not addressed, you should then speak with your financial advisor's supervisor before bringing your problem to the attention of the various regulatory bodies.

|17|

Names, Names and More Names

Monday mornings were usually very hectic in the Connor household because everyone had to be out of the house by seven-thirty. Anna needed to be dropped off at daycare, Ashley and Hilary needed to be at day camp during the summer and the adults needed to be at work. On this particular morning, the kids were ready fifteen minutes early, which was a pleasant surprise.

It was shortly after eight-thirty when Thomas walked into his office. As soon as he saw the huge mound of papers scattered across his desk, he remembered why he had been looking forward to going to the cottage. In order to ensure that he had some time to compile his list of financial advisors, he blocked off an hour and a half in his daily calendar so his assistant knew that he was unavailable from noon until one-thirty. Instead of going out to eat, he would have lunch at his desk so he could start making the calls.

By nine-thirty the office was already buzzing with activity. Thomas liked when people were busy because it meant that business was good. Unlike many industries, software was extremely fickle—one moment you had a product that would revolutionize the world, the next it was yesterday's news. As a senior executive, Thomas wanted the company and its people to flourish.

"Good morning, Thomas," a deep voice bellowed from the doorway. It was the chief financial officer of the company.

"Hi Brad. How was your weekend?" Thomas asked.

"Good. How was yours?"

"We spent the weekend at the cottage with some friends."

"You definitely had the perfect weather for it. Do you have time to go for lunch this afternoon? I wanted to pick your brain on the quarterly projections."

"Actually, I've set aside some time during lunch to take care of some personal business. We're in the process of hiring a financial advisor and I was going to start compiling my list of candidates."

"No problem. How about tomorrow at noon?"

"Sounds good."

"Do you want some friendly advice?" Brad asked.

"Sure," Thomas said.

"When you talk to the candidates to set up an appointment, ask some questions to find out if they're what you're looking for. That will save you a lot of time going forward."

"What do you mean?" Thomas asked.

"When you're on the telephone with each financial advisor, ask questions so you can decide whether or not you'd like to meet them in person. We made the mistake of focusing on quantity rather than quality, which meant that we spent most of our time interviewing people who didn't meet our needs. At one point, we almost stopped interviewing altogether because it was so time consuming."

"Thanks for that. I'll let you know how it goes."

By lunchtime, Thomas was all set to start making his calls. He took the list out of his briefcase and stared at it in bewilderment. He had no clue where to start or what to say. Despite having discussed all of this in detail over the weekend, his mind was a complete blank. At the bottom of the list he noticed that Rachel had included the name of the branch manager of their local bank branch. His name was Peter Lane.

"I haven't spoken with Peter in a few months. He seems like a pretty good person to start with," he thought, as he dialed the number. The phone rang.

"Hi Peter. It's Thomas Connor. How are you doing?"

"Good, Thomas. What a pleasant surprise. We haven't seen you in the branch for quite some time. How are you doing?" he asked.

"Good."

"What about Rachel and the kids?" Peter asked.

"They're great."

"That's nice to hear. What can I do for you?" Peter asked.

"Well, we're in the process of hiring someone to help us with our financial planning and investment management needs. I was wondering if you had anyone at the branch we could talk to?"

"We don't currently have anyone at the branch who has their Certified Financial Planner (CFP) designation. The bank is, however, in the process of hiring financial planners across the country because it has realized that many of our clients are interested in the financial planning process. I do have a close friend that you could call. She has been a CFP for many years and has helped my wife and me with our own retirement planning. She actually just works around the corner from the branch. For investment management, I can refer you to an investment advisor at our wholly owned investment dealer. I've been sending him referrals for years. Both of them are extremely qualified and have my full endorsement."

"At this point, I'm just gathering names. I'm going to be calling everyone before we set up any face-to-face meetings," Thomas said politely.

"No problem. Do you have a pen?" Peter asked. "Their names are Katherine Green and Charles Kaplan."

Thomas wrote down the information as it was given to him. After he hung up the telephone he looked at the first two names on the list.

"That wasn't so bad," he thought. He then started to dial the phone number of the first professional association on his list.

"Thank you for calling Advocis," a pleasant voice answered. "How can I help you?"

"I'm looking for a financial advisor. Is there someone who is able to give me a few names of your members?"

"The easiest way to do this is to log onto our corporate website. We have a section that allows consumers to search our database for qualified insurance specialists and financial planners based on their own selection criteria."

"That sounds easy enough," Thomas said, expecting it to be more complicated. "Thanks for your help."

"You're welcome," the voice answered.

After Thomas hung up the phone, he logged onto the Internet and googled the Advocis web site. Once he was on their site, he found a tab labelled "Find an Advisor". He clicked on this tab, which then took him to a page that allowed him to fill in selection fields such as method of compensation, area of specialty and professional designation. Once he finished filling in his criteria, he clicked on the "Search" button, instructing the site to search its database. Within seconds, more than a dozen names were listed in front of him. "This is great," he thought.

He took the next few minutes to look at the credentials of each candidate. What he noticed was that they were all equally qualified in terms of their professional designations and expertise. They all just worked for different firms. Rather than simply picking three names at random, he referred to the list Rachel had given him. On it were several financial planning companies ranging from independently owned boutiques to large national institutions. He looked at the names of the financial planners on his computer screen and noticed that some of them worked for the companies on his list. He then picked one financial planner who worked for one of the largest financial institutions on his list, another from a medium-sized company and one other from a boutique firm. Their names were Adriana Crane, Carl Rossi and Donna Friedberg.

Now that he had the names of several financial planners, he needed to add the names of a few investment advisors. He started off by visiting the Canadian Securities Institute's website. Within a few minutes of surfing the site, he was directed to the Fellow of the Canadian Securities Institute (FCSI) directory, which listed everyone who held this designation. Although this information was valuable, the directory didn't list its members' titles or areas of expertise. In order to improve his chances of finding some suitable candidates, Thomas decided to take a more proactive approach. He bookmarked this page so he could return to it later. It would be a useful cross-referencing tool.

What he decided to do was call a few of the investment dealers on his list and ask to speak to the manager at the branch that was in or close to his neighbourhood. He would explain that he was interested in hiring an investment advisor and describe the skills and qualifications that he was looking for. With a little luck, the manager would be able to direct him to the right person based on this description.

The first call that he made was to one of the largest investment dealers in the country. There was a branch right in his neighbourhood. When he reached the receptionist at the main switchboard he politely asked for the name of the branch manager and asked her to patch him through.

"Hello, Allen Mercer speaking."

"Hello, Mr Mercer. My name is Thomas Connor. My wife and I are looking for an investment advisor. We're pretty new to this, so I was hoping that you'd be able to refer someone to me."

"It would be my pleasure. Can you give me a general description of your investment objectives? That will help me decide who might be a nice fit. As you may know, this can be important because different investment advisors have different investment styles."

"The most accurate way of describing our investment personality is conservative long-term growth. We're currently in the process of hiring a financial planner and, as soon as we have a financial plan prepared for us, we'd like to hire an investment advisor to manage our investments as outlined in this plan. We're not expecting to earn double-digit returns on a regular basis. We're simply looking for someone who can deliver consistent results in the context of the market."

"It's comforting to hear that you have realistic expectations. What about things like the investment advisor's personality, educational background and experience? Have you given this any thought?"

"Actually, we have. We'd like to work with someone who has at least ten years' experience, holds a professional designation that's related to investment management and is able to provide us with at least one or two references."

"Based on what you've said, one name immediately comes to mind," said Mr. Mercer. "His name is Ian Shaeffer. He joined us straight out of university a little over ten years ago and has been working for the firm ever since. In that time, he has earned the FMA and FCSI designations. He also comes very highly recommended by his clients, so he'll be comfortable with providing you with references."

"How would you describe him?" Thomas asked.

"Ian is very intelligent, energetic and outgoing. More important, he is very professional and conducts himself with a high level of integrity."

"He sounds like someone we'd like to interview. Would you mind giving me his phone number so that I can call him in the next few days to set up a meeting?"

"Certainly."

Thomas wrote the telephone number beside the notes he had taken during the conversation.

"And if it's okay with you, I'll let him know to expect your call," Mr Mercer said.

"That would be fine. I appreciate your taking the time to answer my questions so candidly."

"It was my pleasure. If you have any questions after you talk to Ian, please don't hesitate to call me. If there's anything I can do to make your decision somewhat easier, I'd be happy to help."

"I appreciate it. Thanks again for your time."

As soon as Thomas hung up the phone, it rang. He noticed on the display that it was his assistant and so he answered it.

"Hi. What's up?"

"Rachel is on the other line. Can I put her through?"

"Sure," he answered.

"Hi, honey. I just thought I'd see how your day is going?"

"So far, pretty good. It's funny that you called when you did. I've been busy collecting names of some financial advisors. It's less intimidating than I thought."

"That's nice to hear. Do you think you'll have your entire list done today?" she asked.

"Definitely. I don't think it will take much longer. All I have to do is contact a few more investment dealers and a handful of wealth management firms. Shouldn't be longer than an hour," he said.

"How many names will we have?"

"I think we'll have close to twelve names. I think it's better to have too many rather than too few. We need a diverse group to choose from. I'm going to take some time in the next few days to call each of the candidates directly so that I can screen them. We'll then interview those that are still on our list."

"Is there anything I can do to help?"

"I might need your help to screen some of the candidates. That could take a few hours."

"Just let me know when you need my help. I'll take some time tomorrow afternoon to make a few calls," Rachel offered.

"That would be great. I'd better get back to what I was doing. I'll see you at home."

"Okay. See you tonight."

Thomas turned his attention back to his list. When he saw that he had the names of only two investment advisors, he decided to contact a few more investment dealers from the list that his wife had given him. After speaking with a branch manager at each of these firms, he had two more names—Theo Mueller and Gabriel Woods. Now, all he had left to do was add the names of a few reputable investment counsellors and portfolio managers.

Based on what he had learned in the last few weeks, he knew that many of the wealth management firms had minimums in regards to asset size. He also knew that, depending on the firm, he might be put in touch with a relationship manager rather than the actual portfolio manager. This didn't bother him as long as the relationship manager was well informed on the day-to-day activities of the portfolio management team.

The first firm he called was a highly reputable investment counselling firm. After speaking with the receptionist, he was forwarded to Kim Lennox, an associate with the firm. Thomas introduced himself then started by asking about the firm's minimum account size in order to establish whether he and Rachel would be considered as potential clients.

"Before I get ahead of myself, does your firm have a minimum in regards to account size?"

"If you are interested in having your money managed on a segregated basis, you need at least one million dollars in investable family assets. With two hundred and fifty thousand dollars, you qualify for our pooled accounts. In certain situations, these minimums are flexible."

"What's the difference between having my money invested on a segregated basis and investing in pooled funds?" he asked, just to make sure he understood the difference.

"When you have your money managed on a segregated basis it means that the portfolio manager will use individual securities to construct your portfolio. This means that you'll see your treasury bills, bonds and stocks listed individually on your quarterly statement. With our pooled accounts, your money is still managed by one of our portfolio managers. The difference is that your money is 'pooled' together with that of other investors. This means that you'll see units of the individual pooled funds listed on your portfolio statement rather than individual securities. It also means that your contact at the firm will be with a relationship manager rather than the portfolio manger."

"You mentioned that these minimums are somewhat flexible. How flexible?"

"If, for example, your total investable assets fall somewhere between five hundred thousand and one million dollars, we will consider managing the portfolio on a segregated basis if you are in a financial position to add funds to your portfolio on a regular basis and if you demonstrate that you're committed to a long-term working relationship with the firm."

"Although we don't have the minimum account size, it sounds like we might be suitable candidates to have the minimum asset requirement waived. We are planning to invest a portion of our earnings on a regular basis and we are definitely interested in a long-term relationship. What about the investment process itself? Can we expect to receive an Investment Policy Statement?"

"The first step is to identify your investment objectives, investment horizon and risk tolerance. Once your investor profile has been established, we prepare an Investment Policy Statement for your review. If you are comfortable that the Investment Policy Statement accurately reflects your investment objectives, we then manage your portfolio on a discretionary basis in line with the Investment Policy Statement."

"That sounds like what we're looking for. Can you tell me about your firm's investment philosophy?"

"The best way to describe our philosophy is bottom-up value investing with a bias towards capital preservation. We like to reduce the risk in our portfolios by only investing in companies that have strong and proven fundamentals. This typically results in consistent, above-average, long-term performance."

"Can you do me a favour? Would you fax me the profiles of your portfolio managers? I'm assuming that you have some information regarding their years of experience, professional designations and areas of expertise. I'd also like some information on your long-term performance numbers. If you could include your business card, I'd appreciate it."

"Of course. What's your fax number?" she asked.

After Thomas gave Kim his fax number, he asked one final question.

"As someone who is in the process of hiring a discretionary portfolio manager, can you tell me why I should entrust your firm with my life savings over that of a competitor?"

"I'm glad that you asked because that's a very important question. One of our firm's greatest strengths is our ability to consistently earn above-average rates of return without assuming a great deal of risk. All of our portfolio management decisions are made with capital preservation in mind. Most of our clients are interested in earning predictable returns rather than striving for higher returns and seeing huge swings in the value of their investments. We will never be the top performing investment manager in any given year, but our clients will never experience significant losses either. The firm's reputation was built on this philosophy."

"I appreciate you taking the time to answer my questions."

"My pleasure. I'll fax you the information in the next few minutes. If you have any other questions, please call me directly."

"I appreciate it. Thanks."

Thomas hung up the phone and scribbled down a few notes so that he could refer to them later. After speaking with Kim, he realized that there were several things to consider when choosing an investment counsellor or portfolio manager. In order to make a sound decision, he'd discovered, you must consider the portfolio manager's investment management style, whether your investments will be managed in pooled funds or on a segregated basis and the manager's past performance. He would make sure to ask about these things in the future.

The next call he made was to one of the largest and most highly regarded financial institutions in the world. Although he hadn't had any business dealings with the company in the past, he knew that it was renowned for employing some of the top asset managers in the business. This fact alone made the telephone call worthwhile. After speaking with the receptionist at the head office he was forwarded to a vice-president in the wealth management department.

"Hello, Michael Baum's office," a soft voice answered.

"Hello, my name is Thomas Connor. I'd like to speak with someone regarding your portfolio management services."

"One moment please."

A few moments later Mr. Baum answered the phone. Thomas explained to him that he and his wife wanted to hire a team of investment professionals, starting with a financial planner. He then explained that once they had a financial plan in place, they were interested in having a portfolio manager manage their investments as outlined in the financial plan. The reason for his call was that he wanted to learn more about the firm's discretionary portfolio management services.

"Due to the size of our company, we're well equipped to meet the needs of a diverse group of consumers," Mr. Baum explained. "Depending on the size of your portfolio, you'll have one of three options. These include investing in our broad line of mutual funds, investing in our pooled accounts or having your assets managed on a segregated basis."

"These options seem to be common in the wealth management industry," Thomas observed.

"You're right, they are common. Most discretionary portfolio management firms offer similar services. The only difference is that they may have different minimum required asset levels for investing in their pooled funds and having your portfolio managed on a discretionary basis. Our minimums are somewhat higher than those of most of our competitors."

"How much higher?" Thomas asked.

"In order to have direct access to one of our portfolio managers we require you to have at least three million dollars in family assets. If you have less than this amount, you'll qualify for our pooled funds."

"That's quite a bit of money. Why is the minimum so high?"

"As a result of our dominant global position, we advise some of the wealthiest individuals and largest institutions in the world. As such, we find that it's necessary to maintain high minimum account sizes so that these clients have direct access to our portfolio managers. This doesn't mean that our clients with less than three million dollars in assets receive a lower level of service. Although they don't have direct access to our portfolio managers, they do benefit from their investment management skills through our pooled funds."

"What about the investment management process. Is it similar to that of your competitors?"

"Yes, it is. You'll find that all the top portfolio management firms will carefully walk you through a similar process. In almost every case, this process ends with you receiving an Investment Policy Statement. It's standard practice in the discretionary portfolio management industry."

"What about your investment philosophy?"

"Again, due to our size, we have hundreds of asset managers who work in offices around the world. With this many portfolio managers and investment counsellors it's difficult to adopt a single investment philosophy. Our pooled funds are managed by using the multi-manager approach. This means that the portfolios are managed by a number of portfolio managers, each with his or her own investment style. This gives the investor exposure to a diverse range of investment styles."

"Would you be able to provide me with your performance numbers?"

"The easiest way to look at our past performance is by visiting our website. All of our performance numbers for our portfolios are listed there. You'll also be able to see the holdings for each of our pooled funds. You'll see that our performance is very competitive across all asset classes."

"Can you quickly tell me some of your firm's strengths?"

"One of our strengths is that we have a truly global presence. By maintaining offices around the world, our portfolio management teams make investment decisions based on research that is prepared by analysts and economists working in the region that they are responsible for covering. This allows them to keep a pulse on the local economies, which translates into solid long-term returns. Another of our strengths is that we are one of the largest and most profitable financial institutions in the world. This gives our clients a high level of comfort because they know that their assets are very safe."

"I appreciate you taking the time to speak with me. You've been very helpful."

"It was my pleasure. If you have any questions, please don't hesitate to call me back. I hope that you'll consider working with us in the near future," Mr. Baum said.

"Thank you," Thomas said. "I look forward to speaking with you again."

His list now stood at nine names—four financial planners, three investment advisors and two discretionary investment managers. This didn't include the name of Cindy and Patrick's financial planner, Megan's investment advisor or Isabel and Jacob's portfolio manager. In terms of diversity, he was content with the names he had because they included people who worked for companies ranging from small, independently owned boutiques to large global financial institutions. As a result of this diversity, Thomas was confident that he had the names of some very good candidates. He looked at his watch and realized that it had taken him almost two hours to compile his list of names. Although it wasn't as intimidating as he originally thought, he was relieved that this task was behind him. He couldn't wait to tell Rachel tonight.

~

That night, after the girls were in bed, Thomas and Rachel sat down with glasses of wine in the living room. It was nice to be able to relax together at the end of the day. Thomas reached for his briefcase and pulled out the list of advisors he'd compiled.

"Look what I managed to accomplish this afternoon," he said waving the list with a flourish.

"That's great, honey! Look at all of those names," Rachel replied enthusiastically, taking the paper from her husband. "How long did it end up taking?"

"It took me a little under two hours. It didn't seem that long though."

"What's the strategy now?"

"I think we should first focus on hiring a financial planner. Once we've hired a financial planner and have started that process, we'll then turn our attention to interviewing and hiring an investment advisor or portfolio manager. It makes more sense to meet with these people once we have a clear picture of our situation."

"Good plan. Would you like me to be responsible for calling the financial planners? I could set aside some time tomorrow."

"That would be great."

"So how should I go about calling everyone?"

"As I mentioned, Brad gave me some good advice this morning. He said that we should make sure that we check everyone out over the phone so we don't spend time interviewing candidates who aren't a good fit from the beginning."

"So what you're saying is that we should be thorough?"

"That's a good way of describing it. We have a pretty good idea of what we're looking for, so it shouldn't be too difficult. Like you said, we just have to be thorough."

"What kind of questions should we ask? It's seems important that we're able to make a final decision based on the same set of criteria."

"That's a good point. Just so you know, I've only included the names of people with the years of experience, educational background and professional designations we want in an advisor. What we're trying to establish during the initial phone call is whether the financial advisor specializes in any one area, whether our investor profile is typical of the advisor's clients, and what we can expect in terms of the financial planning process. If, for example, you call a financial advisor and he tells you that he specializes in trading commodities, his typical client is a sixty-five-year-old high–net worth male, and that he isn't familiar with the investment management process other than filling out the new account forms, we'll know it won't be a good fit."

"What if the financial advisor has all the skills that we're looking for but I feel that there might be a personality conflict based on our conversation on the phone? Do we still meet with him or her?" Rachel asked.

"My instinct tells me we should. For all we know, he or she might be having a bad day or we might have caught him or her at a bad time. Although our final decision will be heavily based on how well we think we'll get along with the individual, I think that it's important to give each qualified candidate the opportunity to present themselves in person."

"Okay. Everyone can have a bad day. I'm going to set aside some time at work tomorrow to start working my way through the list. I should have no problem calling everyone."

"Sounds good to me," Thomas replied.

For the rest of the evening, they watched a DVD that Thomas had rented on his way home from work. As soon as it ended shortly after ten, they headed upstairs and went to bed. Tomorrow would prove to be an interesting day.

Key Point

Take detailed notes of the conversations that you have with the various financial professionals. This information will be extremely useful later on in the process.

|18|

The First Call

After a very busy morning that included a conference call, several meetings and an important presentation, the last thing Rachel felt like doing was calling the names on her list. Still, she knew that it had to be done, so she went to her office, sat down at her desk and pulled the list from her bag.

The first financial planner on her list was Katherine Green, the one referred by their bank manager. Rachel dialed her number.

"Hello, Katherine speaking," she answered.

"Hi Katherine. My name is Rachel Connor. Peter Lane suggested that I call you. We're looking for a financial planner because we don't know which way is up in regards to our finances. We're looking for someone with at least ten years' experience and a professional designation related to their particular field who can also give us a few references. I know that you have each of the requirements that we're looking for, but I have a few more questions for you if you have a few minutes."

"Sure. What would you like to know?" Katherine asked.

"Can you tell me a little bit about the financial planning process? I know very little about the process itself."

"It's nice to hear to you referring to financial planning as a process. You'd be surprised at how many consumers and professionals actually skip or gloss over the process. In order to develop a sound financial plan, there are six steps that you need to take. The first step is where the three of us sit down and define the client-planner relationship. This step is important because it lets everyone put their cards on the table—we establish what services I will offer, what it will cost and how decisions will be made."

"That seems logical."

"The second step consists entirely of data gathering. This is where you collect all of your banking and insurance statements, T-4 slips, portfolio statements and anything else I might need to see. We'll also discuss your financial goals in detail."

"We already have everything in one folder, which will make this step a little easier."

"Great! The third step is where I analyze and evaluate your financial status. It's during this step that I do most of the work."

"I like the sound of that," Rachel said.

"The forth step is where I develop and present my financial planning recommendations based on everything we discussed. This is a very important part of the process because it's at this point that I address all of your financial objectives and make recommendations that will address these."

"Is this where we receive a hard copy of the financial plan itself and review it with you?"

"Yes, it is. And this brings us to the fifth step. This is where I actually implement the financial plan. This usually means that I'll refer you to other professionals as needed."

"I'm assuming that this can include accountants, estate lawyers, insurance professionals, investment advisors or portfolio managers?"

"That's right. The sixth and final step in the process is ongoing because this is where we monitor your progress to make sure things are going smoothly. Typically we would do this at least every eighteen months."

"The process sounds very thorough, to say the least. What about your typical client?"

"Most of my clients are under the age of forty-five. Although it's never too late to do some financial planning, once an individual has been in the workforce for more than fifteen years, it's rare for him or her to go through the entire process. Can I ask you a question?"

"Sure," Rachel replied.

"What are you hoping to get out of this process? And why now?"

"For the last few months, I've been somewhat anxious about our financial well-being. I am responsible for all of our household finances and I don't really know if we're on the right track. By taking the appropriate measures, we're hoping to sleep better at night knowing that everything is being well looked after."

"If at some point you'd like to meet in the future, please don't hesitate to call me," Katherine offered.

"Actually, I'd rather not put it off longer than I have to. If you're available this week, it would be nice if my husband and I could come by and meet with you in person."

"What day is best? If it's more convenient for you to meet on the weekend, I'm here next Saturday morning."

"Saturday would be perfect. How about ten o'clock?"

"That sounds good. I'll see you then."

"Would you like us to bring anything?" Rachel asked.

"For the first meeting, just bring yourselves. All we'll be doing is talking."

"Great. I'll see you Saturday morning."

After Rachel hung up the telephone she opened her Daytimer and made a note of their appointment with Katherine. And with that, the first meeting was booked.

The next name on the list was Adriana Crane. She also held her CFP designation and worked for a large financial services company.

"Hello, Adriana Crane's office," a female voice answered.

"Hello, my name is Rachel Connor. My husband and I are looking for a financial planner. I was hoping to speak with Adriana so I could ask her a few questions. Is she available by any chance?"

"One moment please," the voice said.

A few moments later Adriana answered the phone.

"Hello, Adriana speaking."

"Hi Adriana. My husband and I want to find a financial planner. We found your details on the website of one the professional associations of which you are a member, and I thought I'd call to find out if you're taking on any new clients."

"Yes, I am taking new clients. I appreciate you contacting me," Adriana replied.

"Do you mind if I ask you a few questions?" Rachel asked.

"Not at all."

"What can we expect in terms of the financial planning process and your ongoing services?"

"The first thing I'll need from you is a copy of all of your latest portfolio statements. Once I've had a chance to look over your statements, I'll ask you a couple of questions that will help me identify your investment objectives and risk tolerance. Once I have this information, I can then recommend a mix of mutual funds based on your answers that you provided in the questionnaire."

"What about the actual financial planning process itself? Will you be walking us through the six steps? I'm under the impression that the financial planning process is quite rigorous, which is why we need a financial planner in the first place," Rachel said, a little confused.

"Some financial planners will take you through a lot of unnecessary steps. For the most part, I find this process somewhat time-consuming with little benefit. Most of my clients are happy with simply answering a few questions and then investing in our mutual funds."

"Can you recommend any products other than your company's own mutual funds?"

"I can recommend other investment products, but I usually stick to our own line of mutual funds because I'm very familiar with them. I've been recommending them for more than ten years."

"Thank you," said Rachel, realizing that this woman probably wouldn't be right for her. "I appreciate you taking the time to talk to me. If I have any additional questions, I'll give you a call."

"Should I expect to receive copies of your statements?" Adriana asked.

"Actually, we're just in the process of collecting information. If we decide to pursue things further, I'll call and get your fax number. Thanks again."

"You're welcome. Thanks for calling."

Despite the fact that Adriana had her CFP designation and similar work experience to Katherine's, she seemed to offer very little in terms of financial planning. Although Rachel knew that the financial planning industry was highly fragmented, she never expected to find such a discrepancy in the level of service provided by two similar financial planners. If she hadn't taken the time to learn about the profession, she probably wouldn't know the difference between simply answering a few questions and actually taking the time to walk through the financial planning process itself. Rachel was starting to feel as if all the research that she and Thomas had done was really worth the effort.

The third name on the list was Carl Rossi. He also worked for a non-bank-owned firm that was similar in size and reputation to the one that she had just called. Based on the last telephone conversation, Rachel didn't know what to expect and was hoping that the result would be a little more promising.

The telephone conversation with Carl immediately restored her confidence in the calibre of the candidates on her list. From the beginning, Carl talked about the importance of each of the six steps involved in the financial planning process. What impressed her most was that Carl didn't ask to see her statements or how much money they had to invest. His only concern was making sure that Rachel truly understood what financial planning meant and how much work it entailed. By the end of the twenty-minute conversation it was apparent that Carl had no intention of flogging mutual funds or other investment products. The only service he was interested in providing was financial planning and the advice that accompanied it. He was a financial planner in every sense of the word. Rachel looked forward to meeting with him in person and booked an appointment for early Saturday afternoon.

The final call was to Donna Friedberg. Donna was a chartered accountant (CA) and held her RFP designation. She worked at an independent firm that she had established with two other partners. Unlike the other institutions that Rachel had called, Donna wasn't able to recommend investment or insurance products because her firm's sole focus was on accounting and fee-based financial planning. As such, she relied heavily on the services of outside professionals whenever insurance, investment products or legal advice was needed. Rachel was intrigued by the fact that this alleviated any conflicts of interest.

Again, the telephone conversation went extremely well. Donna certainly seemed knowledgeable about the financial planning process because she had been doing it for more than fifteen years. Most of her clients were in their late thirties to mid-forties. Donna, like Carl, stressed that the financial planning process was rigorous and time-consuming. The fact that she was honest and forthright impressed Rachel. During the conversation there was no doubt that Donna might be a good fit, so Rachel scheduled a meeting for the following Monday evening.

Now that she had finished calling everyone, it became apparent to her how busy they would be over the next several weeks. Needless to say, the kids would be spending a lot of time with Grandma and Grandpa. Hopefully they wouldn't eat too many of Grandma's special pickle sandwiches. Then again, pickles never really hurt anyone.

Key Point

Do not hesitate to ask financial professionals a wide variety of questions. Some of these questions may be in regards to experience, educational background and compensation. It is extremely important that all of your questions are answered in a forthright manner.

| 19 |

Interviewing Financial Planners

When Thomas arrived at home he was pleasantly surprised to find Rachel and her parents playing with the girls in the backyard. Dexter was in his usual spot underneath the tree in the back corner taking a nap.

"What a nice surprise! How come you're home so early?" he asked Rachel, who was chasing Ashley around the garden.

"I decided late this afternoon that it would be good to get home at a reasonable hour to see the kids," she answered. "I also thought it would be nice to have Mom and Dad over for dinner," she added, trying to catch her breath.

"How are you doing, John?" Thomas asked his father-in-law who was sitting quietly in a chair in the shade.

"I'm fine. How's work going?"

"It's going well," Thomas replied. "And if you're asking if the technology trend has passed, it hasn't. We're still in business."

"It's just a matter of time," John replied, laughing. "It's just a matter of time. Computers will go the way of the dodo bird."

One of John's favourite pastimes was giving his son-in-law a hard time about anything and everything. Thomas's work was one of his favourite targets because he knew that Thomas took it very seriously. Although John knew that computers weren't actually just a passing trend, he liked to pretend they were. This drove Thomas batty because he was never quite sure if John was kidding.

"Quit teasing him," his wife Lisa said, giving John a little nudge.

Lisa adored her son-in-law and always stuck up for him.

"Thank you, Grandma. It's nice to know someone is watching my back," Thomas said, winking at Ashley who had come over to give her father a hug.

"Rachel told us about all the meetings you have in the next couple of weeks. It sure sounds like you have your work cut out for you," Lisa said.

"We do, but I'm actually looking forward to it. They all had interesting things to say on the phone."

"When's your first meeting?" John asked.

"The first one is scheduled for Saturday morning. We're meeting with all the financial planners first, after which we'll meet with investment advisors, investment counsellors and portfolio managers."

"Let us know if you meet some decent people. If it goes well, we may just have someone look at our finances as well," John said.

"That's not a bad idea," Thomas responded. "I'll let you know how it goes on Saturday."

~

Saturday morning, after the kids were dressed and had eaten some breakfast, Rachel collected all the materials that she thought they might need for the interviews. These included the notes that they had taken on each financial advisor, information on the financial firms they worked for, a list of the questions that they were going to ask and their scrapbook. Although it seemed like a lot to carry, she felt that they'd be better off to be overprepared rather than underprepared. Thomas couldn't agree more.

As soon as John and Lisa arrived to take care of the girls, Thomas and Rachel were out the door. Their first meeting was with Katherine Green, who worked around the corner from their local bank branch. Although they hadn't met Katherine before, they were relieved that their very first interview was with someone who was referred to them by someone they knew very well. It was a nice way to start the interview process.

They arrived at Katherine's office shortly before ten o'clock. Rachel always insisted on being early because she thought it was rude to be late.

Katherine was a short woman in her early to mid forties. She was dressed in a smart black business suit, and her dark blonde hair was pulled back from her face in a loose ponytail. This made her warm smile even more noticeable.

"It's nice to put a face to the name," Rachel said, shaking her hand.

"It's a pleasure meeting you. Please have a seat," she said, motioning to the two chairs. Rachel and Thomas sat down.

"Peter Lane mentioned to me that you helped him and his wife with their own retirement planning," Thomas said.

"That's right. I've known Peter for a long time, and we've been referring our clients to one another for many years."

"The reason that we are here is that we recently decided that we needed to put our finances in order with the help of a financial planner," Rachel admitted.

"It's never too late," Katherine encouraged. "You'll be glad you did. Why don't I start by answering any questions that you may have? If you're new to the financial planning process I'm sure there's a lot you'd like to know."

"Do you mind if we take notes while we talk? It'll give us something to refer to afterwards," Rachel asked.

"Of course not," Katherine answered.

"Why don't you start by telling us a little bit about yourself?" Thomas asked.

"I grew up in Barrie and have a BA in history from Trent University. After earning my degree, I applied for a variety of jobs in the financial services industry because it seemed like a challenging, fast-paced environment. I was eventually hired as a customer service representative at a large mutual fund company. It was during this time that I successfully completed my CFP designation. About a year later, I started a new job as an associate to a senior financial planner at a large, well-known financial planning firm. This eventually led to my current position as a financial planner. I'm married and I have two boys, aged four and six."

"We have three girls," Thomas said with a smile. "It's comforting to know that you have so much experience working in the financial services sector. How much actual financial planning experience do you have?"

"I have almost ten years of practical financial planning experience. During my time as an associate to the senior financial planner I was exposed to every facet of the financial planning process in an environment that was very conducive to learning. I refer to this process as my apprenticeship with one of the best in the industry. When I eventually made the difficult decision to move on, I was more than adequately prepared."

"What made you decide to move on?" Rachel asked curiously.

"I eventually realized that if I wanted to be responsible for my own clients I would have to get out on my own. If I were still working for the same financial planner today, I think I would always have felt like an apprentice regardless of how much responsibility I was given. Although it was a difficult decision, it was the right one."

"If I met one of your clients and told them that I was considering working with you, what do you think they would say about you?" Rachel continued.

"I hope most of my clients would say I'm honest, kind, considerate and reliable. The less obvious descriptions would be disciplined and stern."

"Can you elaborate on the less obvious ones? Although we've only just met, you certainly don't come across as being stern," Thomas said.

"The reason that some of my clients would describe me as disciplined and stern probably stems from the fact that I take my job very seriously. When it comes down to it, most people would rather devote time to pursuits other than financial planning. In many cases, individuals will walk through the entire financial planning process only to abandon it just as they're close to finishing it. In these instances I'll push people to finish the process. This is when my stern and demanding side comes out."

"I'm sure that your clients appreciate it. Do people quit in the middle of the process quite often?" Rachel asked.

"More than you can imagine," Katherine responded with a sigh.

"What can we expect from you in terms of service?"

"As far as the planning process goes, you can expect me to thoroughly take you through each of the six steps in the financial planning process. This entails a great deal of work on your part. At the end of this process I will present you with a detailed financial plan that addresses all of your needs. At that point we'll then focus on implementing the financial plan. This may involve me making investment recommendations as outlined in the plan or bringing in one or more other professionals to help us do this properly. It really all depends on the complexity of your specific situation. Once everything is in place, we'll periodically review your situation to make sure it hasn't changed."

"What can we expect in terms of contact? Can we expect you to call us on a regular basis?" Rachel asked.

"That depends on you. If you'd like me to call at regular intervals, I can call as often as you'd like. It's much more important to schedule meetings on a regular basis so we can review your situation and make changes as needed."

"You've touched upon my next question. If we decide that we'd like to bring in other professionals to help us implement certain areas of the plan, is that all right?"

"I would be more than happy to work with people that you bring into the relationship, providing that they are reliable and professional. How does that sound?"

"That sounds fair and also brings me to my next question. How are you paid? We've read a lot about the various compensation methods in the financial services industry and it's a little confusing," Thomas admitted.

"That's probably the one question that most people are afraid to ask. As far as my compensation is concerned, I am paid a percentage of any fees that you pay from the financial planning process itself and the investment products that you buy."

"Isn't there some pressure for you to recommend your company's proprietary products?" Thomas asked.

"Not at all. I am able to recommend almost any product available in the marketplace. There is no pressure on me to push our company's products. This doesn't mean that I'll never recommend our own products, however. I will only do so if there isn't anything more suitable available to you. Does this make sense?" Katherine asked.

"That's an honest answer; we appreciate that," Rachel said.

"It always pays to be upfront," Katherine said.

For the next thirty minutes Rachel and Thomas asked a wide range of questions, all of which Katherine answered in a straightforward manner. The conversation then turned to more personal matters when they found out that Katherine's parents had a cottage on a lake near theirs. As they were leaving, Rachel told Katherine that they were meeting two other financial planners in order to explore all of their options. Katherine responded by telling them that this was prudent and that their final decision shouldn't be taken lightly. She then thanked them for giving her the opportunity to meet with them and told them that if they thought of any other questions, they should contact her at their earliest convenience. Before they left, she handed them a business card and shook hands with each of them. They now had their first interview under their belts.

After grabbing a quick bite to eat at the local deli, Thomas and Rachel were ready for their meeting with Carl Rossi. Carl's office was located in a modern low-rise building just outside of the downtown financial core. When they arrived at the office, Carl greeted them a few moments after they walked into the lobby. Judging by the slight shades of gray in his hair, he looked to be in his mid to late forties. Although it was Saturday, he was nicely dressed in a dark blue suit, white shirt and patterned blue tie.

"Hello, you must be Rachel and Thomas. It's a pleasure to meet you," he said with a smile.

"Hi Carl. I'm Rachel. We spoke on the phone. This is my husband, Thomas," she said, shaking his hand.

"Why don't we go into my office so we can get started," he said, motioning them down a long hallway.

Once they were in Carl's office they sat down and got comfortable. Rachel pulled out her scrapbook as if it were routine.

"Do you mind if we take notes?" she asked politely. "It will give us something to refer to later."

"Of course not," Carl answered.

Carl's list of credentials was as impressive as his professional demeanour. He had grown up and attended university on the west coast. When he decided that he wanted to pursue a career in financial planning, he completed his CFP designation immediately after earning his bachelor of commerce degree. After he earned his designation, he moved east and started working as an associate financial planner. When he had gained several years of practical experience, he then became responsible for advising and attracting his own clients, and had been doing so for almost fifteen years.

"Carl, when we spoke on the phone, you talked a lot about the importance about the financial planning process itself. Can you elaborate a little on this?"

"There is a lot of confusion about what qualifies as 'financial planning'," said Carl. "For some individuals, financial planning simply means balancing their chequebook. For others, it means investing their money in mutual funds, stocks or bonds. Although financial planning will often encompass these things, a true financial plan addresses all of your financial needs. These can include your cash management needs, investment needs, estate planning needs, retirement needs and so forth. Typically, there are six steps that need to be taken to address all of these needs properly. If you don't take each of these steps, you probably won't have addressed all of your financial needs. This is why most individuals need the help of a professional."

"Where do you fit into the process? Specifically, what can we expect from you?" Thomas asked.

"Simply put, my job is to walk you through the six steps and make sure that all of your needs are addressed. At the end of the process, you can expect to receive a detailed hard copy of a financial plan. Once you receive this, we will then need to implement the plan. This is usually done under my direct supervision with the help of other members of my team."

"That brings me to my next question. Will you work with outside people?" Thomas asked.

"I don't usually use outside help," Carl said. "Within my team I have an investment specialist who is licensed to sell mutual funds and life insurance. He can use our own in-house products or those products offered by our competitors. As far as your estate planning and tax needs are concerned, I've been working with the same two individuals for over ten years."

"Would you be willing to consider using outside help? We're interested in using different people for our financial planning and investment management needs in order to avoid any conflicts of interest that may exist if we rely solely on one individual or a related team of individuals."

"Although that is a legitimate concern, I can assure you that it wouldn't be an issue. The reason why I use the same group is that clients seem to prefer the convenience of one-stop shopping. Also, I've found really good people in whom I have a great deal of confidence. To answer your question, however, I would be willing to work with outside professionals if that's what you preferred. My first and foremost interest is to be given the opportunity to address your financial planning needs. If you decide that you'd like to use outside help to implement the plan, you're welcome to do so."

"In this type of situation, how would you be compensated?" Rachel asked.

"I'm compensated by both fees and commissions depending on my role. In terms of preparing the financial plan, you'll be charged a flat fee based on the complexity of the plan. If you decide that you want to use our services for the investment management process of the plan, you'll pay commissions based on the investments we choose."

"What about for our estate planning needs?"

"If your situation calls for the services of a lawyer or an accountant, you'll pay hourly fees to these individuals. With that said, an estimate of all of the fees will be disclosed to you before we prepare or implement any part of the plan," Carl said.

"Do you specialize in any one particular area?" Rachel asked.

"My focus is on general financial planning. My typical clients tend to be individuals and couples in their early thirties to mid-forties with typical to moderately complex financial needs."

"Would you be able to provide us with references?" Thomas asked.

"Certainly. When you're interested in contacting one or two references let me know. At that point you should give me a profile of an individual or couple you'd like to speak with. I'll give you a list of names, any of which you are welcome to contact," Carl offered.

"If we were to talk to one of your clients who had some constructive criticism about you, what do you think he or she would say?" Thomas asked, catching Carl a little off guard.

"That's a good question. In all my years as a financial planner, I've never been asked that! I think that one criticism would be that it sometimes takes me too long to return telephone calls. In the last several years my practice has grown enormously, so I'm very busy servicing my existing clients and meeting new ones. I'm in the process of hiring additional support staff in order to free up more time in my schedule."

"How many clients do you currently have?" Thomas asked.

"I currently work with nearly five hundred individuals and families."

"Given your busy schedule, what can we expect in terms of contact initiated by you?" Rachel asked.

"You can expect a call from me or someone on my team at least every six months. I also feel that it's important to meet in person every eighteen to twenty-four months in order to make sure that your financial needs haven't changed."

For the next forty minutes, Thomas and Rachel continued to ask a barrage of questions. By the end of the meeting, it was obvious that Carl had a great deal of financial planning expertise, a very successful practice and was extremely professional. The one concern that they had was that Carl seemed to have a lot on his plate. He acknowledged this by admitting that, on occasion, he wasn't always able to return phone calls promptly. In his defence, however, he did say that he was in the process of hiring additional staff. This would likely make a positive difference.

Another concern was that Carl relied on the members in his team to implement financial plans, rather than using the help of outside professionals. Although this would make it easier from a one-stop shopping perspective, they had made the decision from the beginning to work with several different individuals who were the top in their respective fields. By using several unrelated professionals to implement the different components of the financial plan, a system of checks and balances would be in place, which would likely lower the chances of receiving advice that was less than impartial.

Despite these two concerns, Carl had demonstrated that he was very astute in regards to financial planning. His expertise and knowledge of the profession outweighed each of these concerns. He also seemed to use a very structured and organized approach to evaluating and addressing his client's needs. This gave Rachel and Thomas the impression that the process would be a relatively smooth one from beginning to end. With two interviews now completed, they were more than ready for their third meeting on Monday evening.

~

Donna Friedberg's office was located in the north end of the city. When they drove past the address Rachel had written in her book, they thought they had the wrong place because it looked more like a beautiful house than an office building. After parking the car in the street, they walked up to the front door where they saw a small plaque that read Friedberg & Partners Ltd. They pushed the heavy wooden door open to find a reception area with two couches, several chairs and a table with a telephone on it. Beside the phone was a list with the extensions of a dozen or so employees listed in alphabetical order. They dialled Donna's extension, and she answered the phone immediately.

"Hi Donna. It's Rachel and Thomas Connor," Rachel said, introducing herself.

"Hi Rachel. I've been expecting you. I'll be down in a second."

A few minutes later, a woman who looked to be in her fifties came down the stairs. She was dressed in a dark green suit, wore glasses and had a gentle manner. Her wavy, gray hair hung loosely to her shoulders.

"Hi, I'm Donna," she said, offering her hand. "You must be Rachel. And you must be Thomas," she said. "Thank you for coming."

"It's our pleasure. Thank you for seeing us," Rachel said.

Donna took them up the stairs and down a hallway that was beautifully decorated with modern art. The hardwood floor was partially covered by a long, narrow Persian rug that ran past each office right down to the end of the hall. When they came to the last door at the end of the hall, everyone walked in and took a seat.

From the beginning of the conversation, it was evident that Donna was very passionate about her profession. It was this passion that had led her to earn her RFP designation at a very early stage in her career. What was even more impressive was her unassuming demeanour. She was very easy to talk to.

After asking her many of the same questions they had asked the other two candidates, they were pleased to learn that Donna had been a chartered accountant and financial planner for more than fifteen years. After spending almost ten years with an accounting firm, she had decided to start her own company along with two of her former colleagues.

In terms of the services that she offered, she strictly focused on accounting and financial planning. She didn't provide investment advice, estate planning or sell insurance or any other investment products. All this was done with the help of other qualified professionals that were either referred by her or hired by the client.

"Being a CA, how did you get into financial planning?" Rachel asked.

"After working as an accountant for a few years, I found that many of my clients were asking me about financial planning. I was getting so many questions that I decided to earn my RFP designation so that I would be qualified to advise them properly. Also, accounting and financial planning seem to go hand in hand."

"If you don't sell the investment products, how do you make money?" Rachel asked.

"My income comes entirely from accounting and financial planning. I am paid a fixed hourly rate, the same as a lawyer is. This means that the more complex your situation, the more it will cost. I should warn you that my services don't come cheap. It seems that many people are under the impression that a detailed financial plan should cost no more than a few hundred dollars. This isn't the case, however."

"How do we know if we can afford your services? I mean, you could charge us anything you wanted to," Thomas asked.

"My hourly fee is one hundred and fifty dollars. Before I start to work on any financial plan I always provide an estimate of the total cost to the client. This amount can be a little more or a little less depending on each individual case."

"Actually, that's about what I thought. How many hours does a typical financial plan take?" Rachel asked.

"It can take anywhere from six to ten hours. Again, the more complex your situation, the longer it will take. On the other hand, if your situation is extremely simple, it probably doesn't make sense to hire me because your money wouldn't be well spent," Donna said candidly.

"How can we tell if our situation is complex? I've always assumed that our overall situation is relatively straightforward," Thomas said. This caused Rachel to smile because she knew that by "straightforward" he actually meant "cheap".

"Let's assume that you are in your early twenties, have no dependents and have just started your career. This would mean that you're in the cash management stage of life. At this stage, your tax returns and estate planning needs are straightforward, you might not be ready to buy life insurance and you'd have very little money to invest. Your financial needs would, therefore, be fairly simple because your primary goal would be to pay off any outstanding debt and implement a savings program."

"Our situation is more complicated than that," Rachel acknowledged.

"I suspected that it was or else you wouldn't be here. Most of the people who come to see me are usually at a stage in their lives where they realize that they haven't addressed any of their tax, estate planning and retirement needs. In order to address all of these properly, it makes sense to rely on the advice of a professional."

"We haven't dealt with any of those things. Does that make our situation complex?" Thomas asked.

147

"I wouldn't necessarily say complex; it would probably be better described as typical. Of course, I can't be more specific until I actually have a closer look at your individual situation. If you're wondering if you should even be considering hiring a financial planner, all you have to do is ask yourself how you feel about your financial future. If it's uncertain and makes you somewhat anxious, then it's time to do something about it."

"It does and we are," Rachel said without hesitation.

"Then it's a wise decision," Donna replied. "Are you familiar with the six steps of the financial planning process itself?"

"Yes, we're fairly familiar with the process and the six steps. It seems as if this approach is standard in the industry," Thomas said.

"This process is fairly standard in the industry, and there's a good reason for that. The six-step process serves as a solid platform that truly uncovers and addresses your needs."

"Is there any way that your approach to financial planning differs from your competitors?"

"As far as my approach is concerned, it's similar to that of most experienced financial planners. One of the first things you learn in this profession is that financial planning requires a disciplined and practical approach in order to be effective. As such, most planners will use the same tried and tested applications for no other reason than that they work. I do try to differentiate myself from my competitors by helping my clients increase their financial knowledge and by making them feel confident as investors."

"I'm not sure that I quite understand," Thomas said.

"Something I like to do is help my clients understand what they're doing and why they're doing it. I strongly believe that the more knowledgeable you are about financial planning, the less intimidating it becomes. This brings me to my second point. As your financial knowledge increases, so does your confidence. Confident investors tend to make wise investment decisions, whether they are choosing the right financial professional, buying investment products or assessing their risk level."

"That sounds like a good way to help your clients. I agree with your comment on being confident. We've spent a great deal of time learning about the financial services industry and are in a much better position because of it. A little learning goes a long way," Rachel said.

After discussing Donna's relationship with her clients for several more minutes, the conversation turned to Donna's company and the potential disadvantages of dealing with a small, independent firm as opposed to a large financial institution. Thomas felt it was important to raise this subject because he was under the impression that employees at an independent firm might be less accountable for their actions than employees at one of the big banks. Donna addressed this concern head-on, almost as if she knew that it was coming.

"By strictly limiting my services to accounting and financial planning, my clients have to rely on the services of other professionals in order to implement the different components of their plan. These professionals may include lawyers, insurance salespeople, investment advisors and portfolio managers. This means that several professionals will review my recommendations and implement the plan, providing that it makes sense. This not only makes me accountable to you, but also to a number of other professionals in the industry. More important, by relying on the services of outside professionals, I've eliminated any conflict of interest that might exist if I were to implement the plan myself. There's also the fact that my entire livelihood is tied to my company. If I don't provide my clients with the highest level of service imaginable, my reputation and business would be at risk. These things should reassure you that everyone employed at my firm will provide you with the highest level of service while acting with the utmost integrity."

"You've certainly made your point. I never looked at it that way," Thomas admitted.

"I'm glad that you brought it up. It would be a shame if you left here without having had all your questions answered. Are there any other concerns that you'd like me to address?" Donna offered.

"I don't think so," Thomas answered. "You've been very honest."

"If you were in our shoes and had to choose a financial planner, on what would you base your decision?" Rachel asked, pulling no punches.

"If I were in your position, I would base most of my decision on what felt right. If you set the bar high enough in terms of the qualifications of the professionals that you'd consider hiring, you'll end up meeting some of the best people in the industry. If this is the case, all you will really have to go on is a gut feeling because they will all have similar qualifications. I'm fairly certain that once you meet everyone you'll know what feels right. If you don't have a good feeling about any of the people that you interviewed then you should continue interviewing until you do. That's the best advice that I can give you. I hope it helps."

The interview came to a close thirty minutes later. Needless to say, it was a nice way to end their search for a financial planner. All three individuals were equally impressive in very different ways. All that they now had to do was make a difficult decision. Based on the interviews with all three candidates, they were confident that they had met with some of the most qualified planners in the city.

They arrived at home around eight o'clock. While Thomas drove the babysitter home, Rachel checked on the girls who were sleeping soundly in their beds like three little angels. She then went back downstairs and put on the kettle to make some tea.

Thomas was back home a few minutes later. After he took off his shoes, he came into the kitchen and sat down at the table beside Rachel.

"Can you believe that we interviewed our last financial planner tonight?" Thomas said in disbelief.

"Do you feel like making a decision tonight?"

"I wouldn't mind. It would be nice to make a final decision."

"That would be good," Thomas said. "In order to make sure that we don't influence one another by discussing the candidates, let's start by writing down the name of our top pick and a few reasons why we picked him or her. We'll then compare our notes to see if one particular person made an equally good impression on both of us."

"What happens if we each write down a different name?" Rachel asked.

"If that happens we'll have at least narrowed it down to two candidates. We'll then discuss why we chose the one we did. If we have to, we can always refer to our notes and meet with each of the candidates again. We'll then make a decision that we both agree on."

"That sounds like a good idea," Rachel acknowledged.

They each wrote down the name of their preferred candidate and three reasons why they picked that particular individual. Once they were ready, they told each other whom they had chosen. In both cases it was Donna Friedberg.

"I guess that it's true. When it feels right, you just know," Rachel said.

"I had a feeling that we'd agree," Thomas said. "Donna seemed exceptionally well rounded, honest and forthcoming. For whatever reason, I got the sense that we could trust her completely."

"I feel the same way. One thing that put my mind at ease was that she was in a position to offer truly unbiased financial advice. I was also impressed by the fact that she relied on outside help to implement her financial plans."

The longer that they discussed their decision the more apparent it became that they were both very confident and comfortable with their final choice. Although all of the candidates had their individual strengths, it was obvious that Thomas and Rachel felt a special connection with Donna. As far as her credentials were concerned, she had more than fifteen years experience, earned her RFP designation and was well positioned to offer impartial advice. The ability of their financial planner to offer this type of impartiality had been a priority for them from the very beginning. By hiring Donna they knew that her focus would be on gathering data, analyzing and evaluating their financial status, identifying their financial objectives and making recommendations. These recommendations would then be implemented by outside professionals who were subsequently chosen by them. Although Donna charged a fee for her services they both felt that it was a small price to pay to put their financial house in order.

Key Point

Try and make your decision to hire a specific individual shortly after the final meeting. This will ensure that all of the details of your interviews are fresh in your mind.

|20|

The First Hire

Later that night, little Anna woke with a terrible cold, so Thomas stayed home the following day to look after her.

"Do you want me to stay home with you? We can make it a family affair," Rachel said.

"That's sweet of you," Thomas smiled, "but it doesn't make much sense for both of us to stay home."

"You're right. Do you think that we should call Donna and tell her the good news?" Rachel asked.

"I'll give her a call a little later this morning," Thomas said.

"What about the other two financial planners? Should we call them and tell them that we've chosen someone else?"

"It seems like the courteous thing to do. I don't mind telling them because I'm sure they'll understand. I don't want you to worry about calling anyone. I'll take care of it."

"Could you do me a favour? When you speak with Donna can you ask her whether we should interview investment advisors and portfolio managers before or after she's looked at our situation? I just want to confirm that it makes sense to wait until after we have a financial plan in place," Rachel said.

Once Rachel and the other two girls had left for the day, with the house quiet and Anna still sleeping, Thomas decided to have some more coffee and read the morning paper. It wasn't often that he had some time to himself. After about an hour and a half, he decided that he'd better call the financial planners before Anna needed his undivided attention.

The first call he made was to Katherine Green. He started the conversation by mentioning that that they were both impressed with her qualifications and positive attitude. He then told her that despite her solid qualifications they decided to work with someone else. The reason for this was that they felt that it would simply be a better fit. Katherine fully understood their decision and added that she hoped that they would consider her for any other financial needs they might have in the future.

The next call was to Carl Rossi and, as expected, he also was very understanding. After Thomas explained how they had come to their final decision Carl asked if there was anything he could have done differently to win their business. Thomas said that it wasn't one particular thing, but mentioned that they were under the impression that he was too busy to take on new clients. Carl acknowledged this and thanked him for being honest. He then wished him all the best and asked that he keep him in mind in case they were ever interested in a second opinion on their financial affairs.

Although no one likes to be told that they're not the first choice, both financial planners took the news quite well. This was reassuring because Thomas didn't like to hurt anyone's feelings. After speaking with both financial planners he realized that a true professional would understand and accept their final decision and that they had nothing to gain by making him feel uncomfortable about his final choice. It was nice to see such a high degree of professionalism among the candidates. In a perfect world he would work with all of them. That, of course, wasn't realistic.

Now that he had delivered the bad news, he was looking forward to calling Donna and telling her the good news. He dialed her number hoping that she was in the office.

After exchanging pleasantries, Thomas told Donna that he and Rachel were very excited about working with her. Donna said she was glad they'd chosen her and that she looked forward to working with people who were so motivated about getting their financial affairs in order.

"So, what's next?" Thomas asked.

"At this point we're ready to take the first step. What we need to do is establish what you are expecting from me in terms of service. Although we touched upon this during our initial interview, it's really important that we go over it again. Once I'm comfortable that we've covered all the bases, I'll prepare a contract that you'll need to review and sign. This will reduce the possibility of miscommunication in the future. Once you've signed the contract, then we're ready to go on to the next step, which is gathering data and analyzing your financial goals."

"Do you have to meet in person to do this?"

"I would prefer it if we did. It will be a lot easier if we go through everything together. In order to take the second step, you're going to have to fill out a lengthy questionnaire, which I'd like to go through with you in person. We will also have a lengthy conversation so I clearly understand all of your financial goals."

"What kind of questionnaire?" Thomas asked.

"Essentially, what you're going to do is take all the information that you have in your financial scrapbook and put it down on paper. Most people find this task daunting because their information is all over the place. You have everything in one easily accessible file, so it won't take you too long."

"That sounds good. You have no idea how much we're looking forward to getting everything in place."

"I'm looking forward to helping you do it," Donna said.

"Rachel wanted me to ask you a question. Do you think that we should meet with a few investment counsellors and portfolio managers before or after we have a financial plan? I'm thinking that it would make more sense to wait until we have a clear picture of our situation."

"My advice is to interview these people once we're midway through the financial planning process. At that point I should have a good idea of what you have in terms of investable assets. You'll want to have these advisors ready to implement the plan shortly after I present it to you."

"Thanks for the advice. In terms of our next meeting, how does next Tuesday evening work for you?"

"How does six-thirty sound?" Donna suggested after looking at her Daytimer.

"Sounds good. Is there anything that we should bring?"

"Bring all of the information that you brought with you last time. This includes your bank statements, insurance policy, copies of your wills, and so on. I'm going to make copies of all of these things for my file."

"We'll see you on Tuesday. Thanks again."

After Thomas hung up the telephone it was as if a huge weight was lifted off of his shoulders. They had now hired a financial planner in whom they had a great deal of confidence. It was only a matter of time before everything fell into place. After taking a few moments to bask in the joy of this first milestone he turned his attention back to his parental duties and went upstairs to check on Anna. She was still sleeping like a baby.

Key Point

Most financial professionals know that they will not be a perfect fit with every individual they meet. As a professional courtesy, you should be honest and give a valid reason why they were not hired. This information will help them fine-tune their business and will likely result in the financial advisor becoming a more qualified professional.

|21|

The Financial Plan (Part I)

By the time their next meeting with Donna rolled around, the couple started feeling somewhat anxious. They didn't know what to expect and they were worried that they weren't adequately prepared for the meeting.

"I hope we brought everything you asked for," Rachel said when they reached Donna's office, letting her anxiety get the better of her.

"Don't worry if you didn't. I can always get it later," Donna responded. "We have a lot of work ahead of us. Do you have any questions before we get started?"

"Can you tell me what we're going to be doing today?" Thomas asked.

"Essentially, we'll try to get through the first two steps of the financial planning process. The first step is to define the client-planner relationship, which includes things like the services that I provide, how long our professional relationship will last and the costs for my services. I'll then write up a contract that clearly states all of this information. The next step is gathering data. Some financial planners will do this by having you complete a questionnaire before the first meeting. I've found that the information provided in the questionnaire is more thorough and accurate when I take the time to help the client complete it."

"Do we have enough time to do all this today?" Thomas asked.

"I'm sure that we'll get through it. I've allocated about three hours. It probably won't take that long because all you have to do is transfer the information from your scrapbook to the questionnaire. Most people don't have the information so readily at their fingertips. It often takes them weeks to collect all of this information."

"What should we do first?" Rachel said.

"Let's talk about my services and what you're expecting from me. Do you have any questions regarding what I'm going to be doing for you?"

"My understanding is that you will be presenting us with a detailed financial plan that will cover every facet of our financial affairs. This will tell us what we need to do in order to meet our retirement, insurance, estate planning, tax planning and investment management needs. Is that right?" Thomas asked.

"That's right. After we're done, you'll know what you need to do in order to achieve your financial goals. What about after I present you with the final copy of the financial plan?" Donna asked, quizzing the couple.

"You will work with other professionals to implement the different parts of the plan," Rachel answered.

"Right. And what about after the plan is implemented?" Donna asked.

"You'll review our financial affairs on a regular basis as required. This can be once a year, every few years or when we feel our situation has changed," Thomas responded.

"Very good. What about costs? Do you remember what we talked about in terms of compensation?"

"Yes—you charge an hourly rate," Rachel said.

"That's right. I charge one hundred and fifty dollars per hour. After today, I'll be able to give you a better idea of how many hours I think it will take me."

"What about any ongoing fees?" Thomas asked. "If six months down the road I have a quick question based on something that I heard or read, will we be charged for that?"

"Good question. Typically, I won't charge you for keeping in touch. It's part of the ongoing service that I provide. If your question requires that I reassess your situation and an updated financial plan is required, then my hourly rate will apply."

"That seems fair," Thomas agreed.

"What I'll do is print up a contract outlining everything we just talked about while you're completing the questionnaire," said Donna.

"We'll then go through the contract together. If it makes sense then we'll all sign it."

"That was easy," Thomas said. "If everything moves along this quickly, we'll be done in no time."

"Famous last words," Donna said, smiling. "Let's see if you feel the same way after you work through this," she said, handing them each a thick document.

"It looks like I spoke too soon," Thomas laughed, backpedalling.

"Why don't you make yourself comfortable at the table," Donna offered motioning towards the round table in the corner of her office. "That will give you some room to spread out. Can I offer you something to drink? We have coffee, tea, juice and soda."

After Donna left to put on a pot of coffee, Rachel and Thomas moved over to the table so they could start working on the financial planning questionnaire. The first section was fairly straightforward because it asked for personal details such as their name, address, phone numbers, e-mail addresses, birth dates and social insurance numbers. They were also asked to fill out other important information such as the name of their employer, occupation, years of employment and banking information.

The next section was similar to the first, but it focused on the children's personal information. It asked for their names, birth dates and whether any of them were beneficiaries of a Registered Education Savings Plan (RESP). Finally, it also asked them to list each of the kids' hobbies. This last question piqued Thomas's curiosity.

"I wonder why we're being asked to list the kids' hobbies? What could this have to do with financial planning?" Thomas asked his wife.

"I'm not sure. Let's ask Donna."

A short while later Donna came back holding a tray with a pot of coffee, three mugs, some sugar, cream and some cookies.

"How's it going?" she asked as she put the tray on the table in front of them.

"It's going well. I have a question though. How come you're asking us about the kids' hobbies? We don't mind answering, but I'm curious why this is relevant."

"That question always seems to get a response. The reason that I ask that is in many families the kids' hobbies can often become a major expense. If you have three children who are active in a sport such as hockey, it can get quite expensive to buy the equipment, drive them to different tournaments and pay for extras such as hockey camp. It's not uncommon for parents to pay thousands of dollars per year on these extra-curricular activities. The more kids you have, the more money you'll spend on these activities."

"Of course," Thomas replied. "Our girls are still young so we're not at that stage yet."

"Many parents don't realize how much they spend annually on their children. They just spend as money becomes available. This is one of the most overlooked areas of the household budget."

The next section of the questionnaire was the Income Sources and Expenses. This first part of this section asked them to separately list their annual employment, pension and investment income. It also asked to list any bonuses and any other income that they receive on a regular basis. They did this by writing down the information from their T-4 slips. Other than employment income, they didn't earn anything else.

The second part of this section asked them to list their monthly household expenses and any major expenses that they might incur immediately or at some point in the future. They started with their monthly expenses and listed things like groceries, telephone bill, hydro, entertainment costs, mortgage payments and anything else that was a regular monthly expense. They took their time so they were sure not to miss anything.

As far as their current major expenses, the only item that came to mind was possibly buying a new car. They wrote this down along with the possible date of purchase and estimated cost in the appropriate space. Their future major expenses were an entirely different matter because this required some guesswork. They started by listing the obvious ones such as the girls' post-secondary education costs, a bunkie at the cottage and extensive travel after they both retired. That's as far as they got.

"Donna, we need some help as far as the major expenses go," Rachel asked politely.

"What have you listed so far?" Donna asked. They told her what they had written down.

"What about home renovations or landscaping?"

"I don't foresee that we'll be doing any renovating. If anything, we would likely buy a bigger house," Rachel said. "But not any time soon."

"That's a major expense. Make sure to put that down anyway. It would be very helpful if you could give me an idea of when you might move and how much you'd spend on a new house. I know this is hard to predict, but do your best."

Rachel and Thomas briefly talked about when they might move. They then agreed on an amount they'd expect to pay for a house that would likely meet their needs when the kids were older. They wrote this information down.

"What about your parents? Do you think that you might have to support them at some point? Long-term care can get quite expensive," Donna warned.

"That never would have crossed my mind. I could see how some of this would put serious financial pressure on someone if they hadn't prepared for it." Thomas admitted. "I don't anticipate that we'll have to help our parents. They are all financially secure."

"If you can't think of any other expenses, you should move on to the next section. If at some point in the future you believe that you might incur a major expense, make sure to bring it to my attention. I can't stress how important this is."

The next section was the Net Worth Statement. This section was probably the single most important section in the entire questionnaire because it would give Donna a clear picture of their current financial situation. The information provided in this section would serve as a launching pad for everything that would follow. This is why it was important to make sure that this information was accurate.

As with most net worth statements, this one was divided into two parts—Assets and Liabilities. In the asset section, they were asked to list items such as cash, Registered Retirement Savings Plans (RRSPs), non-registered securities, Employee Share Purchase Plans (ESPP), cash surrender values of their insurance policies, real estate, automobiles and other significant personal assets such as the contents of their home. For the most part, they had all of this information at their disposal. They simply transferred all of the amounts from their various bank, discount brokerage and insurance statements. In terms of the value of their cottage and house, they had a reasonable idea what they were worth because they had recently had both properties assessed. In regards to their other personal assets, they made a conservative estimate as to their value and wrote an amount that was somewhat at the lower end just to be safe.

The liabilities section was also fairly straightforward because it asked them to list all of their debts. This included things like credit card balances, personal lines of credit, mortgages, car loans, investment loans and any other amounts owing. Once they were finished listing all of their liabilities they were both a little surprised at the amount.

"Ouch! This number really hits home when you see it written down in one lump sum," Rachel said. "It looks a lot bigger than it feels."

"A lot of my clients have the same reaction," Donna said from behind her desk. "It always looks like a lot when it's all added up. I can't stress enough how important the net worth statement is in the entire financial planning process. In order to reach your goals, it is imperative that you increase your net worth as you grow older. This can be achieved by saving more money, increasing the return on your investments or paying down your liabilities. Every family should manage their finances in much the same manner as a corporation. This is why I prepare a cash flow statement, balance sheet and net worth statement as part of the overall plan. If you adopt this approach, you will always know whether or not you are headed in the right direction simply by referring to your net worth statement."

The net worth statement was followed by the Retirement Planning section. This section required the couple to indicate, to the best of their abilities, what year they expected to retire. It also asked them to list the monthly benefits, if any, they would receive in pension income from their respective companies. They also needed to indicate at what age or on which date the pension plan started. Finally, they were also asked to list how long and how much they were planning on contributing to their Registered Retirement Savings Plan each year. Other than the RRSP information, the couple didn't know much about their respective pension plans, so they referred to their pension statements. After staring at the forms for a few minutes, they weren't any better off—it was as if they were written in a different language. They decided to ask for some help.

"Donna, could you help us decipher our pension statements. We have no idea what they say," Rachel said.

"Of course," Donna replied, getting up from behind her desk. "They can often be confusing."

Donna started by pointing out that most pension statements have very similar formats and list the same information regardless of the company. In most cases, pension statements are divided into several sections, including personal information, salary, credit and contribution information, pension benefits and beneficiary information.

After pointing out each of these areas on their statements, she then took the time to discuss each one in detail. She started by ensuring that all of their personal information was correct. When she saw that it was, she moved on to the next section, which outlined their salary, credit and contribution information. For the most part, this information was straightforward. It simply outlined the details of how much they had contributed to their pension plan and how their benefits were calculated.

The next section was the one that usually caused the most confusion because it contained information on the annual pension the employee had earned to date, a projection of the annual pension the employee would earn under the earliest unreduced retirement option and a projection of the annual pension an employee would receive when he or she becomes eligible for normal retirement at age sixty-five. After explaining that these numbers were simply an estimate of their annual pension benefits at different points in their career, they made a lot more sense. In simple terms, these numbers identified how much you would earn if you retired early, when you could retire without reducing your pension and how much you would earn if you worked until your normal retirement date.

The final section listed the beneficiary information and outlined the survivor benefits that this beneficiary was entitled to upon death of the pensioner. This information was also fairly straightforward.

After Donna was finished walking the couple through their statements she asked them if they had any questions. The only question they had was in regards to some of the wording in their statements. It was something that they never understood.

"How come our pension statements use the words 'projection' and 'estimate'? Does this mean that we won't know what our exact benefit is until we retire?" Rachel asked.

"There are two types of pension plans. The first type is called a Defined Benefit Pension Plan. Under this type of plan, a formula determines the benefit for which an employee qualifies and the employer contributes whatever is necessary to provide the promised benefit. There are four different ways an employer will contribute to this type of plan: through a flat amount formula, a flat percentage of earnings formula, a flat amount per year of service formula and a percentage of earnings per year of service formula. Each of these various formulas has pros and cons depending on your specific situation. The advantage of the defined benefit plan, however, is that you'll know what your pension benefit will be upon retirement."

"Is this the type of pension we have?" Thomas asked.

"No. Your pension plan is a Defined Contribution Pension Plan. Under this type of plan, the contributions to the plan are fixed. Your actual pension benefit will vary depending on the amount of the contributions you make, the investment returns of the plan's assets, the age at which you started participating in the plan and the age at which you retire. The most important characteristic of this type of plan is that you won't know what your benefit is because the plan itself is affected by investment returns. If the rate of return of the plan's assets are above average over the long term, your benefit will be higher as well. Of course, if the investment returns are poor then you'll receive less income during your retirement. This is why they provide you with estimates instead of actual figures. The information on your pension statement is based on assumptions and historical rates of return."

"Which plans are more common?"

"Most government agencies, educational institutions and major corporations use defined benefit plans. Smaller companies tend to use defined contribution plans because they are less costly to establish and maintain. Depending on the company, the contributions can sometimes be generous, which is good. Also, if you contribute, your contributions to the plan are tax-deductible up to the RRSP limits. Keep in mind that this reduces your RRSP deduction limit."

"I feel as though I'm now an expert on pension plans," Rachel said proudly.

"The more you learn, the better off you'll be," Donna answered. "You are both doing a great job of taking in all the information."

Now that they had a thorough understanding of their pension benefits they were able to transfer the numbers from their statements to the financial planning worksheet. They were now ready to move on to the next section, Estate Planning.

The questions asked in this section were fairly general in nature. They were asked whether or not they each had a will, when they were last updated and whether they had powers of attorney in place. In terms of their insurance policies, they were asked to list the policy type, the value of the policy, the insured and the beneficiary of each policy. Again, they simply took the information from their insurance statements and wrote the information down in the appropriate space.

This brought them to the final section of the questionnaire, which was titled General Information. This space was reserved for additional information, such as the name of the couple's banker, accountant, lawyer, insurance agent and any other professional advisors that they worked with. It also asked them to list some of their favourite activities, interests, hobbies and favourite charitable foundations. Finally, there was a space that asked them to list their top three financial goals. In no particular order of preference, they listed paying for their kids' post-secondary education, retiring comfortably and leaving each of their daughters a sizeable inheritance. With a few final strokes of their pens, they were done.

"Donna, it looks as though we're done," Thomas announced.

"Perfect timing. I'm just finishing up writing our contract. We'll go through everything together. Could you do me a favour though?"

"Sure," Rachel said.

"Can one of you go to the photocopy room and copy all of your statements? I'll need a copy of everything for my file."

"I'll go," Thomas said. "Where is it?"

"It's the third room on your left down the hall," Donna said. "Thank you."

While Thomas was busy copying all of their statements, Rachel took the opportunity to review their answers one last time. She knew that the information that they provided was important and wanted to make sure that they didn't leave anything out. After scanning all of their answers she decided that they had done a pretty decent job.

"I've just printed three copies of the contract," Donna said, reaching for the printer.

A few moments later Thomas walked back into the office holding two separate stacks of paper. He handed the originals to Rachel who then put them back in her scrapbook. The other pile went to Donna.

"I didn't know what you wanted, so I just copied everything," Thomas said.

"I appreciate it. It's always better to have too much information rather than too little. Are you ready to go through the contract?"

The couple indicated that they were and sat back down in their seats in front of Donna's desk. She then handed them each a copy of the contract.

"There is nothing in the contract that we haven't yet discussed. Essentially, it recaps everything that we talked about in terms of the scope of my service, costs involved and any additional ongoing services. Please read through it and make sure that we haven't left anything out. As I mentioned before, the purpose of the contract is to avoid any surprises later on."

While Rachel and Thomas read the contract, Donna reviewed their answers in the financial planning questionnaire. As expected, the couple had done an excellent job of filling in all of the required information. Other than a few minor things, she was very pleased with the detail of the information they provided.

"This is great," Donna said. "I don't think you left a single thing out. Do you have any questions about the contract?"

"I don't think so," Rachel answered. "As you said, it pretty much covers everything we talked about. I'm ready to sign it."

"So am I," Thomas said.

After they had each signed the contract, Donna made a photocopy of it and the questionnaire and handed the documents to Rachel.

"Make sure you keep a copy of everything that I give you," Donna instructed. "You may want to refer back to some of the information later on."

"What's next on the agenda?" Thomas asked eagerly.

"That's it for today. The next step is analyzing and evaluating your financial status after going through all of the information in the questionnaire. This will take about a week, during which time I may have some additional questions for you. After this, I'll put all of my findings down on paper and we'll go through them together."

"That sounds good. We'll wait to hear from you. Once we do, we'll set up another meeting here in the office," Rachel suggested.

"Perfect. I should have something to show you by next week. You should expect a call from me no later than Monday."

Key Point

The task of gathering all of your financial data can be daunting. It is an extremely important step in the financial planning process and, as a result, you must allocate a realistic amount of time to getting all of this information together.

| 22 |

The Financial Plan (Part II)

As promised, Donna's phone call came on Monday evening and, once again, the couple found themselves in her office on another Tuesday night. They were both looking forward to hearing what she had to say, so they got right down to business.

"So how does it look?" Rachel asked, expecting the worst.

"From my preliminary analysis, I can tell you that you're in good financial shape."

"Really? That's a relief," Rachel answered, feeling as if a huge weight had been lifted off of her shoulders.

"It's not all good news, however," Donna added quickly. "From a net worth standpoint, you are in pretty good shape because you both earn very high incomes and have managed to keep your liabilities relatively low. As a result, your net worth is higher than most people your age. From a financial planning standpoint, however, your affairs are in complete disarray. There is no structure to your finances, whatsoever. Essentially, what's been happening is that you have more money coming in than going out, which is a nice problem to have. This has masked many areas that need attention, however."

"Can you give us an example?" Thomas asked.

"The most obvious example is the current state of your investments. Your money is scattered across so many different investment products in so many different accounts that it's almost impossible to keep on top of everything. I counted nine different investment accounts in total. Another problem is that it looks as though you haven't been effectively minimizing your taxes."

"That's our fault," Thomas said. "We've been doing our own taxes so we could save some money."

"I've prepared a preliminary plan that deals with each issue in an organized manner. It will address your cash management, retirement, tax and estate planning needs," said Donna. "And you will probably find that proper planning will save you even more money than trying to do it all yourselves."

"What do you mean by preliminary plan?" Rachel asked.

"I always present my clients with a rough version of their financial plan first because it gives them the opportunity to address any issues that may arise before the final copy is made up. Aside from the way it looks, there is usually very little difference between the recommendations in the preliminary plan and the final draft. However, if you have any questions or concerns with any of the information, you should bring them to my attention during today's meeting."

"Where do we start?" Thomas asked.

Donna passed them each a copy of the rough draft. It looked to be at least twenty-five pages thick.

"Let's start by looking at the table of contents. This way you'll know what to expect as we go through the document."

The Table of Contents consisted of eight different sections: Introduction, Budget & Savings Planning, Retirement Planning, Investment Management, Insurance Planning, Estate Planning, Tax Planning and Conclusion. These sections were further subdivided into subsections that addressed each specific need.

"As far as the **Introduction** is concerned, I think it's pretty self-explanatory. The one thing that I'd like to bring your attention is that I've listed your top three financial goals in this section. In the questionnaire you indicated that these are paying for your children's post-secondary education, retiring comfortably and leaving each of the kids a nice inheritance. The reason that I'm pointing this out is that the purpose of this entire document is to serve as a roadmap to achieving each of these goals. If you have any other financial goals, it's important that you bring them to my attention now so we can address them."

"We actually talked about our goals after we got home the night we first met and we agreed that if we could do all that, we'd be thrilled," Rachel said.

"It's nice to know that you've given it some thought. As you can see, the Introduction also includes a general definition of financial planning, a description of your overall financial health, which is stated as being good, and a list of the areas that require the most attention."

"As you said, it's pretty straightforward," Thomas agreed.

Budget & Savings Planning

"The Budget & Savings section is next. This section always gets a lot of interest because its subsections cover your Net Worth, Cash Management and Credit & Debt Analysis needs."

"Why do people find this section so interesting?" Rachel asked.

"It's primarily because they finally know exactly what they are worth and how much money they spend on a monthly basis. If you look at the first chart, which is the Net Worth Statement, you'll see all of your assets and liabilities listed down to the penny. The number in the bottom right-hand corner is your current net worth. As you can see, you're not doing too badly. It's important to mention that you should be calculating your net worth on an annual basis. That way you'll know if you're heading in the right direction year after year."

"Not bad," Thomas said. "What about this second chart?"

"This is a Cash Flow Statement. The purpose of this statement is to provide you with a clear idea of your cash flow over a twelve-month period. As I mentioned earlier, most people don't have the slightest clue about how much money is coming in or going out. This statement is designed to tell you exactly that. It shows you how much money is coming in every month through employment, investment or rental income and how much is going out to cover all of your expenses."

"I can't believe how detailed the information is. It lists all of our regular expenses, including things like our phone bill, hydro costs and entertainment expenses. I also can't believe how much we spend every year," said Thomas. "At least now we know where the money is going."

"It has to be detailed because one of the most effective ways of increasing your net worth is by reducing your expenses. If you can reduce your non-essential expenses and some of your fixed expenses you'll increase your savings rate, thereby increasing your net worth."

"That makes sense," Rachel said. "I see that you made a few suggestions here."

"Even though you have positive cash flow, there is still a lot of room to reduce your monthly expenses," Donna pointed out. "If you look under discretionary or non-essential expenses, for instance, you'll see that you spend almost eight hundred dollars per month on dining out. You may not realize it, but this is actually very high. Most couples don't spend that much. If you were simply to reduce this expense by half you would save almost five thousand dollars per year."

"We rarely even think about how much we spend in restaurants. When you look at it as an annual expense, it seems so excessive," Thomas admitted, feeling a little bit embarrassed.

"A second area for potential improvement is the amount of money that you spend on clothing. It is also relatively high compared to many other couples your age."

Thomas gave Rachel a quick glance suggesting that this item should be directed towards her. Thomas was allergic to shopping malls. The only time he went out and bought new clothes was when Rachel forced him to go with her. He was glad the amount he spent online buying books wasn't mentioned, however.

"I admit that certainly does look like a lot of money to spend on clothing," Rachel said, staring at the line item. "I'll try and spend less on new clothes," she offered.

"I'm not trying to be critical," Donna reassured her. "It's my job to point out where your money is going so that you can make informed decisions about what you spend it on. I'm on pretty friendly terms with Holt Renfrew myself," she laughed, and then continued. "Now that we've touched on how you can potentially reduce some of your expenses, I might as well mention what you might want to do with these savings. You listed your first financial goal as saving for each of the girls' post-secondary education. Aside from purchasing a home or cottage, this is usually one of the greatest financial hurdles parents face. You have three kids all fairly close in age, so the costs associated with university will be condensed over a very short period of time."

"I've always assumed we would simply cash in some of our investments to pay for university," Rachel said. "My concern has always been that we would deplete most of our investments all at once, however."

"Although selling your investments at that time would be an easy way to address this financial goal, it wouldn't be the wisest. As with most financial decisions, tax is always an important factor to consider. One of the most common investment vehicles currently used for saving for a child's education is the Registered Education Savings Plan (RESP). Over the years, the federal government has made these plans quite attractive. One reason for their increasing popularity is that the federal government now pays an annual grant up to a maximum of five hundred dollars for each child. These grants are based on how much money you contribute to the plan in any given year. Another advantage is that any money that is invested in the plan grows tax-free until it is withdrawn once the child starts attending university. There are some limitations to the plans, which I've outlined below."

"How much will we have to save for each child?" Thomas asked.

"It is estimated that twenty years from now a post-secondary four-year degree will cost approximately seventy-five thousand dollars. This includes tuition, books and accommodation. In order to send all three girls to university, I have calculated that you'll have to save roughly two hundred dollars per month per child. After taking the federal grant into account, a seven per cent annual rate of return and a two per cent inflation rate, you'll have saved enough money if you do that. This should serve as a good incentive to be more aware of how much money you're spending every month."

The third subsection in Budget and Savings section was Credit & Debt Analysis. This section was also fairly straightforward. It simply listed all of their debts, taken directly from their net worth statement, and showed how much annual interest each loan was costing them.

"The reason that I've included this section is that you'll want to review this number every year and try to keep it as close to zero as possible. I find that most of my clients are motivated to pay down their liabilities once they see how much it's costing them to maintain their loans. In your particular case, I'm recommending that you use some of your non-registered assets and pay off your few remaining debts entirely."

"The reason we haven't paid down these debts is that it was comforting having money invested outside of our registered plans," Rachel explained.

"Is your peace of mind worth paying this much in interest?" Donna asked, pointing to the total amount of interest they had paid the previous year.

"No, it isn't," Rachel said.

"That's why I'm recommending that you pay off these debts. You should keep in mind that you both have significant holdings in the Employee Share Purchase Plans (ESPP) of your respective companies. Your investments in these plans represent a significant portion of your total net worth. It's never a good idea to hold all of your eggs in one basket. My suggestion is to use some of this money so you're debt free. How do you feel about this?"

"I'm not sure. I always thought that I'd hold all of my shares until I retired or the firm was bought by a competitor," Thomas said.

"I thought the same thing," Rachel said. "But I see your point."

"This is why I like to go through the preliminary plan first. It gives me a chance to address any concerns ahead of time."

"Couldn't we use our other investments to pay off our debts?" Rachel asked.

"You could, but that wouldn't help in diversifying your assets because the shares in your respective companies would represent an even larger percentage of your total assets. The strategy behind selling a portion of your shares is two-fold—paying off your debt and better diversifying your assets. Also, all of your other investments are in your Registered Retirement Savings Plans (RRSPs). If you withdraw this money you will have to pay tax on the amount withdrawn. This wouldn't be a wise decision."

"Donna, we're looking to you to get us in the best financial shape possible. If this is your suggestion then we'll gladly take your advice," Rachel said.

Thomas nodded in agreement.

"Another reason that I'm suggesting that you sell a portion of your shares is that the tax consequences will be minimal. You each have some capital losses that you've been carrying forward for many years. These can be applied towards any capital gains that are triggered on the sale of the shares. I've addressed this in the tax planning section of the plan. If we can increase your diversification, pay off your debt and do this without paying much tax, it makes good financial sense."

The last paragraph of the Credit & Debt Analysis section addressed the couple's capacity to take on debt in the future. This information was important to know in case they ever needed to borrow money from the bank. The calculation that most financial institutions use to assess the maximum acceptable level of debt an individual can take on is called the Total Debt Service Ratio (TDS). Donna took a few moments and explained that this calculation was done by dividing the sum of their monthly mortgage payments, property taxes, heating costs and any other debt payments by their total gross household income. The couple's TDS came in at a little over twelve per cent, which meant that they were well below the forty per cent threshold at which point most financial institutions would no longer lend money. This meant that if they approached a financial institution for a loan and their financial situation hadn't changed much, they would almost certainly qualify.

Retirement Planning

The third section is often considered to be the most important aspect of any sound long-term financial plan—retirement planning. If individuals aren't meticulous when planning for their retirement, they can find themselves in financial hardship after they stop working. Rachel knew this, and it was what had caused her sleepless nights and started the financial planning process in the first place.

In terms of planning for their retirement, Donna outlined three important steps that needed to be taken in order to meet their goals. These steps consisted of evaluating their current retirement assets, establishing how much in savings they needed in order to maintain or improve their current standard of living when they stopped working and developing an investment strategy to meet their income needs during retirement.

To evaluate their current retirement assets, Donna showed them a spreadsheet that listed all of their current retirement assets individually. This included their pension benefits, registered retirement savings plans and non-registered investments that were earmarked for the long term. When they saw the total they had in current retirement assets they were surprised.

"Is that what we currently have in retirement assets?" Thomas asked, pointing to the total at the bottom right-hand corner of the spreadsheet.

"Yes. As you can see, you each have a little over one hundred and ten thousand dollars in your pension plans. This isn't money that you can simply access at any time, however. At retirement the total value will be used to buy an annuity or, in some cases, can be transferred to a Life Income Fund (LIF). Both of these vehicles are designed to provide you with a stream of income during your retirement. We will address how much income I anticipate you'll earn from these plans in your next section."

Thomas and Rachel both nodded to indicate that they were with her so far.

"In regards to your RRSPs, you've done a good job of saving money. You currently have a little over three hundred and twenty-five thousand dollars between you. I'm assuming that this is because you've been contributing money to your respective plans each year?"

"We started contributing when we first started working. That was back in our early twenties, which seems like an awfully long time ago now," Rachel replied, smiling.

"In addition to this, you also have money in your respective Employee Share Purchase Plans. As I mentioned in the Credit & Debt Planning section, I'm recommending that you take some of this money to pay off your various liabilities, including the balance remaining on your mortgage, your personal lines of credit and your various credit cards. If the interest that you pay on these liabilities isn't tax-deductible, it makes no sense to keep these loans outstanding."

Thomas and Rachel nodded again to indicate that this also made sense.

"After we cash in a portion of your shares and pay off these debts, you'll have a combined total of two hundred and forty thousand dollars in your respective ESPPs. I still feel that your overall net worth is too concentrated in the shares of your respective companies, so I'll address the risks associated with this later on in the Investment Planning section."

"Is this what we have in total current retirement assets?" Thomas asked, pointing to the number at the bottom right-hand corner of the spreadsheet.

"Yes, that's correct. After subtracting the amount that we are going to use to pay off your liabilities, you have just over seven hundred and eighty-five thousand dollars in retirement assets."

"That seems like a lot of money," Rachel acknowledged.

"It is a lot. There's one thing that you have to keep in mind, however—taxes. If you were to collapse your registered plans and sell all the shares in your Employee Share Purchase Plans, you would have to pay more than one hundred and fifty thousand dollars to the Canada Revenue Agency. This is why it's always important to always consider any tax consequences before making any financial decisions."

"The Tax Man always gets his share," Thomas said, ruefully.

The next subsection was the nuts and bolts of the Retirement Planning section because this is where the financial planner had to accurately estimate how much money a client would need in order to maintain a similar or improved standard of living during his or her retirement. This was always challenging because there were many outside factors that had to be taken into consideration. These included things such as the inflation rate, investment performance, interest rates and taxes. Another important factor in assessing an individual's retirement needs was acknowledging that everyone has different spending habits. If, for instance, a couple planned on taking a trip around the world as soon as they stopped working, they would likely need significantly more in savings than people who simply wanted to spend most of their time at the cottage. Then, of course, there were also all of the expenses that many individuals fail to plan for. These include major expenses like their children's weddings, the possibility of the kids wanting to attend graduate school without a scholarship and personal long-term care costs. Donna took time to explain all of this so that Thomas and Rachel had a clear understanding of the information she was about to present to them.

"A generally accepted rule of thumb is that an individual will spend about seventy per cent of their current expenditure level during their retirement. In the last several years, however, I've found that many couples retired much earlier, were in better health and, as a result, were much more active than retirees twenty years ago. In order to support their more active lifestyles, they tend to need a higher level of income," Donna explained.

"So how much will we need?" Thomas asked reluctantly.

"If you look at the next section, I'll show you how I've estimated your future income needs. As I mentioned, I am somewhat more aggressive in terms of estimating the level of income my clients will eventually need because of their increased activity level. In your first five years of retirement, I've assumed that you'll need about eighty per cent of your current level of income. This should allow you to live comfortably and do all of the things you'd like to do after you retire. You'll notice that I've estimated that you'll need about seventy per cent of your current income during your sixties. This is because as you get older, you'll typically spend less money every year. During your early seventies and beyond, you'll likely only need to live on about fifty per cent of your current income. The reason why most individuals tend to spend less as they age is because they spend less on clothing, dining out, driving the car, and so on."

Donna took them through her next spreadsheet. The first thing they noticed was that all of their current monthly and annual expenses were neatly listed along the left-hand side of the page under a heading aptly named Current Expenses. These amounts were taken directly from their financial questionnaire, so they were numbers that they recognized. Immediately to the right of this column were three additional columns. They were labelled Retirement Expenses (Age 55 to 60), Retirement Expenses (Age 60 to 70) and Retirement Expenses (Age 70 Plus). Below each of these headings were dollar amounts that corresponded to each of the expenses listed on the left. For example, under automobile expenses the current amount allocated was six thousand five hundred dollars per year. During the first five years of retirement, from the ages of fifty-five to sixty, this number dropped to four thousand five hundred dollars. It then dropped to three thousand dollars under the Retirement Expenses (Age 60 to 70) column and stayed there for the remainder of their retirement. In almost each case, their expenses dropped as they grew older. The one obvious exception was medical expenses. These increased as they aged. At the bottom of each column the expenses were totalled, giving them the total amount of money Donna expected them to spend each year.

"Essentially, what this spreadsheet shows is an estimate of your annual expenses at various stages during your retirement. They are based as a percentage of your after-tax income and on your current expenses as listed by you in the questionnaire. As you can see, all of the expenses listed in the second column titled Retirement Expenses (Age 55 to 60) are roughly eighty per cent of your current expenses. In the next column, they are roughly seventy per cent, and in the final column, they are fifty per cent."

"Obviously, as you grow older you tend to spend less. That's pretty interesting," Thomas said referring to the numbers.

"I knew you'd like it," Donna replied. "Everyone seems to get a kick out of seeing how much they'll spend when they're older."

"It doesn't look as if these numbers have been adjusted for inflation. Are these amounts in today's dollars?" Rachel asked.

"Very impressive," Donna responded. "Most people wouldn't even think to ask that question. The numbers that you see here are in today's dollars. The reason for this is that the numbers are more meaningful if you can conceptualize your purchasing power. If these amounts were all adjusted for inflation they wouldn't make any sense to you. Of course, it's extremely important to take inflation into account, which I've done on the next page."

On the next spreadsheet, all of the expenses were adjusted for a two per cent annual rate of inflation.

"I can't believe how expensive things will be when we retire," Thomas said lightheartedly.

"You'd be surprised how many people forget to take inflation into account," Donna warned.

Now that they had an idea of how much money they would spend during their retirement, they were ready to know how much they needed to save in order to provide them with enough investment income to cover their retirement expenses. This calculation was fairly complicated because there were many factors that once again needed to be taken into account. These included factors such as their expected retirement date, marginal tax rate, rate of return on their investments and the inflation rate. Due to the complexity of these calculations, most financial planners rely on forecasting software to arrive at the results rather than trying to calculate the amount themselves.

In order to ensure that the information that Donna presented to the couple was relevant to their specific situation, she had made certain assumptions based on the information that they provided in the questionnaire. The first assumption was that they both wanted the option to retire at the age of fifty-five. This didn't necessarily mean that they would stop working at this age; it just meant that they were interested in seeing if it was a possibility. In all likelihood they would both work into their late fifties or early sixties. Another assumption Donna made was that they would contribute the maximum allowable amount to each of their respective registered retirement savings plans until the age of fifty-five. As far as the rate of return was concerned, Donna assumed that their investments would grow at seven per cent annually and that the inflation rate during this period would be two per cent. In regards to the shares in their respective companies, she assumed that they would be taxed at a capital gains rate of twenty-three per cent. All of these assumptions were clearly listed at the beginning of the section preceding the results.

"Before we get to the specifics, I want to take a moment to show you how I arrived at the various numbers. As we saw in the previous section, I've estimated that you'll need about eighty per cent of your current pre-tax income to cover all of your expenses from the age of fifty-five to sixty. Your latest T-4 slips stated that you earned a total combined income of two hundred and eighty thousand dollars. If you take eighty per cent of this, you get two hundred and twenty four thousand dollars. Does that make sense so far?"

"Yes," Thomas and Rachel said together.

"Very good. The next thing we need to do is establish how much money you will need to save in order to provide you with enough investment income if you decide to retire at the age of fifty-five. In your particular case, the amount that you need to save is higher than most individuals because you indicated that one of your most important financial goals was to leave each of the kids a sizeable inheritance. As such, I've assumed that you will want to save enough money so that you can pay your expenses without having to touch the principal. Is that a fair assumption?"

"As long as we can afford to do so," Rachel confirmed.

"Let's have a look at the numbers then. In the first five years after retirement, you'll need to earn roughly eighty per cent of your current salary in order to maintain the same standard of living. We've already established that this means you'll need to earn two hundred and twenty four thousand dollars per year. In order to calculate the total amount of savings you'll need to generate this amount, I simply divided two hundred and twenty-four thousand dollars by seven per cent, the assumed long-term annualized rate of return. This calculation gives you three million two hundred thousand dollars. This is, of course, in today's dollars and will have to be adjusted to reflect inflation."

"Is that the magic number?" Thomas asked.

"That's the magic number."

"Is that realistic?" Rachel asked. "It seems like an awful lot of money to save by the time we turn fifty-five."

"It will take some discipline on your part, but it's achievable. Let me show you how we will get you there."

Donna took a few moments to reiterate that most individuals achieved their retirement goals in one of three ways—saving in a non-registered account, contributing to an RRSP or participating in a company pension plan. Regardless of how an individual saved for retirement, it was extremely important that the funds were properly invested so that over the long term they earned a rate of return that was significantly higher than the rate of inflation. In addition to inadequate savings rates, poor investment performance was one of the most common reasons why individuals were ill prepared for retirement. It was for this reason that Donna always encouraged her clients to use the services of an investment professional rather than doing it themselves.

In terms of the couple's Canada Pension Plan benefits, Donna explained that she did not take their monthly benefits into consideration because she wanted to establish a plan that required the couple to save on their own. When they turned sixty-five, her suggestion was to simply reduce the amount of money that they would withdraw from their registered plans by the amount of their annual CPP benefit. The advantage of this is that this money would continue to grow tax-free in their registered plans.

By using retirement forecasting software, Donna was able to evaluate how much money the couple needed to save annually, how long they needed to save and at what rate their investments needed to grow. Both Rachel and Thomas were impressed with the detailed report that was presented to them because it outlined exactly what they needed to do to achieve their retirement goals and, more important, it confirmed whether their goals were realistic or not.

"The Retirement Savings Plan and the Retirement Income Report are very important pieces of information. That's why it's very important that you both understand exactly what is being stated and the assumptions on which the results are based," Donna said sternly. They both nodded.

"As you can see, I've divided the information into three different sections. Each section separately addresses your various savings strategies—your Employee Share Purchase Plans, Registered Retirement Savings Plans and Defined Contribution Pension Plans. The report outlines whether you'll be able to save the three million two hundred thousand dollars needed in order to retire at the age of fifty-five. As mentioned earlier, I've assumed a seven per cent annual rate of return and two per cent inflation rate."

The first section addressed the couple's non-registered investments, which consisted primarily of their Employee Share Purchase Plans. As with most ESPPs, employees are given the opportunity to allocate a fixed percentage of their salary to buy shares in the company that they work for. In some cases, they are allowed to buy the shares at a discount and, in other cases, the employer pays for a portion of the purchase price on behalf of their employees.

"Over the last several years, it looks as though you've each been contributing about ten thousand dollars per year to your Employee Share Purchase Plans. As such, I've assumed that you will continue making contributions to each of your plans and I've assumed that you'll be contributing at least twenty thousand dollars combined each year going forward."

"That sounds about right," Thomas said.

With this said, let's have a look at what we've come up with. After plugging in the various numbers and assumptions into the Retirement Forecaster, you end up with this figure," Donna said pointing at the number.

"I would have thought it would have been more than eight hundred and thirteen thousand dollars," Rachel admitted. "Shouldn't it be higher considering we're contributing twenty thousand dollars per year for the next sixteen or seventeen years?"

"The reason why I started with your non-registered assets is because I wanted to make a point. More specifically, I wanted to show you how taxes and inflation can rear their ugly heads. I've assumed that you'll be paying capital gains tax at a rate of twenty-three per cent every year going forward. This may or may not be the case because you may not sell a majority of your shares until you retire. Also, the eight hundred and thirteen thousand dollars has been adjusted to reflect inflation. The actual dollar value of these combined plans when you're fifty-five will be in the neighbourhood of one million one hundred and sixty-five thousand. At that time, however, this will only be able to buy you eight hundred and thirteen thousand dollars worth of goods and services in today's dollars because of inflation."

"Just to make sure that I understand, we'll have the equivalent of eight hundred and thirteen thousand dollars in non-registered assets when we retire?" Thomas asked.

"That's correct. Of course the amount may be higher if you defer the taxes payable for several years. It essentially all depends on when you realize the capital gains of your shares. If you don't sell any of your shares until you retire, you'll have more money but your tax bill will also be higher. We'll address this in more detail in the tax planning section of the plan. Let's have a look at your registered plans. I think after you see the results, you'll appreciate the importance of deferring and minimizing your taxes."

The assumptions that Donna made when forecasting the future value of the couple's registered assets were similar to those made with regard to their non-registered assets. There were two important differences, however. In terms of their tax rate, it was no longer taken into account because the money invested within a registered plan grew tax-free until it was transferred to a Registered Retirement Income Fund (RRIF) and the first withdrawal had to be made at the age of seventy-one. The other assumption was that they would both maximize their RRSP contributions while respecting the contribution limits set by the Canada Revenue Agency (CRA) and taking the Pension Adjustment (PA) into account. This meant that their contributions would increase over time as allowed by the CRA. In terms of current assets, they had a combined total of a little over three hundred and twenty-five thousand dollars in their Registered Retirement Savings Plans and two hundred and twenty thousand in their Defined Contribution Pension Plans.

As a result of the tax-deferral nature of registered plans, whether it is a pension plan or RRSP, the assets within these plans appreciate faster than those in non-registered accounts. This fact was evident as soon as the couple saw what their registered plans would grow to by the time they turned fifty-five.

"That's amazing!" Thomas said, as soon as he saw the forecasted value of their RRSPs.

The combined value of their RRSPs when they turned fifty-five would be a little over two million two hundred twenty thousand dollars. After taking inflation into account, this was the same as having one million five hundred and sixty thousand dollars today.

"Tax deferral certainly makes a difference," Rachel acknowledged. "Are the numbers the same for our Defined Contribution Pension Plans?"

"No, the numbers are somewhat lower. As you may or may not know, you aren't allowed to contribute the maximum allowable amount to each plan. You can make your maximum annual contribution to one, the other or divide it between both plans. I have assumed that the only contributions that will be made to your employer-sponsored pension plan going forward will be the three per cent of your salary that your employers are making on your behalf."

"Why aren't we allowed to contribute the maximum allowable amount to both?" Thomas asked.

"In order to make sure that all taxpayers at comparable income levels have access to comparable tax assistance, the federal government limits the overall amount that you can contribute to one or more pensions. The CRA does this by relying on something called the Pension Adjustment. The PA is the value of the benefits earned under an employer-sponsored retirement plan such as your Defined Contribution Pension Plan. The PA you earn in a calendar year for participating in one or more of these arrangements will reduce your RRSP contribution room for the next calendar year. For Defined Contribution Pension Plans, the PA is the total of all employer and employee contributions for the year. A person's RRSP contribution room is reduced by the value of the previous year's PA. This means that you can only contribute a total of eighteen per cent of your gross annual income regardless of how many pension plans you belong to."

"So how much have we been contributing to our respective retirement plans?" Rachel asked.

"It looks as though you've been contributing half of the maximum allowable amount to each plan. With regard to your pension plans, both of your employers have been contributing three per cent of your gross annual income. It looks as though you've been contributing another six per cent on your own."

"That explains why our RRSP contribution limits were always lower than the maximum limits that I read about in the newspaper," Rachel said. "I've never really understood why."

"That's exactly why," Donna replied.

"You said that our companies are each contributing three per cent of our income on our behalf. Is that common?" Thomas asked.

"The fact that both of your employers are contributing three per cent to your respective plans is nothing more than a coincidence. There are no standard rules in regards to how much an employer contributes to the company pension plan. The only requirement is that they have to contribute at least one per cent of their employees' gross salary every year in order to maintain the plan and it can't be more than eighteen percent of their gross salary. Some employers will match their employees' contributions one for one and others will contribute a fixed percentage thereof. Some plans require that the employees contribute to the plan and others restrict their employees from contributing altogether. Pension plans come in all different shapes and sizes. If you ever have questions regarding your pension you can speak to the human resources department of your company."

"Is there any reason why we wouldn't want our employers to continue contributing three per cent of our salary on our behalf?"

"Absolutely not. In your particular case, they will contribute a fixed percentage of your salary whether you contribute or not. As I mentioned earlier, we should make a decision as to which plan you would like to make your contributions to going forward. There are distinct advantages to each plan, so we should do whatever best suits your particular situation."

"What are some of the differences between our pension plans and our RRSPs?" Thomas pressed.

"One of the most attractive features of investing money in a pension plan is that proceeds invested in the plan are creditor proof. If, for some reason, you become insolvent, your creditors won't have access to the funds in your pension plan. They would, however, have access to the funds inside of your RRSP. This may change in the near future, however."

"What would be a disadvantage in contributing all the money to our pension plans?"

"The main disadvantage is that you can't readily access the funds inside your plan until retirement. This means that once you contribute the money it's locked in until you stop working. Once you do retire, your income will come from a Life Annuity, Locked-In Retirement Income Fund (LRIF) or Life Income Fund (LIF). Again, there are maximums to how much you can withdraw each year. With an RRSP and RRIF there are no limits in regards to the amount you can take out. Your only consideration with regard to these types of plans would be the tax implications."

"It sounds as though contributing money to an RRSP would be a better option for us because they offer more flexibility in terms of accessing the funds," Rachel said, thinking out loud. "I don't anticipate that creditor protection will be something that we will have to worry about. Of course, now that I've said that, we'll probably go bankrupt tomorrow."

"I don't think creditor protection is or should be a high priority for you. If you were running your own business, it would be a different story. In your particular case, your employers will contribute three per cent of your salary regardless of whether or not you contribute. The advantages of being able to access the funds and have full control over how the money is invested should be more important than protecting the proceeds from creditors. Also, a good portion of your retirement assets are already creditor protected because of the money that you already have in each of your pension plans."

"So what will the plans be worth assuming that only contributions that will be made are the three per cent of our annual salary?" Rachel asked skeptically.

The combined amount of the pension plans was one million one hundred and sixty-five thousand dollars. After adjusting the number for inflation, it equalled just over eight hundred and twenty-six thousand dollars.

Thomas took a moment to look at the inflation-adjusted value of their RRSPs and added the number in front of him. "This means that when we turn fifty-five we'll have around two million three hundred and ninety thousand dollars in inflation adjusted registered assets."

"And if you add the eight hundred and thirteen thousand dollars adjusted for inflation in non-registered assets that we'll have saved, the total comes to three million two hundred thousand dollars," Rachel said, after adding the numbers in her head.

"Now comes my favourite part," Donna said. "Do you remember how much money I estimated that you'll need in order to meet your retirement goals?"

Rachel and Thomas flipped back to the page that estimated their future retirement needs and immediately saw that they needed to save three million two hundred thousand dollars adjusted for inflation in order to retire at the age of fifty-five.

"How much money will you save?" Donna asked rhetorically.

After Thomas read the number out loud, a smile broke across his face.

"So how does it feel?" Donna asked.

"It feels good," Thomas said.

"It certainly feels great," Rachel added.

The last page of the Retirement Planning section summarized all of the information found in the preceding pages in an easy-to-read chart that they could refer back to later. By simply referring to this spreadsheet every so often, they would remind themselves how much money they needed in terms of retirement income, the current value of their retirement assets and what they needed in terms of retirement assets in the future. Regardless of how they looked at the numbers, it was apparent to them that they would be able to achieve their goals as long as they stuck to the plan. This piece of information alone made all of their hard work well worth it.

Investment Management

Now that Rachel and Thomas knew how much money they needed to save in order to retire at the age of fifty-five, they needed to establish how the money should be invested. As Donna had mentioned earlier, inferior long-term investment performance was one of the many pitfalls of being inadequately prepared for your retirement.

As far as Donna's services were concerned, she didn't make specific investment recommendations herself. She did, however, recommend a specific Asset Allocation Model that would likely earn the annual rate of seven per cent that she used as one of the assumptions in her analysis. This Asset Allocation Model was based on the historical rates of return of each different asset class—cash, fixed income and equities.

"As you know, I'm not qualified to select the actual investments themselves. As such, I always recommend that my clients use the services of a professional investment manager such as an investment advisor, investment counsellor or a portfolio manager. During one of our telephone conversations, Thomas asked me when you should start interviewing various investment managers. Now that you have a much better picture of your financial situation, you should start interviewing potential candidates as soon as you're ready."

"In terms of the investment planning, you'll tell us how we should diversify our investments, right?" Rachel asked.

"That's correct. Right now your investments are scattered across far too many areas. Also, I'm not comfortable with the amount of money you have invested in your share plans."

"What do you suggest?" Rachel asked, looking for guidance.

"Given that you will probably both work at your respective companies for many years, you will be investing in your ESPPs for quite some time. What I don't want is for your shares to represent an increasingly disproportionate amount of your net worth. It's not prudent, which is why I'm suggesting that you sell an additional one hundred thousand dollars worth and invest the proceeds in a properly diversified portfolio. Going forward, I would then like you to commit to making sure that your combined positions in your respective companies never represent more than one half of your financial assets. You'll be somewhat restricted as to when you can sell your shares, but in the long run you should be able to find yourself within these limits. What do you think of my suggestion?"

"To be quite honest, I'm not sure how I feel about it. I've heard of people losing lots of money because the business that they own becomes insolvent. I've never even entertained the thought of this happening to a company that I work for," Rachel replied.

"One aspect of my job is to help you make difficult decisions that could potentially affect your future net worth for better or worse. I'm suggesting this as a precaution in order to preserve your current assets in case either of the companies that you work for becomes insolvent."

"As someone who works in the technology field, I've had friends who have seen their companies go up in smoke almost overnight. Therefore, I'm not opposed to following your advice," Thomas said.

"If you're comfortable with it, then so am I," Rachel said.

"What is your suggestion in regards to diversifying the proceeds of the sale of the shares and our other retirement savings?" Thomas asked.

"In order to achieve your goals, I'm recommending that the asset allocation of all of your registered and non-registered assets should be five per cent in cash, thirty-five per cent in bonds, twenty per cent in Canadian equities, twenty per cent in US equities and twenty per cent in International equities. This is the optimal asset mix that should provide us with an average annual long-term rate of return of at least seven per cent. For comparison purposes, I've included a pie chart of the current asset allocation of your investments and my recommended asset allocation."

All of the information was neatly presented in two pie charts accompanied by a description of each individual asset class and its long-term historical performance. As far as their current asset mix and prescribed asset mix was concerned, it was like night and day. Currently, they were almost entirely invested in stocks. This explained why the value of their investments had been bouncing around like a yo-yo over the last few years.

"In terms of the investment process, what else can we expect from you?"

"If you need help in making a final decision on the right investment manager, I can help you do that. I can also help you with monitoring your portfolio's performance. For the most part, however, a good investment manager will do this for you," Donna replied.

"Do you have anyone with whom you work on a regular basis?" Thomas asked.

"I have a handful of investment managers that I refer clients to. They are all very different in terms of the services they offer, area of expertise and personality. Again, all of them are very good at what they do. I'll provide you with their names as soon as you're ready.

Insurance Planning

"Now that you know what it will take for you to meet your retirement goals, let's discuss what we need to do to protect you from a sudden loss of income. As far as insurance is concerned, I'm recommending that you increase your coverage. You currently each have one hundred and fifty thousand dollars in coverage, which is provided to you by each of your employers. Unfortunately, this isn't enough should something happen to one or both of you."

"We had a feeling that this was the case. A close friend of ours told us that at the very least, we each need at least one million five hundred thousand dollars in coverage," Rachel admitted.

"Your friend is absolutely right. Do you know why he said this?"

"Jacob said that if something were to happen to either of us, we would need to replace the loss of after-tax income. This would be about ninety thousand dollars per year based on each of our current gross annual incomes. At an average rate of return of seven per cent per year, a one million five hundred thousand dollar policy would provide us with enough money to pay the bills until the kids were grown."

"That's right. As you know, taxes play an important role in most financial decisions. Although the initial one million five hundred thousand dollar payout would be tax-free, any investment income earned on this amount is taxable. This means that the face amount of the policy would actually need to be a little higher."

"He said the exact same thing. He also said that we should consider taking out additional insurance to pay the taxes on our Registered Retirement Savings Plans and capital gains tax on our non-registered investments and cottage," Rachel continued.

"This Jacob is very well informed," Donna said. "As far as the amount of insurance is concerned, I'm recommending that you each take out an additional one million five hundred thousand dollar policy. This can be either a Universal Life or Term to 100 policy. After taking out this additional insurance, you'll each have one million six hundred and fifty thousand dollars in coverage. This will adequately meet your needs because, after you pay off your debts, you will require less income to cover your expenses going forward."

"What's the difference between these two types of insurance policies?" Thomas asked.

"Universal Life is unique in that it consists of two parts—term insurance and an investment account. With each premium, a portion is used to cover administrative expenses and cost of insurance. Any amount in addition to these expenses is credited to an investment account where the money can be invested in a broad range of investment vehicles usually in the form of mutual funds. The attractive feature about the investment account is that the money grows tax-free until it is withdrawn. This is why it is suitable for those investors who have additional savings above and beyond their RRSPs. The downside of this type of policy is that it costs quite a bit more than simple term insurance."

"Does Term to 100 have any special features?" Rachel asked.

"No. It is a standard life insurance policy that gives you coverage until you die. You pay a fixed premium and, if something happens to you, it pays your beneficiary the face amount that was originally purchased. This type of policy is very popular because it is relatively affordable."

"Is there anything else as far as insurance is concerned?"

"That's about it. Just so you know, I've also had a look at your disability insurance and found that each of your employers provides you with very good coverage in the event you become disabled and can no longer work. I've listed the details of your coverage in this section here," Donna said, pointing to the page in front of her. "If one of you becomes disabled, your disability insurance will kick in after three months and provide you with an income until you are once again able to go to work."

Estate Planning

This is another area that is often overlooked by many individuals, even though it is extremely important. In most cases, proper estate planning is essential for anyone who wants to ensure that the majority of their estate is passed on to their desired beneficiaries, whether it be family members, close friends or favourite charities. An estate plan can be as simple as having an updated will or it can be as complicated as having several legal trusts established that require that the assets of an estate be distributed over several generations. In any case, an estate plan should ensure that the assets are distributed to the appropriate beneficiaries while taking steps to minimize taxes. Regardless of the complexity of your estate planning needs, you should always rely on a legal professional to prepare the appropriate documents in order to ensure that all of your wishes have been well documented.

The starting point for most estate plans is to draw up a will that reflects the desires of the individual. A will is important because it documents the intentions of the testator—the person making the will—and identifies each beneficiary and the assets that they are entitled to once the individual passes away.

Another reason a will is important is that it names an executor, whose primary role is to ensure and oversee that the deceased's assets are distributed according to the will's instructions. This person is usually a close friend, family member or a trusted professional who is familiar with the individual's specific situation. When choosing an executor, you should be confident that that person has good judgment and a high level of integrity. You should also make certain that the individual you name has agreed to be the executor of the estate and you should name an alternate executor should the original executor predecease you or become incompetent. As far as the compensation of the executor is concerned, it should be negotiated beforehand. If this isn't done the courts will set the compensation from a schedule of allowable tariffs, which may be inadequate for the amount of work involved in settling the estate. Typically, the compensation is set at several percentage points of the total value of the estate but can also be set at a predetermined, fixed amount.

As far as the actual will is concerned, there are several items that should always be included. In most provinces, a will contains six basic clauses that identify the instructions of the testator. These clauses identify the executor, revoke all former wills and codicils, appoint the executor and describe his or her occupation and address, instruct the executor to pay all just debts and identify in detail which beneficiary is to receive specific assets and the residue of the estate. In addition to these standard clauses, there is also the possibility of adding optional clauses. These clauses can state such wishes as the type of funeral you'd like to have, where you would like to be buried or whether you would like to be cremated.

After having drafted a proper will, the second most important document is the power of attorney. A personal power of attorney is different from a will in that it can appoint someone to make decisions of a personal nature in the event that the individual becomes mentally incapable of doing so on their own accord. If for example, Rachel outlives Thomas but is no longer capable of making her own decisions due to mental incapacity, a personal power of attorney will name the individual who is legally allowed to make any decisions on her behalf.

The third most important aspect of estate planning is reducing the amount of probate and taxes payable at death. In terms of reducing probate, you can do one of three things—hold assets jointly so that when one of the joint owners dies the other automatically gets title, transfer ownership of property prior to death or make a major charitable donation. All of these options will result in lower probate fees and taxes payable, thereby leaving a larger portion of the estate to an individual's named beneficiaries.

"I've had a look at each of your wills and they are quite outdated," Donna said matter-of-factly. "You haven't drafted powers of attorney either. We need to do that right away."

"I actually prepared our wills myself with one of those do-it-yourself kits," Thomas said. "At the time I was under the impression they would serve us fine."

"Those kits are all right providing your situation is relatively simple. Once you have children and want your assets to be distributed properly, it's better to have a professional do it for you. As far as my recommendations are concerned, you should meet with an estate lawyer who will draft updated wills and powers of attorney on your behalf. You should also hold all of your assets jointly, which, for the most part, you already do. What you may want to do is start thinking about whom you would like to name as an executor and who will have power of attorney over your affairs in the event of incapacitation. You also need to think about guardians for your children, in case something happens to both of you. That way you'll have the names ready when you meet with a lawyer."

"Do you have an estate lawyer that you can refer us to?" Rachel asked.

"Yes, I actually work closely with several estate lawyers. All of them do excellent work. You should get in touch with them in the next few weeks at the very latest."

Tax Planning

"Before we have a look at the last section of the financial plan, I think it's important to mention that over the years, the Canada Revenue Agency has made it extremely difficult to minimize taxes. In the past, there were legal loopholes that enabled individuals to minimize their taxes, but, unfortunately, most of them have been closed or eliminated. This is why it's even more important to take advantage of all of the tax-reducing strategies that are still available."

"Can you give us some examples of some of the strategies still available?" Thomas asked.

"Actually, I've listed all the strategies that apply to your specific situation in this section. The first and most widely used tax savings strategy is contributing money to your Registered Retirement Savings Plan. When you make a contribution to an RRSP you get a tax credit for the contribution made. Also, when you contribute money to an RRSP the investments grow tax free inside the plan. We've already discussed the merits of RRSPs in the Retirement Planning section so we won't go into much detail in this section."

"We both have a good understanding of the mechanics of RRSPs. What else can we do to pay less tax?" Rachel asked.

"There's another way that we can use the RRSPs to your advantage. This is by holding a majority of your interest-bearing investments such as bonds, mortgage-backed securities and GICs inside your RRSP rather than outside."

"How does this help us minimize tax?" Thomas asked, confused.

"Interest income is taxed at the highest rate, whereas dividends and capital gains are taxed at a lower rate. As such, it makes sense to hold a good portion of your interest-bearing investments in a registered account. It's important to mention that you have to take several things into consideration before you move all of your fixed-income investments into your RRSP. Before you make any changes you should take interest rates, volatility of the stock market and your income needs into account. If interest rates are low and the stock markets are expected to be active over an extended period of time, for example, it doesn't necessarily make sense to hold all of your interest-bearing investments inside a registered plan because they are paying you very little interest and your equities may end up generating significant capital gains if your investment manager is even moderately active. In your particular case, I'm satisfied with how the investments are diversified among your various accounts based on my asset allocation recommendations."

"Any other suggestions?"

"Another strategy is to eliminate all of the non-deductible interest on debt. As I mentioned earlier, if you borrow money to invest in stocks, bonds, real estate or a variety of other types of investments, the interest on these loans is tax-deductible. That means that if you have money invested outside of your registered plans and still have a mortgage, it makes sense to pay off the mortgage and then borrow the money and invest it. The only hurdle that most people have trouble getting over is investing borrowed money. It takes some getting used to," Donna said candidly.

"In our particular case, we're selling some of the shares in our Employee Share Purchase Plans and paying off the mortgage, so we can't take advantage of this, can we?"

"If we do what I've prescribed then you won't have a mortgage to worry about," Donna answered.

"When we sell our shares, won't we have to pay tax on the capital gains? If this is the case, doesn't it defeat the whole purpose of trying to reduce our taxes?" Thomas probed.

"It's nice to see that you're becoming more aware of any taxes that you might have to pay—it's a good habit to get into. In addition to better diversifying your assets, the other reason that I'm recommending that you sell a portion of your shares to pay off your debts is that the capital gains taxes that you will owe will be partially offset by the capital losses that each of you have been carrying forward for many years. Do you remember where these losses are from?" Donna asked, curious.

"Many years ago, when we both starting working, we tried dabbling the stock market on our own. We invested in a few small, speculative companies and, needless to say, we ended up losing quite a bit of money," Rachel said.

"Well, not all is lost. The losses that you incurred back then can be applied towards any capital gains in the future. Although the losses won't cover all of the gains, they will cover a good portion of them so the capital gains taxes will be reduced significantly."

"I'm quite surprised that the losses can still be used. I would have assumed that they would have expired or become unusable after a certain period of time," Thomas suggested.

"Actually, many people don't know that you can carry the losses forward indefinitely. A lot of individuals even forget that they have them and fail to take advantage of them."

"I think we would have been guilty of that," Rachel reluctantly admitted.

"As far as other tax-saving strategies are concerned, we may want to consider tax-friendly investments such as Limited Partnerships. These types of investments usually come with a certain amount of risk, so it's very important that you have the merits of these investments evaluated by a qualified investment professional. From a tax standpoint, they are often attractive. I'm not in a position to evaluate them as an investment, however."

"Is it safe to assume that you will help us prepare our annual tax returns?" Rachel asked.

"I'd be happy to provide you with accounting services. In fact, it makes sense because of my familiarity with your overall situation. My accounting fees aren't included in the financial planning process, so there will be additional costs for me to prepare your returns and provide ongoing tax advice."

"That's fine. I wasn't expecting it to be included because filing our annual returns wasn't mentioned in the financial planning contract as being included in the initial fees," Rachel said.

"You have no idea how reassuring it is to see your level of attention to detail," Donna said.

The last section of the financial plan neatly summarized all of the key facts, figures and recommendations that were made throughout the plan, so that the information was readily available in case either of them needed to refer back to it at some point in the future. It also included a copy of the financial planning agreement, which could be referred back to later.

"So," Donna asked. "What do you think?"

"Firstly, I can't believe that we're done. It feels great," Rachel admitted. "Secondly, I'm really happy with the amount of detailed information you've presented to us. It feels as if no stone was left unturned."

"That's nice to hear. What about you, Thomas?"

"I feel the same way. I can't believe that we didn't do this years ago," he added, looking over at Rachel to gauge her reaction. She smiled.

"Most people feel that way after they've gone through the exercise. It's not over though. We still have a lot to do."

"What do you mean?" Rachel asked.

"After you sign off on the preliminary plan, I'll prepare your final copy for you. The information won't be much different, but the document itself will be more polished. If nothing has changed during this time then we have to start implementing the plan."

"What's the first thing we need to do?" Rachel asked.

"The first thing you need to do is start looking for someone to manage your money. This person will play an important role in helping you achieve your goals because many of the assumptions made in the plan assume that your financial assets will appreciate at a reasonable rate above the rate of inflation. Although it may seem easy to manage your own money during good market cycles, most individuals aren't in a position to properly manage their money during bad market cycles."

"We agree completely, which is why we've already started compiling a list of names of investment advisors, investment counsellors and portfolio managers," Thomas said. "We have absolutely no interest in managing our own money."

"If you can do me a favour and let me know when you've hired someone, I'd appreciate it. It's likely that I'll have frequent contact with this individual, so I'd like to call to introduce myself sooner rather than later. If you need me to refer you to someone, don't hesitate to ask. In the meantime, expect a final copy of the financial plan in the next week or so."

"Thanks, Donna. We appreciate it," Rachel said. "We'll talk to you in the next couple of weeks to let you know when we're ready to put things in motion."

Key Point

A well prepared financial plan should address all of your financial needs including Budget & Savings Planning, Retirement Planning, Investment Management, Insurance Planning, Estate Planning and Tax Planning.

| 23 |

The Investment Advisors

After their meeting with Donna, Rachel and Thomas decided to let a week go by before calling and scheduling any interviews with the various investment advisors and portfolio managers on the list. The last thing that they wanted to do was make the process so daunting that they might want to abandon it midway through. After taking some time to think about other things, they were both very eager to once again get underway.

Rachel and Thomas were very pleased that they had found Donna, and they hoped that their next hiring decision would be as easy.

As they had done with the financial planners, they started by calling someone with whom they were somewhat familiar. In this case it was Charles Kaplan, the investment advisor who had been referred to them by the manager of their local bank branch. He worked for the full-service investment dealer that was wholly owned by their bank.

When he phoned Charles, Thomas explained that they had just finished working with a financial planner and were now looking for someone to manage their assets in accordance with the plan. He also mentioned that even though they had been dealing with the branch for many years they were going to be interviewing several candidates, all of whom worked at different firms. Thomas felt that it was important to be upfront about this so that Charles didn't assume that he was the only candidate being interviewed.

"I'm glad you told me that you're meeting several candidates. This is reassuring because it tells me that you're taking the process seriously," said Charles. "In terms of my experience, I have been an investment advisor with the firm for more than ten years. During that time, I have earned my Financial Management Advisor (FMA) designation. I also have my Level I and II Life Insurance license, which allows me to advise clients on their insurance needs."

"Is it common for an investment advisor to have his insurance license?" Thomas asked.

"In the last few years it has been become more common," Charles explained. "Although I don't sell a lot of insurance, it's nice to have written the exams because it enabled me to learn more about the insurance business."

"Why don't we start by you telling me about your investment philosophy?"

"The cornerstone of any sound investment strategy is diversifying your assets across a broad range of investments. I also believe that investors should invest in companies that have sound fundamentals and strong balance sheets. Something I find all too common is that novice investors tend to accept too much risk based on their profile," Charles said.

"Can you describe your typical client?"

"I'd say that my typical client would be between the ages of forty and sixty. A majority of my clients are referred to me by the bank, so they are fairly conservative in terms of their risk profile. They include business owners, professionals and retirees."

"Do you have any one area of expertise?"

"That would be managing people's assets in accordance with their investment objectives and risk profiles. I don't specialize in any one type of investment or sector of the economy. I tend to focus more on the process itself."

"That sounds good. Peter told me that you've done a great job for clients at the branch. Can we set up a meeting some time next week? Are you free during the evenings by any chance?"

Charles said he was and they arranged to meet the following Tuesday at five-thirty. The next name on his list was Ian Schaeffer. He had been referred by the manager of an investment dealer with a branch in their neighbourhood. Thomas dialled the number and after a few rings he was forwarded to Ian's voice mail. After leaving a message, Thomas hung up the phone and moved on to the next name on his list, Theo Mueller.

When Thomas was gathering names, he had made a conscious effort to contact firms of various sizes because he thought it would be prudent to see what services different-sized firms had to offer. Theo Mueller worked at a medium-sized, independently owned firm. After speaking with him, Thomas was glad he'd called.

Theo Mueller had been working in the investment industry for over fifteen years. He started out working at a credit union, which gave him the opportunity to learn everything he needed to know about the financial services industry. In terms of financial acumen, he was very well versed on a wide range of investment-related topics. More importantly, he also placed a great deal of importance on the investment management process. Thomas had liked everything he heard during the telephone conversation, so he scheduled a meeting for Wednesday evening.

The next call that Thomas made was to Gabriel Woods who worked at a small, independently owned investment dealer. Thomas had been given his name by Gabriel's branch manager. After several rings, Gabriel answered the phone himself.

Thomas took a few moments to introduce himself and explain why he was calling, but a few minutes into the conversation he started to get a sense that Gabriel might not be a good fit based on their investment objectives.

"How would you describe your investment personality?" Thomas asked.

"The most accurate description would be aggressive growth. My area of expertise is in emerging mining, biotechnology and technology stocks. In fact, most of my recommendations are from this sector."

"These types of companies are typically considered to be high risk, aren't they?"

"Yes. Most of these companies are very speculative in nature," Gabriel answered candidly.

"How would you describe your typical client?" Thomas asked.

"Most of my clients are speculative investors. They are sophisticated investors who are aware of the risks and rewards of investing in these areas. I typically manage the money that they have allocated to aggressive growth. This can be anywhere from ten to twenty-five per cent of their overall holdings. Depending on the client, it's sometimes even higher."

"I appreciate your time, Gabriel. We're really looking for someone who is more conservative in nature. We are just in the early stages of finding a compatible investment advisor, so we're not in a financial position where we're comfortable with accepting a high level of risk."

"Then I'm definitely not the right person to help you," Gabriel said pleasantly. "But, if at some point in the future you're ready to consider more aggressive investments, please call me."

"I appreciate you taking the time to talk to me. Thank you."

Almost immediately after he put the phone back in its cradle it rang. Thomas picked it up on the first ring.

It was Ian Shaeffer returning Thomas's call. Thomas explained what he and Rachel were looking for and asked Ian about his experience.

"The company hired me immediately after I graduated from university, which was about ten years ago. It's hard to believe it's been that long already."

"Do you walk your clients through a formal process before advising them on their investments?"

"Yes, I do. The process consists of several steps that address all facets of your financial situation. Typically, I will take you through these steps after I have gathered all of the preliminary information. If I didn't walk you through a formal process, I wouldn't have the slightest clue about your overall financial situation."

The conversation continued for another twenty minutes during which Thomas was impressed with everything he heard. He was looking forward to meeting Ian in person because he seemed outgoing, energetic and very personable. It was a nice way to end the telephone interview process. He was looking forward to telling Rachel about the three meetings that he had scheduled. Given the initial conversations that he had with each candidate, Thomas was certain that they would find someone who would be the perfect fit.

Key Point

Investment Advisors sometimes have specific areas of expertise. Make sure to interview those that specialize in an area that is complementary to your specific investment objectives.

|24|

Interviewing Investment Advisors

It was shortly before five-thirty on Tuesday evening when Rachel and Thomas arrived at Charles's office in the heart of the financial district. The lobby of the building was still bustling with employees leaving work. Finding the appropriate bank of elevators, the couple travelled up to the thirty-sixth floor. When the doors opened they stepped into an attractively decorated reception area that was accented in dark wood, glass and stone. The walls boasted several modern paintings and the floor was covered by two beautiful Persian rugs. A pretty young woman wearing a headset sat behind the desk, and when she saw Rachel and Thomas she welcomed them with a warm smile.

"You must be Mr. and Mrs. Connor. Charles is expecting you. Why don't you have a seat and he'll be with you in a few moments."

Shortly thereafter a tall, well-dressed man came through the door located to the right of the receptionist's desk, holding out his hand.

After quick introductions, they walked to Charles's office. The first thing that caught Thomas's attention when he sat down were the numerous pictures of Charles's wife and three young daughters.

"I see that we have something in common," Thomas said, pointing to the pictures on his desk. "I'd be willing to bet that you don't get to watch TSN very often either," he added.

"The last time I watched sports on TV was when the Blue Jays won the World Series," Charles laughed.

Getting down to business, he said: "Peter mentioned that you are in the process of interviewing financial planners, investment advisors and portfolio managers."

"That's right. We've actually already hired a financial planner. She drew up our financial plan a couple of weeks ago. We're now looking for someone to help us implement the investment component of the plan," Rachel said. "That's the reason we're here."

"I appreciate the opportunity. Where would you like to start?"

"Why don't we start by discussing your role as an investment advisor? What can we expect from you when we're eventually ready to invest our money?" Thomas asked.

"My role is to provide you with investment solutions that will help you achieve your financial goals. I accomplish this by walking you through a process that's similar to the financial planning process. The main difference is that I'll focus specifically on your investment management needs as opposed to your general financial needs."

"What would the first step be?" Rachel asked.

"The first step involves data gathering, which includes evaluating your investment objectives, time horizon, risk tolerance, tax status, investment knowledge and any unique circumstances that you may have. In your particular case, the final draft of your financial plan will address all of these issues. As a result, I'll rely heavily on the information that's presented to me providing that it has been prepared by a qualified financial planner."

"What do you mean by qualified?" Rachel asked curiously.

"By qualified I mean someone who has their PFP, CFP or RFP designation and I prefer them to have had at least ten years of experience."

"Based on that definition, our financial planner is more than qualified," Thomas said.

"That's good to know. You've obviously been doing some research," Charles acknowledged.

"What comes after you've finished collecting and analyzing the data?" Rachel asked.

"After I've done this, I'll then present you with an investment proposal that outlines the individual securities, asset mix and an estimate of the fees that you'll pay. Once you've had an opportunity to review the investment proposal, we'll go over it together so I can answer any questions that you may have."

"And if everything looks good?" Thomas asked.

"After I get your approval, I'll begin by slowly assembling the portfolio. This might take a few days, weeks or even months depending on the prevalent economic conditions," Charles explained.

"What can we expect from you on an ongoing basis?"

"An important part of my job is keeping you abreast of any significant changes in the economy, monitoring your portfolio on a daily basis and making investment recommendations as needed. This doesn't mean you should expect me to call you every time the stock market is up or down a few points. I'll call you in a timely fashion whenever it's in your best interest to make a change to the portfolio."

"What about performance? How will we know if our portfolio is performing well?"

"Once a year we will sit down and review your investments. We'll use this as an opportunity to discuss any changes in your financial situation that may require your portfolio to be modified," Charles said.

"How are you different from other investment advisors we'll meet? Is there anything that you bring to the table that maybe your competitors don't?" Rachel asked bluntly.

"Although my primary role is that of an investment advisor, I also consider myself to be a coach because I spend a great deal of time educating my clients on a wide range of investment-related topics. I believe that an educated investor is easier to work with because they tend to appreciate the complexity of the investment management process. This approach also helps foster a strong relationship between me and my clients, which is extremely important in this business."

"What about your company itself? Are there any benefits to dealing with your company as opposed to another financial institution?" Thomas asked.

"Two of our greatest strengths are our top-rated research department and our economic strategy team. Our analysts and economists are some of the best in the industry. Another key strength is the strict ethical standards we're expected to adhere to. Although we're not the largest firm in the country, we are one of the most respected."

"What products are you licensed to sell?" Thomas asked.

"I can sell mutual funds, stocks, options and life insurance. As I mentioned on the telephone, I also earned my Financial Management Advisor (FMA) designation, which gives me a good understanding of the financial planning process. I have to stress, however, that financial planning isn't my forte. I leave financial planning to financial planners."

"If one of us calls you, when can we expect you to return our call?"

"I have an excellent support staff, so you can expect me to call you back within a few hours. If I'm out of the office when you call, I'll call you back first thing the next morning."

"Are you limited to selling your firm's proprietary products?" Rachel asked.

"Not at all," Charles assured her. "I can recommend almost any investment that is available in the market. I can even sell GICs that are issued by many of our competitors. If another institution is offering higher GIC rates, I can usually buy them for you."

"I didn't know that. It sounds like there is very little pressure on you to sell proprietary products," Rachel acknowledged, writing down the information on her notepad.

"May I ask how are you paid? I'm assuming that it's different from financial planners?" Thomas asked.

"There are two ways that investment advisors are paid—either through commission or with fees based on assets under management. Currently, most investment advisors still earn commissions on the products they sell. In the last few years, however, there has been a gradual shift towards fee-based accounts. Fee-based accounts have been well received because they tend to align the interests of the client and the investment advisor. Under this arrangement, the client pays a fee based on a percentage of their assets. This can typically range from one per cent to two and a half per cent depending on the account size. Most of my income is earned through fees."

"That sounds similar to the way investment counselling and portfolio management companies charge their clients," Thomas acknowledged.

"You're right, it is similar. I should also mention that another advantage of fee-based accounts is that the fee is usually tax deductible if it's paid outside of non-registered accounts. If you're in a high tax bracket this can make a significant difference. Of course, don't expect this to last forever. The Canada Revenue Agency has a habit of eliminating tax deductibility on items as they become more popular with the general public."

"One of the decisions that we're eventually going to have to make is whether we're going to work with an investment advisor or a portfolio manager. In your opinion, are there any advantages to working with you as opposed to a reputable wealth management firm?" Rachel asked.

"The general school of thought seems to be that ultra high–net worth individuals are better off entrusting their financial assets to investment counsellors and portfolio managers because they are more qualified in terms of managing money. Although the requirements for being licensed as an investment counsellor or portfolio manager are very demanding, I've always placed a higher level of importance on years of experience. It also really comes down to what kind of professional relationship you're interested in."

"What do you mean?" Rachel prodded.

"Although many discretionary portfolio managers have excellent credentials, it doesn't necessarily mean that they'll be more proficient in meeting your needs. There are many investment advisors who have a great deal of experience managing money and they often yield equally impressive results."

"Other than licensing requirements, how are you different, then?"

"The difference is that our role is advisory in nature, which means that we can't simply make changes to the portfolio as we see fit. I'm required to contact you before any changes are made. This means that there tends to be much more personal contact involved in our relationship. A lot of individuals appreciate this because it allows them to learn about the investment management process. As I mentioned earlier, I spend a great deal of time educating my clients on a wide range of investment-related topics. This is something that you likely won't get if you work with a discretionary portfolio manager."

"How will we know what's right for us?" Thomas asked.

"It will depend on a variety of factors such as the amount of money you have to invest, how much involvement you'd like to have and who you think is better positioned to meet your financial goals. I'd like to stress that you don't necessarily have to choose one over the other. It's not uncommon for someone to split his or her financial assets between an investment advisor and a portfolio manager. This would give you the opportunity to see which approach you prefer."

"The thought of using two different people for our investment management needs never even crossed my mind," Rachel admitted.

"There's nothing wrong with working with that approach," Charles said. "If it works for you then that's all that matters."

After another forty minutes of casual conversation about various investment trends, the interview came to an end and Charles walked Rachel and Thomas to the elevators. As soon the elevator doors closed they smiled at each other, indicating that they were both impressed. Charles had demonstrated a high degree of professionalism, confidence and expertise. He seemed like someone they could trust to advise them on their investments. If the rest of the investment advisors were anything like Charles, they would eventually have to make another extremely difficult decision.

~

Next on their interview list was Theo Mueller who worked for an independent, medium-sized firm. He was in his late forties to early fifties and had many years of experience under his belt. During the initial telephone conversation he had seemed to place a great deal of importance on the investment management process itself. Although this was a common theme among all the professionals that they had spoken to so far, Theo really seemed to focus on it.

They arrived at Theo's office at around six-thirty on Wednesday evening. His office was also located in the financial district, only four blocks from where they had met Charles the previous night.

As with most of the other offices that they had visited, Theo's reception area was nicely decorated with touches of sandblasted glass and stainless steel. Due to the time, there wasn't a receptionist to welcome them, so they took a seat on the sofa. A few minutes later, an older gentleman with gray hair walked through the glass doors at the far end of the reception area. It was Theo.

"Hello, you must be Rachel and Thomas?" he asked in a soft voice. Rachel and Thomas stood up and introduced themselves.

"Would you prefer to sit in my office or the boardroom? If we sit in the boardroom I can put on some coffee," he offered graciously.

"A cup of coffee would be nice," Rachel said.

Theo escorted the couple through the glass doors, down a short hallway and into the boardroom. While Thomas and Rachel took a seat at the end of the table, Theo went into the kitchen, which was off of the boardroom, and put on a pot of coffee. He then returned holding a tray with three mugs and spoons, some cream and sugar.

"It'll take a few minutes for the coffee to brew. Why don't we get started by you telling me a little bit about yourselves?"

Thomas and Rachel proceeded to tell him everything about their situation without leaving out a single detail. As soon as they had finished, Theo politely excused himself and went back into the kitchen. He then returned with a pot of coffee, filled everyone's mug and quietly took his seat.

"So where were we?" Theo asked. Rachel politely reminded him.

"It sounds to me as though you're taking the appropriate steps to put your finances in order. Have you found the process intimidating in any way?"

"Actually, so far everything has gone quite smoothly. We've also met some good people along the way. Why do you ask?"

"It seems as though you have a good grip on things and that you're not interested in rushing into anything. You'd be surprised at how many people transfer their money to me without ever having met me in person," Theo said.

"We're fairly new to the whole process so we're taking it slowly until we reach a certain comfort level," Thomas said.

"May I ask how you got my name? Most of my new clients come from referrals," Theo asked, curious.

"I actually called your branch manager and gave him a brief description of our situation. He then recommended that I contact you because he thought you might be a good fit," Thomas said.

"Is there any particular reason why you called our firm?"

"We wanted to interview professionals from a wide variety of companies rather than just focusing on the bank-owned investment dealers. After doing some homework, I learned that your firm is one of the most reputable independent investment dealers in the country."

"I'm glad that you called us because we're in a position to offer you the same services that are offered by our bank-owned competitors. Unless you have specific questions on our firm, I won't go into detail because our reputation speaks for itself."

"I do have one question about your firm. Are your clients protected by the Canadian Investor Protection Fund?" Rachel asked.

"Yes, they are. The same limits apply to all firms that are members of the CIPF regardless of their size."

"What about yourself? How long have you been an investment advisor?" Rachel asked, trying to break the ice.

"I've been doing this for almost fifteen years."

"What about prior to that?" Rachel prodded.

"I worked as the branch manager for a large credit union."

"Do you specialize in any particular area?" Thomas asked.

"Not really. I advise a broad group of clients, so it really depends on their specific needs."

"Do you take new clients through an investment management process?" Thomas asked.

"Yes, I do. It's similar to that of most other seasoned professionals."

"At some point we're going to have to make a decision in terms of who we're going to hire. Is there anything that you bring to the table that the other investment advisors may not?" Thomas asked in an attempt to get him to open up a little.

"I think my greatest asset is my experience. I've been doing this for a very long time, so I'm confident that I'd meet all of your expectations."

"What products are you licensed to sell?"

"Almost every product that's available in the marketplace. I'm also licensed to sell life insurance, but I don't really sell much of that."

"Can you describe your typical client?" Rachel asked.

"I can't really say that I have a typical client. I work with a wide range of individuals, all of whom have different needs. The one thing that they may have in common is that they are quite conservative."

"What do you think your best clients would say about you?" Thomas asked.

"I think they would describe me as being level-headed. I pride myself on doing what's in my clients' best interests and I think they know that," Theo said.

"Why don't you tell us about the last client that you helped? What, for example, was his or her investor profile? And what about his or her investment objectives? Also, what investment solutions did you provide him or her with?" Rachel asked.

"The last clients that I helped were a couple in their late fifties who had received a large inheritance. After the estate was settled, I presented them with an investment proposal based on their specific objectives. Once they saw what I was proposing, they gave me the go-ahead to manage their portfolio in accordance with the proposal and I have continued to do so ever since."

The interview continued in this manner for another twenty minutes and, although they gave Theo every opportunity to let his personality shine through, they left the office feeling that they hadn't really learned very much about him. This didn't mean that he was no longer a candidate. It simply meant that they would have to meet him again before being in a position to decide if he would be a good fit. Maybe if he were given a second opportunity he would open up a little more. After all, Thomas and Rachel decided, maybe he was better with money than with people.

~

Their next meeting was with Ian Schaeffer. Ian worked for a large investment dealer with branches in hundreds of communities across the country. His office was located on the ground floor of a low-rise building on a main street right in their neighbourhood.

Ian's office was somewhat smaller than the other offices that they had visited because the firm consisted of just six employees including the branch manger, three investment advisors and two support staff. As they walked through the front door they both thought that it seemed like a nice place to work because of its cozy atmosphere.

Despite it being shortly after eight o'clock at night, there were still three people working at their desks. As soon as Ian saw the couple walk through the front door, he quickly came out of his office and welcomed them.

During the initial telephone call, Thomas had found Ian to be very energetic and enthusiastic, so he was looking forward to meeting him. Almost immediately, Thomas and Rachel knew that they would be in for a treat. From the moment he shook their hands it was obvious that he was very charming and personable. They also knew that they would have very little trouble getting him to come out of his shell.

"Good to meet you in person, Ian," Thomas said. "This is my wife, Rachel."

"Come in, come in. I've been looking forward to this since we spoke on the phone. I always enjoy meeting new people. Let's go into my office."

The first thing that they noticed when they walked into Ian's office were the newspapers, books and research reports stacked everywhere. Some of the piles of paper were so high they could have been considered hazardous.

"Please excuse the mess. The branch manager is always telling me to clean up before I bring prospects or clients into my office. The only problem is that if I put them away I'll just have to take them back out," Ian explained. "I have a couple of hard hats in my desk drawer if that would make you feel safer," he added with a grin.

Thomas and Rachel smiled. They always appreciated a good sense of humour.

"I don't think that it's necessary. This isn't nearly as bad as our eldest daughter's bedroom," Thomas answered.

Something else that they noticed immediately was that Ian's walls were covered with the framed certificates of all of the courses he had successfully completed and the designations he had earned. This included the certificate for the Canadian Securities Course (CSC), Financial Management Advisor (FMA) and Fellow of the Canadian Securities Institute (FCSI) designations. It was obvious that he was proud of having earned them, which was nice to see.

"It's nice to see your designations on your wall. It demonstrates that you are dedicated to your profession. It must have taken a lot of work." Thomas said.

"It did indeed. Over the years, the courses have become increasingly difficult because of the sheer number of people interested in working in the securities industry. The regulatory bodies have been raising the bar lately in order to try to ensure that consumers are receiving the highest level of service available."

"So, how long have you been an investment advisor?" Rachel started off.

"I'm about a year shy of my tenth anniversary," Ian answered. "I was hired as soon as I graduated from university."

"Did you work as an associate to a more senior investment advisor during the first few years?"

"Actually, I didn't. The branch manager hired me because I already had quite a bit of investment experience. I have my father to thank for that because he introduced me to the financial markets when I was very young."

"That sounds a little bit like a friend of ours," Rachel said, thinking of Megan. "She also started investing at a very young age."

"I think I was about fourteen or fifteen when I bought shares in Coca-Cola. After that, I was hooked. In fact, I still own the shares to this day and have done quite well by holding onto them," Ian said.

"Was that the reason why you were hired so young?" Thomas asked.

"Another reason is that I had received my bachelor of arts in economics. This gave me a solid foundation to work from. I also completed the Canadian Securities Course while I was still at university, demonstrating that I was able to grasp the material before entering the industry."

"How many clients do you currently work with?" Thomas asked.

"I work with about two hundred and fifty families. I don't really have a typical client in terms of their asset size. For the most part, they're just nice, everyday people."

"Do you have an assistant to help you with administration?"

"Yes. Her name is Rebecca. I've been working with her for the last five years and she's absolutely fantastic. To be quite honest, I'd be lost without her."

"What part of your job do you enjoy most? It seems as though there are so many facets to the work."

"I think my favourite part of the job is managing money. I've always enjoyed making investment decisions, and it's even more enjoyable when I'm helping someone else achieve their financial goals."

"Speaking of investment decisions, what kind of research do you do before recommending an investment?" Thomas questioned.

"The first thing I do is make sure that the investment is in line with your risk tolerance. If I decide that it is suitable, I'll then assess the merits of the investment by reading quarterly reports, annual reports and research reports from various research analysts and bond rating agencies."

"Have you ever made a bad recommendation?" Thomas asked, interested to see what the answer would be.

"I would be lying if I said no. One of the first things that individuals need to learn before investing their money is that, on occasion, they'll make a bad investment. No matter how strong a balance sheet looks or how quickly a company is growing its earnings, there is always the possibility that something could go wrong. It simply goes with the territory."

"What do you think some of your strengths are in comparison to your competitors?" Rachel asked for the third time that week.

"I think that I would have to say that I'm a friendly guy, which allows me to make the investment process less intimidating. Most of my clients are very comfortable approaching me. I think this helps

215

reduce the anxiety associated with working with a financial professional."

"What about one of your weaknesses? Can you think of any?"

"I think one of my weaknesses is that I'm not overly concerned with the first impression that I give when I meet new people. The papers piled up all over my office are a perfect example. I probably should have taken the time to tidy up a bit considering that we've never met before. For better or worse, I tend to assume that individuals will see past this, but I'm sure some don't."

For the next forty-five minutes Ian continued to demonstrate his extensive knowledge of the investment management process, capital markets and economy. What made speaking with him so interesting was that he did it with an enthusiasm that they hadn't yet encountered. It was obvious that he was passionate about his work.

"You answered some of those tough questions very honestly. And for the record, we don't care how messy your office is as long as you are good at what you do."

"Thank you. I appreciate that." Ian said sincerely. "But just to be sure that you don't get lost on the way, I'll escort you out," he said flashing his pleasant smile.

When they left Ian's office they were both very pleased with how the interview had gone. Ian seemed great: personable, energetic and knowledgeable. It was apparent that he would be very easy to get along with. They also knew, however, that their final decision shouldn't be based on personality alone. There were many other factors that needed to be taken into consideration. After such a long day, however, they both felt that they could wait until the weekend before making any final decisions. They were due to have dinner with Megan on Saturday and thought talking things over with her might help them choose.

~

By the time Saturday arrived, Rachel and Thomas were ready for a quiet evening out. Many years before, Megan had purchased a condominium in one of the most sought-after neighbourhoods in the city. Hers was one of three apartments made when the owner of a century-old mansion subdivided his house into three separate homes. The resulting flats were beautiful, with high ceilings, fireplaces and private terraces overlooking a lush garden.

"The garden looks great, doesn't it?" Rachel commented, as she and Thomas walked along the stone path to the east side of Megan's house on Saturday night.

Megan greeted them at the door holding a bottle of wine and corkscrew.

"Just in time," she said smiling. "I need a pair of strong hands to open the wine. Can you get this, Rachel?"

"Very funny," Thomas laughed, taking the bottle and corkscrew from her.

When they were settled on the terrace with their glasses of wine and some delicious hors d'oeuvres that Megan had made, she asked them about their progress.

"Two of the meetings went very well. One of the meetings, however, was mediocre at best," Rachel said.

"Why? What was wrong?" Megan asked.

"We got the impression that the investment advisor wasn't that interested in taking on new clients," Rachel replied, thinking of Theo's low-key approach. "It may have been because he was having a bad day, but from a personality standpoint, we don't think it would be a good fit."

"Personality is important. You will have a lot of contact with whomever you hire, so it's important that you like the person."

"The other two men seemed like excellent candidates. We think that we would enjoy working with either of them," Thomas said. "Therein lies another problem."

"What do you mean? You should be thrilled that you have a tough choice to make. A lot of people simply work with the first person that comes along only to see the relationship fall apart a few years later."

"I guess you're right, but how do we make that choice? Both candidates are equally well qualified in terms of experience. Also, from our initial meetings we really like them both."

"One way of helping you make a better decision is to gauge the quality of their work," Megan suggested.

"How?" Thomas asked.

"You may want to ask each candidate to present you with an investment proposal. That way you'll be able to base your final decision on their personality, qualifications and on the quality of their work. This should make your final choice a little easier because you'll have a good idea of what each candidate is proposing."

"That is a great suggestion. How did you come up with it?" Rachel wondered out loud.

"It's common practice in the portfolio management business. If you were an institution or ultra high–net worth individual, most portfolio managers would present you with an investment proposal. This would either be in the form of a formal presentation or a hard document. There's no reason why you can't ask the candidates that you are meeting to do the same for you. Have you met with any investment counsellors or portfolio managers yet?"

"Not yet. We have a list of names. We were going to start meeting with them next week."

"That's a good idea. You'll find that most discretionary money managers will present you with a proposal that is extremely detailed. I think that you'll find it really informative. It may help you decide whether you want to go the advisory route or discretionary wealth management route."

"We're not sure yet what we are going to do. We'll decide after we've met with everyone."

"By the way, how did the financial planning go?"

"It is a great exercise to go through. We now know exactly where we stand. It's very reassuring," Rachel admitted.

After a few more minutes on the subject of Donna Friedberg and the financial plan she prepared for them, the subject changed to Rachel and Megan's new client, and money managers were forgotten for the rest of a very enjoyable evening.

~

On Monday, Rachel decided to take Megan's advice and called Charles and Ian to ask each of them for an investment proposal. She said that she was interested in getting an idea of the specific recommendations they would make in terms of meeting their investment objectives. Although both men graciously agreed to do this, they said that they couldn't make any recommendations until after they had established Rachel and Thomas's investor profile.

Charles asked if he could come by the house after work so he could gather the information in person. Ian also suggested that they meet in person. So, Rachel scheduled consecutive meetings at home on the following Wednesday and Thursday. She appreciated that both men were willing to come to her house because it made the week much more manageable.

After the meetings, it was apparent that both investment advisors had very similar styles in regards to identifying the couple's goals, risk tolerance and investment objectives. They asked many of the same questions about time horizon, acceptable level of risk, investment knowledge and overall financial position. Although Rachel and Thomas didn't realize the importance of the questions being asked at the time, they later learned that the answers they gave were extremely important because they served as the foundation of the Know Your Client Rule. Under provincial and federal legislation, this rule requires all investment advisors to collect adequate information about their clients before making any investment recommendations on their behalf. It was specifically designed to assess the overall suitability of particular investments for different types of investors based on their personal profile.

As part of the goal discovery process, each investment advisor also asked for a copy of the couple's financial plan. This helped them immensely because all of the information was presented in an easy-to-read document. More important, the information had been prepared by another financial professional, which meant that it was probably an accurate snapshot of the couple's overall financial situation. After quickly reviewing the document with the couple both Charles and Ian said that their financial plan was extremely well done. Rachel and Thomas appreciated this a great deal.

In terms of preparation, the investment advisors needed at least one week to put together their respective proposals. This was more than fair because the couple wanted to give each advisor ample time to prepare a high-quality document. In fact, if they needed more time to prepare they were welcome to take it, Thomas had said.

Before ending each meeting, Rachel and Thomas thanked the advisor for his time and told him that they were looking forward to receiving the proposal and going through it in detail. They also told them to call them at their convenience if they needed any additional information. With that, the ball was now in their court.

Key Point

Do not hesitate to ask for a sample of a potential financial advisor's work. You are hiring them, after all.

|25|

Investment Counsellors and Portfolio Managers

On Friday morning, Thomas decided to keep the momentum going by calling the various contacts that he had made at the discretionary portfolio management firms. After speaking with Kim Lennox and Michael Baum, he set up meetings in the late afternoon on the following Monday. He then called Jacob to take him up on the offer to meet with the portfolio manager who managed Jacob and Isabel's money. Jacob was glad that he called and gave him Jack Marshall's number. Thomas called Jack immediately and, as soon as he answered the phone, it was obvious that he was expecting Thomas's call.

"Hi, Thomas. Jacob told me that either you or your wife would be calling. I'm glad you did. How are you?"

"I'm doing well, thank you. I'm sorry to bother you. I know you're busy."

"Don't worry about it. If you're a friend of Jacob's, you are a friend of mine."

"I appreciate it. We're in the process of hiring someone to manage our portfolio. We haven't decided whether we're going to do the investment advisory route or the discretionary portfolio management route, which is why Jacob suggested I should call you."

"That's always a tough decision. For starters, you should establish whether or not your portfolio is large enough to be directly managed by a portfolio manager. Most discretionary wealth management firms have minimums in terms of the size of the portfolios they are willing to manage."

"I know. I've heard it's anywhere from two hundred and fifty thousand to over two million dollars."

"That's right. The second factor is the amount of involvement you'd like to have in the investment management process. Some individuals like to have some say in terms of the investments they hold, while others prefer to leave all of the decisions up to a professional."

"We haven't met with any portfolio managers yet, though we have some meetings scheduled for next week. In the mean time, I was hoping that you could tell me everything I need to know about discretionary wealth management before those meetings, so that I will be able to make an informed decision."

"How's your golf game?" Jack asked matter-of-factly.

"Let's just say I like the game of golf, but the game of golf doesn't like me. I do try hard though."

"Why don't we play at my club tomorrow morning? That will gives me eighteen holes to tell you everything I know. I've been working in the industry for a long time, so I'm familiar with many of the firms and the people who run them."

"That sounds great. Are you sure you don't mind? I don't want to impose," said Thomas, thinking of his fairly unused golf clubs.

"Don't be silly. If I didn't want to play, I wouldn't have offered. Besides, I don't get the opportunity to play as often as I'd like, so it would be nice to get out on the course tomorrow. Why don't we meet at the club at eight-thirty tomorrow morning? We don't have to book a tee-off time, which means we can simply walk on."

Thomas arrived at the golf club shortly after eight in the morning. After passing through a tall set of iron gates, he followed a long, winding road that was lined with mature oaks. When the road eventually came to an end, he saw a beautiful stone clubhouse that dated back to the turn of the last century. As he approached the building, a young man motioned for him to park his car directly in front of the entrance. He stopped the car in the appropriate spot, stepped out and told the attendant that he was Jack Marshall's guest. The employee then politely asked Thomas for the keys to his car so he could take his golf clubs out of the trunk. He then gave the car keys to another man who was responsible for parking the car.

"Would you like your clubs cleaned before you tee off, Mr Connor?" the young man asked.

"Thank you, but I don't think that's necessary," Thomas answered, knowing how seldom he had played lately. Suddenly, he felt butterflies in his stomach.

While he waited for Jack to arrive, Thomas decided to hit some balls on the driving range. A dozen decent shots later, he was feeling better about his game. Back in the clubhouse, he saw a gentleman walking across the room towards him. He looked to be in his mid-fifties, was very well dressed and seemed to have a pleasant face and a nice manner about him. As he approached Thomas, he held out his hand.

"Hello, Thomas. I'm Jack. It's great that you could come this morning."

Thomas shook hands and thanked him for the invitation. "It looks like a beautiful course," he added. "I'm hoping not to embarrass myself."

"Actually, I'm surprised you look so calm. Most of the guests are usually out on the driving range frantically hitting as many balls as they can before teeing off."

"Guilty as charged." Thomas admitted, turning a little red. "I just hit my last ball a few minutes ago."

Both men laughed. Jack then told him that he appreciated Thomas's honesty. Many people wouldn't have let on that they were a little anxious.

"I feel as though I know you," Jack admitted. "Jacob and Isabel think so much of you and Rachel and your little girls."

"They are great friends and have been an enormous help. When we started out on our quest for financial advice we didn't know very much about the financial services industry. We've come a long way and we owe a lot of the credit to them."

"That's one of the reasons why I wanted to meet you. They told me that you have both been very dedicated to learning as much as you can and that you are taking your finances seriously. If I can help in any way, I'm glad to do it."

The men grabbed their clubs and chatted on their way to the first tee. After taking a few moments to stretch, Jack asked his guest whether he'd like to hit first or second. Thomas politely obliged by walking up to the tee and teeing up his ball. As he was taking his practice swings all he could think about was not duffing the ball. Once he was ready, he calmly stepped up to his ball, swung his club back slowly and brought it down in one smooth motion. This resulted in the ball flying nicely down the middle of the fairway. When he saw where it landed he sighed quietly with relief. The butterflies were gone.

"What a nice drive!" Jack said, before hitting the ball quite a distance past Thomas's. "I have a feeling we're going to have a great round today."

After putting their drivers back in their bags the two men headed down the fairway.

"How much do you know about discretionary portfolio management?" Jack asked, getting right to the point.

"What I've learned so far is that discretionary portfolio management is suitable for those investors who want to hand over the day-to-day management of their investments to a professional because they aren't interested in managing their own affairs, they are too busy or their finances are too complicated."

"That's right. A discretionary portfolio manager or investment counsellor will manage an individual's portfolio on the client's behalf in exchange for a management fee. This fee is typically a percentage of the assets being managed. In order to manage money on a discretionary basis, however, the professional has to be licensed to do this."

"What should I look for in a wealth management firm?"

"There are a few things you need to consider, such as size, reputation, past performance and management style. If, for instance, you find it reassuring to have your money managed by a globally recognized financial institution then you would probably want to consider the portfolio management department at an investment bank.

If, however, you prefer more personalized service then you would likely have your money managed by a boutique firm."

"Is one better than the other?" Thomas asked as he approached his ball.

"It's not a question of being better. It has more to do with your personal preference. It is very important, however, that the firm has an excellent reputation, a management style that you are comfortable with and solid performance numbers. Again, these will all vary from firm to firm."

"I've learned a little bit about the various management styles. Are management styles really that important?"

"Management style is important because different management styles will yield different results in various market conditions. My management style, for instance, is bottom-up value. This investment style typically yields slow and steady results over the long term. A momentum manager, on the other hand, can yield quick results in the short term. There is, however, a higher level of volatility associated with this style. It's important that your money is managed in a way that meets your specific risk tolerances and investment objectives. Any qualified portfolio manager will assess your investment objectives and risk tolerances before they manage your money."

Thomas used too much force and chipped his next shot well past the flag. After a second chip shot the ball landed on the green despite being a fair distance from the hole. He wasn't a particularly strong putter and he ended up with a seven on the hole. Jack ended up with what looked like an easy birdie. After replacing the flag, they walked to the second tee.

"What about performance numbers? I'm under the impression that we should simply hire whomever has yielded the best long-term results? Does this make sense?"

"There is no doubt that performance numbers are important. They have to be taken in context, however," Jack cautioned. "The first factor that you should consider is to compare the portfolio manager's performance to a meaningful benchmark. If, for instance, the portfolio manager manages US stocks then you should compare his or her results to a broad US index such as the S&P 500. If the PM matches the index's performance with less volatility or if the PM consistently outperforms the index over the long term then he or she has done a very good job."

"That makes sense," Thomas acknowledged.

"Something else that you should consider is how the returns of the portfolio have been achieved. If you have a PM who has yielded above-average results but the return is due to the appreciation of one or two stocks, this isn't meaningful in assessing the PM's capability. You want to make sure that the returns of the portfolio are a result of the overall asset mix rather than just one or two positions."

"That also makes sense," Thomas repeated.

"In terms of performance, I think that you'll find that most of the top money managers in the industry yield very similar results over the longer term. Once you have narrowed it down to a handful of top-rated managers, your decision will likely be heavily based on the quality of your relationship with the portfolio manager or relationship manager rather than the numbers."

"That's something else I don't quite understand. What is the role of a relationship manager?"

"At many wealth management firms your primary contact is with a relationship manager. This individual will assess your risk tolerance and investment objectives, develop an asset allocation model and keep you abreast of any changes made in your portfolio. They usually work very closely with the portfolio management team and inform you about any decisions the team makes."

By the fifth hole, it was turning out to be a beautiful day. The sun was shining brightly and the temperature was in the low to mid twenties. As Thomas expected, the course was in fantastic shape.

"As I mentioned when we spoke on the phone, I've already made a few contacts at several discretionary wealth management firms and have a few interviews scheduled for Monday. Is there anything I need to know before I meet with them?" Thomas asked.

"If you haven't already done so, you'll want to gather information on the firm's history, employees, investment pools, investment styles, performance numbers and minimum account sizes. After you've received this information, go through it before you meet with them.

That way you'll be well prepared for your interview. All of this information is easily accessible because it can usually be found on the firm's website. Or you can simply call the firm and they will send you an information package."

"I've already done that, but haven't had the chance to go through the information yet. Jack, what about you? How long have you been managing money?"

"I've been a PM for almost twenty years. I started out working in the wealth management division of a medium-sized insurance company. Then I moved to a major pension fund in my early thirties and eventually became one of the fund's portfolio managers. After a little over ten years with that corporation, I left to start my own firm and have been doing this ever since."

"How many employees do you have?"

"We have eighteen employees including three portfolio managers, five analysts and two equity traders. The rest of the employees do our admin."

"Why did you decide to start your own firm?"

"When I worked at the pension fund I was managing money on behalf of tens of thousands of plan participants without ever knowing them. My preference was to manage money directly for high–net worth investors, foundations and corporations. This gave me the opportunity to have some personal contact with the individuals whose money I was managing."

"So you still meet with all of your clients fairly regularly?" Thomas asked.

"Absolutely—it's one of my favourite aspects of my job. All of my clients know they can simply pick up the phone and call me any time. If, for one reason or another, a client wants to meet with me, they know that I'm always available."

"How much money do you have under administration?"

"We manage a little over two billion dollars. When I first started the company almost all of the money I was managing was on behalf of friends, family and former colleagues. After a few years, the business started to grow primarily through referrals."

"Do you still accept new clients?" Thomas asked.

"We don't actively seek new clients through marketing efforts, but we do accept referrals from our existing clients."

"I'm assuming that you also have minimum account sizes?"

"Although most of our clients are ultra high–net worth individuals, we do manage money for clients who don't fall into this category. The reason that we don't strictly adhere to the seven figure minimum is that some of our clients are referred to us by family and close friends. As such, they may not necessarily have several million dollars to invest but still need prudent financial advice. In your particular case, for example, we have a close mutual friend in Jacob. He indicated that you could really use some help, which is why I offered to meet with you. Regardless of your financial situation, I'm going to offer you as much help as I can because you were referred to me by one of my closest friends—who also happens to be one of my best clients. It wouldn't be a smart business decision to tell Jacob that I can't meet with you because you don't meet our minimum account size requirement. Fortunately, due to our firm's small size, we can still effectively service a broad range of clients."

"That seems like a very nice way to do business. I'm sure that all of your friends appreciate this."

"I'm extremely happy with our firm. It has a great atmosphere and we manage money for great people. I'm very proud of what I have built from scratch and wouldn't change a thing. I think that our clients can sense this."

The sixth hole was a short par three. Although the distance to the hole was only one hundred and ten yards there was one small catch—the hole was on an island. This didn't seem to faze Jack in the least because with one smooth stroke he was on the green a few feet away from the hole.

"You make it look so easy," Thomas acknowledged.

"If you knew how many balls I've lost in the water over the years you'd know that I'm secretly thrilled with that shot. I'm just trying not to show it." Both men laughed.

"Here goes nothing," Thomas announced out loud as he approached the tee.

Although he hit the ball cleanly, it still landed in the water well short of the green. This caused water rings to ripple outwards from where the ball hit, serving as a reminder of the penalty stroke he would have to take.

"If at first you don't succeed," Thomas said before take his second swing.

This time the ball landed on the green only to spin backward and land in the water a second time.

"I think I'll lay up," Thomas said. "This is could get expensive," he added, referring to the two balls that he just lost.

The hole ended with Jack getting a birdie and Thomas scoring a seven. Thomas didn't let it bother him though. In all the years he had been playing golf, the one thing he had learned was to not take the sport too seriously.

By the time they finished the ninth hole Thomas had scored two pars of his own. This made him all but forget about the seven he had scored a few holes back. Thomas started the tenth hole by picking up exactly where he left off by smashing the ball two hundred and fifty yards down the middle of the fairway. With a little concentration he was confident that he could improve his score over the last nine holes, providing that the degree of difficulty of the back nine was similar to that of the front nine. And he really didn't care that much how he played, it was nice to be getting a little exercise on such a beautiful day.

"If Rachel and I were interested in having you manage our money, what would be the next step?" Thomas asked, hoping that he wasn't imposing.

"The procedure is essentially the same for every client. We would start by assessing your financial needs and goals. We would then decide on an optimal asset mix based on a careful analysis of these objectives and present you with an Investment Policy Statement. Once you've signed off on the Investment Policy Statement, we would manage your money in accordance with this statement."

"What if we've already clearly identified our financial needs? The only reason that I ask is that we've recently had a financial plan prepared for us that covers all of this information."

"If you've recently had a detailed financial plan prepared for you then we can use the information that you've already been presented with. A skilled financial planner will clearly identify all of your needs and financial goals in great detail. All we would need to do is reassess your risk tolerance so we are comfortable in recommending the appropriate asset mix. It's highly probable that the asset mix that we recommend will almost be identical to the mix recommended in your financial plan, providing that your situation hasn't changed."

"The one thing that I've learned throughout this entire process is that the various financial professionals all adhere to a similar process. It's almost as if all of you have learned from the same book."

"In a way we have. As I'm sure you know, most top financial professionals have earned a professional designation in their respective fields. Acquiring these designations require a great deal of time, effort and dedication. More important, they teach candidates how to effectively advise individuals on their finances, whether it be financial planning, investment advice or discretionary portfolio management needs. In each field, there is a unique process that ensures that all of an individual's needs are properly addressed. This process has to be learned much in the same way professionals in other fields have to learn their trades."

"Which professional designation do you have?" Thomas asked.

"I earned my Chartered Financial Analyst (CFA) designation almost fifteen years ago. In order to manage money on a discretionary basis you need to have earned your CFA or your Canadian Investment Manager (CIM) designation. The CFA is globally recognized, whereas the CIM is designed to meet the licensing requirements for Canadian portfolio managers who work for member firms of the Investment Industry Regulatory Organization of Canada."

As the game progressed, Thomas found he was playing a lot better than he had earlier in the morning. In fact, it was as though a completely different golfer had emerged. After bogeying the tenth, eleventh and twelfth holes he parred the thirteenth and fourteenth. He then managed to birdie the fifteenth hole, which he followed with a double bogey on the sixteenth. The elevated green on the seventeenth hole caused him some problems and resulted in an eight. This brought him to the eighteenth and final hole, which was one of the nicest holes he had ever seen. He wasn't about to let the rolling hills, crater-like bunkers and lush surroundings distract him, however.

"I appreciate you taking the time to meet with me today," Thomas told his host. "It was a great way to spend the day. It was lovely to play such a beautiful course."

"The day's not over yet," laughed Jack. "We still have to get through this fairly long par five. As you can see, the treeline makes the fairway very narrow. There is a water hazard on the left side about two hundred and twenty-five yards out. There are also a couple of deep bunkers that you will want to avoid on the right side of the fairway. If you land in one of those, you'll need your mining gear to get your ball—they are that deep. Aside from that, it's smooth sailing," Jack added with a smile.

Despite hoping to go out in style, it simply wasn't in the cards on this particular day. Needless to say, the eighteenth hole ate Thomas alive. In fact, it was probably one for the record books. Not only did his ball get lost in the trees, he also managed to find the water hazard and ended up hitting into the bunker twice. By the time he had managed to get the ball on the green he had taken ten shots.

"That certainly wasn't pretty," Thomas said shaking his head.

"Don't let it bother you. I've played some of the top courses in the world and this is one of the most difficult holes I've seen. Try to make up for it by sinking this twenty-foot putt," Jack responded with encouragement.

After carefully lining up the ball, Thomas took a deep breath and putted the ball in the direction of the hole. As it rolled towards its target it looked as though it was going to stop on the edge of the hole. Surprisingly, it somehow managed to find the momentum and drop. At that moment the previous ten shots were meaningless.

"Nice putt!" Jack said. "What a great way to end the round."

Thomas picked up his ball and thanked him for a great game. The men shook hands and made their way to the clubhouse for lunch. Over the meal, they discussed their families, careers and hobbies and found out that they had a lot in common. The conversation eventually turned back to financial matters. When it did, the first question Thomas asked was about the management fees that he should expect to pay. Although he had a fairly good idea of how the fees were charged, he didn't really know how much he would be charged.

As a general rule of thumb, he was told to expect to pay up to two per cent for assets totalling less than five hundred thousand dollars. For amounts over five hundred thousand dollars but less than one million dollars, it would cost between one to one and a half per cent. On amounts over one million dollars, the fee was usually between one to one and a quarter per cent. For these amounts above one million dollars, the fee dropped marginally as the assets under administration increased. He was also told that the fees were tax-deductible in non-registered accounts. This wasn't the case for the management fees charged by mutual funds or pooled funds.

Now that he understood the costs that were involved with discretionary investment management, Thomas broached the subject of performance. As expected, Jack's long-term performance numbers were very competitive with those found in the industry. Although he was by no means an expert in terms of analyzing the performance of various portfolio managers, Thomas had done enough preliminary research on the topic to know whether or not an investment manager's long-term returns were competitive.

Aside from these two issues, Thomas didn't really have any other questions for Jack. It seemed that he would be a perfect manager for his and Rachel's money. But, Thomas didn't want to impose on him. He knew that one of the main reasons that Jack had met with him was that he was a close friend of Jacob and Isabel's. He really had to say something, otherwise he'd feel uncomfortable.

"Jack, although I'm a little uncomfortable asking this, I was wondering if you would be willing to manage a portion of our financial assets? I don't want you to say yes simply because we're friends with Jacob and Isabel because that would make me feel as if I were imposing. If you currently aren't taking on any new clients, I completely understand."

"Of course, I wouldn't mind. For the record, we probably would have never met if it weren't for Jacob making the introduction. But now that we have met and I've seen how serious you are regarding your financial affairs, I'd be more than happy to help you. Before you make any decisions, however, I want you to meet with a few other portfolio managers. Just because I manage money for a mutual friend doesn't mean that we will be a perfect fit. I'd feel better if you met a few other professionals before making your final decision. After that, if you decide that I would be the best fit then I'd be happy to take you on as a client. Does that make sense?"

"It makes complete sense. I appreciate your professionalism. In the long run it's probably prudent if I meet with a few other candidates."

Although Thomas was confident that Jack would be an excellent manager, he understood why he was being encouraged to meet with a few other people. Regardless of the outcome, he appreciated the fact that Jack had taken the time to meet with him on a Saturday morning. In the big scheme of things, Thomas and Rachel weren't significant clients for Jack, but he took the time to meet with him anyway as a favour to Jacob and Isabel. Thomas appreciated it.

After lunch ended, the two men stood up, shook hands and thanked each other one last time. As they walked out of the clubhouse to their cars, they were both thinking about how much they had enjoyed the day. Although neither of them had expected to make a new friend, it looked as though they had. Thomas was looking forward to introducing Jack to Rachel. He also had to make sure to thank Jacob and Isabel for making the introduction.

Key Point

Investment Counsellors and Portfolio Managers tend to have their own unique investment management style. Try to have a good understanding of the various investment styles and hire someone who has a style that is complementary to your specific investment objectives.

|26|

Choosing an Investment Advisor

On Monday afternoon, both Thomas and Rachel left work early and attended back-to-back meetings with Kim Lennox and Michael Baum. Although Kim worked for a boutique investment counselling firm and Michael worked for a large global investment bank, their processes of assessing an individual's investor profile were almost identical. The process always started by identifying an investor's investment objectives, investment horizon and risk tolerance. Once an investor profile was established, the client would receive an Investment Policy Statement based on his or her specific profile. If the client approved of the information contained in the IPS, then their financial assets would be managed in accordance with the statement. Both Kim and Michael stressed the importance of this document, as do most portfolio managers and investment counsellors.

Although their processes were very similar, there were some noticeable differences between the two candidates Rachel and Thomas interviewed. These differences were predominantly reflected by the firms that they worked for. One of the attractive features of Michael's company was its global presence. The sheer size and reputable name of the institution conveyed a level of stability and strength that wasn't easily matched by many other financial institutions. Kim's firm didn't have the global presence that some individuals might find attractive, but it did have the potential to provide a highly personalized level of service that larger firms might find difficult to offer. These differences didn't affect either firm's ability to manage money because both companies had excellent long-term performance numbers. These differences might, however, matter to certain individuals because everyone has their own personal preference regarding the type of financial institution that they prefer to deal with. Some people prefer big, while others prefer small.

In Rachel and Thomas's case, they focused on finding someone with whom they could foster a solid long-term relationship. They didn't necessarily have any specific preferences in regards to the firm itself as long as it was well established and had a solid reputation. Jack also met all of their criteria and, as a result of being referred to them by someone whom they respected, it made complete sense to meet with him a second time. If, for one reason or another, they felt that it might be prudent to meet with Kim or Michael again, they would do so before making a long-term commitment. For the moment, however, they were both looking forward to seeing what Jack could do for them.

When Rachel and Thomas arrived home after their meetings with Kim and Michael, there was an envelope waiting for them in their mailbox. It was the investment proposal from Charles Kaplan. As they entered the house they were greeted by a very unfamiliar noise—complete silence.

"Where is everyone? Weren't your parents coming over to watch the kids?" Thomas asked his wife.

"It looks as though we have a few hours to ourselves," Rachel said, reading the note left on the kitchen table. "Mom and Dad took the kids out to dinner."

"What a nice surprise! What do you feel like having for dinner?" Thomas asked. "How about we order in?"

"Why don't we order Thai and go through the investment proposal?" Rachel suggested.

As they leafed through their individual copies of the investment proposal they could see that it was extremely well done; a lot of time had gone into preparing it. The document consisted of twenty-two pages, divided into eight different sections: Introduction, Features & Benefits, Products & Services, Current Asset Allocation, Recommended Asset Allocation, Model Portfolio, Costs Involved and Conclusion.

The **Introduction** started by identifying the couple's investment objectives and risk tolerances as dictated by their investor profile. It also addressed how Charles would meet these objectives by implementing the strategies outlined in the proposal. Although the information in this section was short, it was to the point and left very little room for misinterpretation. Rachel and Thomas liked this.

The **Features & Benefits** section highlighted some of the firm's strengths, including its highly rated research department and solid reputation in the financial services industry. It also highlighted Charles's extensive work experience, the licenses and professional designations that he held and his investment philosophy.

The third section was the **Products & Services** section. It outlined such things as the types of registered and non-registered accounts the firm offered, investment products that could be purchased, interest rates that would be earned on balances and charged on debits and a handful of other unique services that would likely be of interest to them at some point in the future. Although Rachel and Thomas were somewhat familiar with the information contained in the first three sections it was nice to have it readily available at their fingertips.

The **Current Asset Allocation** section was relatively straightforward in that it provided a snapshot of their current asset mix. The information was presented to them through the use of a coloured pie chart. The pie chart was very effective because it was immediately obvious that their current portfolio was far too heavily weighted in equities.

"Donna was right. We do have too much money invested in stocks," Thomas said. "I think that we're taking on too much risk."

"Have a look at the next page," Rachel instructed. "Charles has separately listed all of our investments and has shown what percentage each one represents of our overall portfolio. Our high percentage of stocks is primarily a result of our shares held in our Employee Share Purchase Plans. Donna brought this to our attention and suggested we reduce our holdings in our share purchase plans. Do you remember that?"

"Yes, I remember. Obviously it's something we need to address soon if they both think it's an issue," Thomas said.

236

"I agree. It makes complete sense."

The next section outlined their **Recommended Asset Allocation**. This section showed the optimal asset mix that would meet their financial needs. This information was also displayed in the form of a pie chart. In addition, it clearly identified every change that needed to be made to their existing portfolio so that it better reflected their risk tolerance and investment objectives. All of the suggestions were explained in detail and were presented to them in a clear, easy-to-read format. This section concluded with some additional issues that Charles felt needed to be addressed. Some of these suggestions included reducing the number of mutual funds they owned, reducing their heavy weighting in stocks, investing their cash balances in short-term notes such as treasury bills or commercial paper in order to earn higher interest and consolidating all of their accounts with one institution so that they were more easily managed. The couple agreed that every one of these recommendations made complete sense.

The information presented in the Recommended Asset Allocation section flowed neatly into the **Model Portfolio** section. The material on the next three pages was relatively straightforward because it simply listed the specific investments that would serve as the foundation of their portfolio. These investments were neatly divided across all three asset classes: cash, fixed-income and equities. The percentage that was allocated to each of these asset classes reflected the recommended asset mix that Charles had outlined earlier. After Thomas and Rachel finished going through this information, they realized that all of the information in the later sections were based on recommendations made earlier. It was as if all the pieces of the puzzle were coming together, and it was simply a matter of looking at the big picture.

The **Costs Involved** were covered in the next section. Although the couple knew that costs would eventually need to be discussed, they were pleasantly surprised that they were so plainly addressed in the investment proposal. More important, Charles had taken the time to give an overall estimate of what it would cost to assemble the Model Portfolio and maintain it on an ongoing basis. He also outlined the differences between the cost of investing in individual securities, mutual funds and WRAP accounts. After reading this section, Thomas and Rachel had a fairly good idea of what fees they would pay to have Charles advise them on their investments. This was very important to know before making any final decisions.

The final section of the investment proposal was the **Conclusion**. It summed up all the important pieces of information that had been outlined throughout the document and briefly reiterated the strategy that was being proposed to meet their investment objectives and financial goals. After they each finished reading this section, they closed their proposals and placed them on the table.

"What do you think?" Thomas asked his wife, offering her the last spring roll.

"I can honestly say that I'm impressed. This is extremely well done," Rachel acknowledged.

"I agree. I honestly didn't expect that the information would be presented in so much detail. Charles pretty much covered everything. I feel as though I now know exactly what we need to do with our investments in order to achieve our financial goals."

"I do too. Let's wait until we receive Ian's proposal before we make any decisions. It might simply be that this type of quality is standard in the financial industry," Rachel suggested.

"You're right. We will wait and see what Ian put together. If it compares to the proposal Charles put together for us, we'll certainly have a difficult decision to make."

Key Point

If you are in the process of hiring a professional to manage your investments, you should expect to receive a high-quality document outlining the services that you will receive, the investment strategy that will be implemented and the costs that will be incurred.

| 27 |

Advisory vs. Discretionary

Ian's proposal arrived later the following week. After reviewing it, Thomas and Rachel were somewhat disappointed. Ian's investment proposal consisted of nothing more than three short sections—a cover letter, a list of their current investments and a list of the investments that Ian was recommending. After reviewing the information, they had no idea why Ian was making any of his recommendations because there was no explanation accompanying them. As such, they didn't know how he would help them achieve their financial goals. This didn't sit well with either Thomas or Rachel, which was unfortunate because Ian had a great personality and had seemed like someone they would really have enjoyed working with. At this stage in the game, however, the quality of an individual's work meant everything to them.

Based on the fact that Charles was courteous, professional, demonstrated a high level of integrity and a sound understanding of their financial goals, Thomas and Rachel decided that Charles was the most suitable candidate to advise them on their investments. After calling Ian to thank him for his efforts, the only decision that they had to make was whether they were going to have their money managed on an advisory basis, discretionary basis or a combination of both. In order to make this final decision, they thought it would be wise to meet with Jack Marshall together. After everything that Thomas had told Rachel about Jack, she was very much looking forward to the meeting.

Thomas and Rachel were now so close to having all of their financial affairs in place that they didn't want to slow down. After they met with Jack they would be able to make their final decision about the type of money management relationship they would enter. They

239

scheduled the meeting for early Thursday evening at Jack's office, which was also in the downtown core. In fact, it was only a few blocks away from the centre of it all, the former stock exchange.

Much of the meeting was spent discussing Thomas and Rachel's life goals. Although Jack and Thomas had already talked about this in detail on the golf course, it was important for Jack to discuss it with Rachel in order to make sure that her financial goals were the same as her husband's. One of the most dangerous assumptions that a financial professional can make is that a husband and wife both have identical financial goals. On occasion, the exact opposite is true. As such, it was extremely important for Jack to make certain that everyone was on the same page.

Jack spoke openly about the services that he offered, his investment style and several similar case studies of clients that he had helped. Thomas and Rachel, on the other hand, talked about their past investment experiences, overall investment knowledge, when they wanted to retire, some of the things they wanted to do after they retired and how much money they were hoping to leave each of their daughters. All of this information was already at Jack's fingertips because Thomas had mailed him a copy of the financial plan that Donna had prepared for them.

As the meeting came to a close, Jack discussed how the discretionary process worked. Although the couple had a good understanding of the difference between working with someone in an advisory capacity and someone in a discretionary capacity, they both found it helpful to hear the difference between the two relationships one more time.

In an advisory relationship, they would ultimately be the ones accepting any advice given to them regarding the investments bought and sold. In a discretionary relationship, however, a portfolio manager makes all of the investment decisions on their behalf—as long as these decisions are within the boundaries of the Investment Policy Statement. Jack emphasized once again that the Investment Policy Statement would be the single most important document that they would receive from him because it established a framework within which he would manage their investments. They would be asked to review it and then sign a contract indicating that they understood and agreed with the framework under which their investments would be managed. The meeting ended with all three of them agreeing that they would receive the Investment Policy Statement within the next ten days. Once they had the opportunity to review the document, they would then meet again to go over any questions or concerns that they might have.

The Investment Policy Statement arrived by courier several days after their meeting and, as expected, the information was presented to them in a highly professional manner. It focused almost entirely on the framework under which their financial assets would be managed. This information was outlined over twelve sections, all of which were relatively straightforward: Introduction, Investment Objective, Management Style, Qualitative & Quantitative Constraints, Research Sources, Tax Issues, Cash Flow Requirements, Specified Restrictions, Conflicts of Interest, Regulatory Compliance, Management Parameters and Reference Portfolio and Conclusion.

The **Introduction** started by explaining how a written long-term investment policy would protect the couple's portfolio from ad hoc revisions of a sound long-term investment strategy. It also explained how it would clarify their overall investment plan and clearly articulate their investment objectives and constraints, thus providing a benchmark with which to evaluate their portfolio manager. This meant that misunderstandings would be less likely to arise going forward. In addition, the IPS would clearly articulate the investment policies and procedures, establish stringent guidelines for the prudent investment of their financial assets, describe suitable investments that could be included in the portfolio and list any constraints that they may have brought to Jack's attention during the initial interviews.

The **Investment Objective** section was very brief and to the point. It stated that the objective of the portfolio was growth with a bias towards capital preservation, which would be achieved by investing in securities of Canadian, US and international-based companies. This information was based on the couple's primary investment objective, which was identified in their financial plan and through the various data that Jack had collected during their initial interviews.

The **Management Style** section described the team's particular investment style, which was bottom-up value. More specifically, this section described the various criteria each security would have to meet in terms of the various value and leverage ratios.

The **Qualitative & Quantitative Constraints** was the most technical section in the Investment Policy Statement. It was divided into five subsections: Asset Classes Eligible for Investment, Number of Securities, Diversification, Constraints by Asset Class and Holding Period & Investment Horizon. These five subsections served as the core of the Investment Policy Statement by clearly defining the boundaries within which the team would manage their portfolio. Some of these criteria included the minimum acceptable market cap of stocks that could be considered for inclusion, debt ratings of various fixed income products and the maximum allowable concentration of any one class of security within the portfolio. If, for any reason, Jack included a security that fell outside of these parameters, he would be in default of the IPS.

The **Research Sources** simply listed the various sources that would be used for research purposes. This included the research departments of the various investment dealers, debt rating agencies, independent research analysts and Jack's own "in-house" research.

The **Tax Issues** section listed any tax issues that needed to be considered when managing the portfolio. It also stated that revenues from the portfolio would be taxed in the hands of the investor at the client's corporate or marginal tax rate as dictated by the Canada Revenue Agency.

The **Cash Flow Requirements** section listed any short, medium or long-term cash flow needs that Thomas and Rachel had identified during the interview process. If, for one reason or another, the couple anticipated a change in their cash flow needs, they would immediately bring this to Jack's attention.

In the past decade, it had become increasingly common for individual and institutional investors to identify securities that they would rather avoid even if it meant portfolio returns might be compromised. Some of these companies included those that neglect or destroy the environment, negligently diminish the quality of life of individuals through their involvement in the tobacco, alcohol or gambling industries or promote conflict between individuals through their involvement in the arms industry. The **Specified Restrictions** section listed any companies that the clients didn't want included in the portfolio. Rachel and Thomas had not specified any of these restrictions.

The **Conflict of Interest** section stated that all investment activities must be conducted in accordance with the Code of Ethics and Standards of Professional Conduct adopted by the Canadian Securities Institute.

The **Regulatory Compliance** section stated that the portfolio would be managed in accordance with applicable legislation, including the Income Tax Act (Canada). More specifically, it outlined how various financial instruments would be taxed in terms of interest, dividends and capital gains.

The **Management Parameters and Reference Portfolio** outlined the parameters of the portfolio's recommended asset mix. It was imperative that the portfolio's asset allocation always adhered to the minimum and maximum allowable percentages described in this section. This ensured that the portfolio would always be well diversified and prevented the portfolio manager from becoming too heavily concentrated in any one of the three main asset classes—cash, fixed income and equities. These parameters would allow the manager to be underweighted or overweighted in any asset class as long as it was within the stated parameters. In Thomas and Rachel's particular case, their cash position could range anywhere from two per cent to thirty per cent, their fixed income position could range from ten per cent to seventy per cent and their total equity position could range from twenty per cent to seventy per cent. In addition to outlining the team's asset allocation parameters, this section also identified the Reference Portfolio. The Reference Portfolio served as the benchmark against which its performance would be measured. If they matched the benchmark's performance with less volatility or outperformed the benchmark on a consistent basis the team would be doing an excellent job.

The **Conclusion** briefly summed up all of the information in the previous sections and reiterated the purpose and overall importance of the Investment Policy Statement. It also listed the contact information of key employees at the firm.

After they finished reviewing the document in its entirety, Thomas and Rachel knew exactly how their portfolio would be managed if they handed it over to Jack and his team. More specifically, they knew that their portfolio would be well diversified across a broad range of high-quality securities in an asset mix that would meet their specific investment objectives. What they found most appealing about this type of relationship was that it was very hands-off and left them with very little to worry about. The disadvantage of this type of relationship was that they wouldn't be given much of an opportunity to learn about the investment management process because they wouldn't be involved in the investment decision process itself. Although this wasn't a priority, it was something that they had to consider before making a final choice. Regardless of their decision, they both agreed that they had come an incredibly long way in this entire process and had now narrowed the list down to two final candidates. They were both very proud of this.

Key Point

The Investment Policy Statement is an extremely important document because it sets the parameters within which investment counsellors and portfolio managers must manage their clients' financial assets.

|28|

The Final Decision

Although several days had passed since they had received the Investment Policy Statement from Jack, they had not yet made a decision. In order to help them get over this final hurdle, Rachel decided to ask Megan for a little more help and walked down to her office to see if she was available.

"Hi, do you have a second?" Rachel asked, poking her head into the doorway.

"Sure, have a seat. I've been working on this deliverable for the last three hours and could use a break. My eyes are going buggy from staring at my computer screen for so long."

"Thomas and I need some help. As you know, we're down to making a final decision in terms of hiring an investment manager. We've narrowed it down to two final candidates—Charles and Jack."

"Isn't Charles the investment advisor that you spoke so highly about? Wasn't he referred to you by the branch manager at your bank?" Megan asked.

"That's right. He has done a great job and is very professional."

"And Jack Marshall is the other candidate?" Megan asked.

"That's right. Needless to say, Jack is excellent. If we handed our portfolio over to him we'd know that all of our financial goals would be met and we would never have to worry about our finances again. As you know, he was referred to us by Jacob and Isabel, both of whom we trust implicitly."

"So what's preventing you from making a final decision? Are you worried about hurting someone's feelings? I know Jack and he'd certainly understand if you decided to go with Charles," Megan said, assuming this was the problem.

"Not at all. We've had to gently let down quite a few candidates to get to this point," Rachel said. "No, the reason that we're having trouble making a final decision is that we're simply not sure under which type of arrangement we'd like to have our money managed. On the one hand, we would like to be moderately involved in the decision-making process because it will give us some control over our financial affairs and enable us to learn about the investment management process along the way. If we want that, we choose Charles. On the other hand, the thought of handing the day-to-day management of our portfolio over to Jack is extremely appealing because we'd never have to worry about our investments again."

"I still don't understand why the decision is so difficult," Megan said.

"Why, do you see an obvious choice?" Rachel asked, somewhat confused.

"It seems obvious to me. Why don't you simply hire both? You could have Charles advise you on a portion of your assets and hand over the day-to-day management of your remaining assets to Jack. It's obvious that you aren't sure which type of relationship you would be more comfortable with. This is totally understandable because you've never worked with an investment professional before, so you don't really know what to expect. If you work with both of them for a period of time you'll be in a much better position to make an informed decision. Maybe you'll prefer the advisory route, maybe you'll prefer the discretionary route or maybe you'll prefer a combination of both. There is nothing wrong with using the services of more than one financial professional. In time, your preference of one over the other may become apparent by itself."

"That makes a lot of sense. You mentioned this before, but I wasn't sure if it was all that common," Rachel admitted.

"It's an important decision. My suggestion is to work with both Charles and Jack. I can tell you with a great deal of confidence that they would both prefer managing a portion of your assets rather than none at all. You might even find that you'll work with both of these guys until you are old and gray."

As usual, Megan was extremely helpful in making sense of what didn't necessarily have to be a difficult decision. She had a knack for looking at things in the most logical way. As a result, Thomas and Rachel made a final decision to hire both Charles and Jack. In their particular situation this made the most sense and seemed as though it was the right decision.

The first person they phoned was Charles. He had worked extremely hard and they thought that he would appreciate hearing that they wanted to meet a second time to go through his proposal together. As a professional courtesy, they told him at the beginning of the conversation that they were considering having their assets managed by two different professionals. After explaining why they were considering this type of arrangement, Charles seemed to understand their reasoning.

At their second meeting, Charles took the time to go through the investment proposal that had earned him the job. As he carefully took them through the information, he explained in detail why he made each recommendation. By the time they were done, no stone was left unturned. After he had answered the few remaining questions they had, Rachel told him that they were impressed with the proposal and that it was extremely well done. She also acknowledged that he seemed to have a very good understanding of their investment objectives and financial goals. As such, they wanted to hire him to administer their non-registered assets and RESPs. Although their non-registered accounts represented only a quarter of their investable assets, they played an important role in ensuring that the couple would retire comfortably. Charles was aware of this and appreciated the fact that they trusted him to advise them on all of their retirement needs.

The first step they took was to complete a New Client File application form for each of them. This document was extremely important because it listed all of their personal information, financial information, risk tolerances and investment objectives. It also outlined all of the rules and regulations involved in opening and maintaining an account. After these files were completed, the couple then signed the various agreements for each account and showed Charles their photo ID, an important step to avoid fraud.

247

As a long-term strategy, Thomas and Rachel agreed that they would adopt the asset allocation model that was outlined in the financial plan that Donna had prepared for them and that Charles confirmed to be suitable. As soon as their accounts had been transferred over they agreed that they would meet to discuss investing their money in accordance with all of the suggestions he had made in the investment proposal. He agreed and told them that it might take several weeks or even months to make all of the necessary portfolio changes. They understood that he was at the mercy of the prevailing economic conditions and asked him to take all of the time he needed to invest their money properly.

In terms of the amount of contact they would have, they decided that for the first couple of years, they should meet in person at least every six to twelve months. They also agreed to speak on the telephone or through e-mail as often as needed. This was in addition to any information that Charles mailed to them on a regular basis.

They then turned their attention towards fees. After discussing the various fee structures available to them, they decided to pay a percentage-of-assets fee rather than paying a commission on each transaction. This meant that the administration fees would be tax-deductible if they were paid outside of a registered account. This would save them money because they were both in the highest marginal rate and would get a good portion of the money back when they filed their tax returns each year. As the meeting came to a close, all three felt that they were entering into a promising new relationship. They took a few more minutes to iron out some additional details and then said goodbye. As Thomas and Rachel left Charles's office they both knew that they had made an excellent choice.

The day after their meeting with Charles, Thomas and Rachel called Jack to tell him that they were interested in hiring him to manage their money. As a professional courtesy, they told him that they were going to work with an investment advisor who would administer their non-registered accounts because it would provide them with better insight into the investment management process. More specifically, they wanted to make sure that Jack was comfortable with managing only a large portion of their assets as opposed to all of them, especially since they didn't have the firm's required minimum asset requirements. But Jack said that he was more than happy to take them on as clients given that they were such close friends of Isabel and Jacob. He did have one stipulation, which was that they had to commit to growing their assets through savings so they would come closer to the minimum. They both agreed that this was a reasonable expectation and in the best interests of everyone. They also scheduled a time to meet at Jack's the following morning to finalize all the details.

During this meeting, Jack took the time to walk them through the Investment Policy Statement. After they had all of their questions answered, he surprised them by taking them around the office and introducing them to the employees of the firm. As he made the introductions, he explained exactly what role each individual played within the firm and what role they would have in managing their assets. After having met the various individuals it was apparent that the top money managers often relied on the support of a group of highly talented individuals. They were confident that their money was in the right hands.

In order to proceed, they were again required to complete a number of forms to open their new accounts. Most of the forms were similar to those they had completed with Charles with one exception—the discretionary management contract. This contract outlined that the couple was authorizing a portfolio manager to manage their money on a discretionary basis as long as it was in accordance with the Investment Policy Statement. This meant that every investment decision would be made by members of the firm rather than the clients themselves. The contract also stated the annual management fee that would be paid by them and that this fee was a fixed percentage of the total assets that were being managed.

In order to initiate the transfer of their RRSPs, Jack had them sign several T-2033 forms. Once the transfer forms were handed in to their financial institution's back office, the transfer to their new accounts would take place within several weeks. Once all of their assets were transferred, Jack would go ahead and invest the money as he saw fit as long as it was in accordance with the IPS.

In terms of contact, they would meet once a year to review their portfolio's asset allocation and performance. In between meetings, Jack made it clear that he would be readily available whenever they needed to speak or meet with him. Given the nature of the relationship, however, they didn't expect to be in contact with him more than four times per year. It was reassuring that he was always available, however.

Before wrapping up the meeting, the one remaining question they had concerned how they would know what investments were being made at any given time. Jack acknowledged that this was an excellent question and explained that after each transaction a confirmation slip describing the security and amount bought or sold would be mailed to them. In addition, they would receive their portfolio statement on a quarterly basis. This would summarize every transaction made in the period and list all of their current holdings. This type of reporting is required of every investment management firm in the industry, with the only difference being how well the information is presented. In addition, they would receive a statement outlining the performance of their investments on a quarterly basis. This would keep them up-to-date in regards to how they were doing.

The meeting ended after about an hour and a half. During this time, they managed to sort out all of the minor details, fill out the required forms and initiate the transfer of their registered accounts. Both Thomas and Rachel had a difficult time believing that everything was finally in place. Looking back, they couldn't believe all the work they had had to do to get to this point. In many ways it was quite mind-boggling. Now all they had left to do was wait for the transfers to take place. In the meantime, they would treat their friends to a celebratory dinner. This was the least they could do given how much help they'd had getting to where they were now.

> ## Key Point
>
> **Establish a mutually agreed upon standard of service from the onset of the relationship. This will reduce any misunderstandings during the course of your working relationship and will ensure that the level of service remains consistent.**

|29|

Mission Accomplished

As a special thank you, Rachel and Thomas hosted a dinner in a private room at one of the city's best restaurants. It was expensive but they were happy to treat their friends because, without them, they would never have been able to get their financial affairs in order. The evening included the chef's famous tasting menu, accompanied by the sommelier's favourite wines. The room itself was gorgeous, with beautiful china and extravagant arrangements of flowers. The finishing touch was the unsurpassed view of the city through the window wall that spanned across the entire room. Although the restaurant was extremely busy, they couldn't hear the patrons in the main room because of the heavy wooden French doors that separated them from the other guests. This provided the hosts with the intimate setting they were after.

"I'd like to propose a toast," Megan said holding up her glass. "I'd like to congratulate Thomas and Rachel for a job well done!"

"To a job well done!" everyone around the table said together.

"So how does it feel?" Patrick asked. "You guys must be thrilled."

"We're both pretty happy with what we've accomplished. Looking back, I'm actually quite surprised we made it. It seems like such a long time ago when I strong-armed you-know-who to get our financial affairs in order. It's a huge load off my shoulders to say the least," Rachel admitted.

"It does feel good," Thomas agreed. "I've certainly learned more than I imagined. When we started this whole process I wouldn't have recognized a financial plan if it came up and bit me on the nose. Not only do I now know exactly what goes into a financial plan, I can accurately describe the contents of an Investment Policy Statement.

It's quite incredible when you think about it. It almost makes me wonder if I could manage all of our investments on my own," he added, fishing for a reaction.

"You wouldn't dare," Cindy said.

"You're right, I wouldn't. I have seen firsthand how much work goes into financial planning, investment advisory and discretionary investment management. There is so much information that you need to keep on top of. I don't have any interest in monitoring changes in the provincial and federal budgets, shifts in the economy, budgeting, insurance planning, tax planning or investment management. I couldn't possibly do all of that on my own. I'd have to do the work of several financial professionals."

"Thomas, I think your do-it-yourself days are coming to an end," Jacob said.

"I wouldn't say that," Thomas replied. "There's always going to be a roof that needs to be fixed," he said with a chuckle.

After the team of waiters came in and served the lobster bisque, the conversation turned back to financial matters.

"What is the most important thing that you learned during this whole process?" Isabel asked.

"I think it's the fact that everyone needs a plan," Rachel answered. "Without a plan, there is really no way of knowing where you're headed. The fact that we didn't have a plan is what caused me to not sleep at night. I haven't lost a minute of sleep since we had a financial plan prepared for us and made arrangements to have our money managed by professionals. The need to plan your financial future is extremely important regardless of your age, background, socio-economic level or investment knowledge."

"What I found most interesting is that each person we hired emphasized how important the planning process was. They each had a different approach in regards to planning, but they all placed a great deal of importance on the planning aspect nevertheless," Thomas added.

"I have a question," Rachel said. "Now that we have essentially entrusted our financial affairs to a group of investment professionals, what should we expect going forward?"

253

"If you've hired the right professionals, you only really need to evaluate whether you are hitting your financial goals every few years, keep your financial advisors abreast of any changes in your financial situation and stay committed to any savings plan that was established. The professionals that you hired will do the rest," Megan advised.

"It's important to mention that you aren't going to achieve your goals in a straight line," Jacob warned. "There are a lot of factors out of everyone's control that will affect your results. Over the longer-term you have to remember to stay the course. If your goals are realistic, you'll be able to achieve them."

"Jacob, that's an excellent point. It's extremely important to have and maintain realistic expectations. It isn't a financial professional's responsibility to make you rich beyond your wildest dreams. His job is to help you achieve realistic goals," Cindy added.

"I have another question," Rachel said. "How do we know if the financial professionals we hired are doing a good job? Are there any signs that we should look for indicating that they are doing a poor job?"

"It all comes back to your financial plan. As you know, your financial plan has a section that sets your financial targets every year until well into your retirement. Although you aren't going to achieve your annual targets in a straight line, you should come close to achieving your five-year targets. If you feel that your investment manager isn't achieving these targets then you have a reason to challenge his or her performance. There are a few stipulations, however. The first is that you must assess your results in the context of the prevailing economic landscape. If, for instance, there is a global recession, you probably won't achieve your goals until the recession has passed. On the other hand, if your timing is such that you experience an incredible period of growth and surpass your first five-year target by a huge margin, you shouldn't be too quick to deem your financial advisor a financial wizard. Again, you have to evaluate his or her performance in the context of the market," Jacob explained.

"What's another stipulation?" Rachel asked. "Does it by any chance rest on our shoulders?"

"It does indeed. As I'm sure you've heard many times before, you have to stay committed to the savings program or debt reduction that you initially established with your financial planner. If you don't stick to it, you shouldn't expect your investment manager to achieve miracles. If your savings commitment needs to change for some reason, you should sit down with your financial planner and reassess your targets to see how your retirement may be affected."

"How often should we refer to the financial plan?" Thomas asked.

"As often as you need to," Megan replied. "It will serve as your roadmap for the future."

"I guess we should place a great deal of importance on the various documents that we received," Thomas said.

"Yes, they are all very important. In fact, in the future you'll probably refer to them quite often, so keep them where you can easily find them," Megan suggested.

Before Thomas had the opportunity to ask another question, the team of waiters returned to clear the soup bowls. A few moments later they returned with large plates elegantly displaying watercress salad topped with fresh berries and a poppy seed dressing.

"Is there anything else we need to do in terms of reaching our goals?"

"The only other thing that comes to mind is that you have to ensure that you have correctly identified your risk tolerance. Although a top financial professional will do everything he or she can to assess your risk tolerance, an individual's appetite for risk can change very quickly when stock markets become volatile. If you are uncomfortable with the volatility of your portfolio then you have probably overstated your tolerance for risk. The misidentification of a client's acceptable level of risk is one of the most common reasons problems arise later on. Ultimately, only you truly know your acceptable level of risk," Jacob answered.

"That's a very good point. I'm confident that we clearly identified our acceptable level of risk. They all asked us a slew of questions regarding our attitudes towards risk and we answered each question honestly."

"It sounds like they did a very thorough job," Isabel said. "That's the sign of someone who takes their job seriously. I'm sure you are in good hands."

"What are you going to do now that your finances are in order? You'll need a new project!" Cindy observed.

"The first item on our agenda is a one-week holiday at the cottage, which I think is a vacation well deserved," Rachel sighed.

"It's definitely something you have earned. We're all very proud of you guys and wish you a stress-free financial future," Megan said.

"And before you know it," Patrick said. "You'll be helping everyone else."

As the evening progressed, they enjoyed the rest of the tasting menu, including roasted caribou with potatoes and mixed vegetables, a sampling of pastries for dessert and an extensive cheese plate. The evening ended with coffee and brandy over great conversation.

On the way home in the taxi, Thomas and Rachel talked about how much they enjoyed spending the evening with their friends. Although it wasn't too late, they wanted to do nothing more than get home and climb into bed. As far as they were concerned, it was the perfect way to end what had turned out to be a busy couple of months.

After they arrived at home, Rachel took off her shoes as she walked through the door and headed straight to the living room. She then took the financial plan, investment proposal and Investment Policy Statement from the table and took them upstairs to their office where she placed them safely in the desk drawer. As she closed the drawer she couldn't help but think about everything they had learned about the financial industry and all the people they had met. Despite it being a busy couple of months, she felt such a sense of relief that they had finally put their family finances in order. The fact that she had three professionally prepared documents outlining how they would achieve their financial goals put her at ease. More important, if she ever needed to refer to the information, it would always be readily available. This also gave her an overwhelming sense of reassurance.

Although it had taken a great deal of time, a lot of work and required difficult decisions to be made, she was confident that their financial future rested in the hands of some of the most capable professionals in the financial services industry. She climbed into bed, knowing that the newspaper headlines that used to keep her awake at night were now nothing more than words on paper.

~ The End ~

Appendix A

Professional Financial Designations

Chartered Accountant (CA)

An accountant who has successfully completed the education, examination and experience requirements of the Institute of Chartered Accountants and is a member in good standing of his or her provincial institute. Members are subject to a code of professional ethics/conduct, mandatory continuing education and mandatory professional liability insurance in respect of any public accounting practice.

Chartered Financial Analyst (CFA)

A designation held primarily by institutional money managers and stock analysts, the CFA is issued upon passing exams administered by the US-based CFA Institute.

Certified Financial Planner (CFP)

An international designation administered in Canada by the Financial Planners' Standards Council of Canada. CFPs must meet a uniform set of standards with respect to care and continuing education, experience (two years minimum), professional conduct and agree to report infractions to the Financial Planners Standards Council (FPSC).

Certified General Accountant (CGA)

An accountant who has successfully completed the education, examination and experience requirements of the Certified General Accountants Association and is a member in good standing of his or her provincial association. Members are subject to a code of professional ethics/conduct, mandatory continuing education and mandatory professional liability insurance in respect of any public accounting practice.

Chartered Financial Consultant (ChFC)

An individual who has passed exams administered by the Canadian Association of Insurance and Financial Advisors (CAIFA), indicating that he or she is a financial advisor with knowledge of wealth accumulation and retirement planning.

Chartered Professional (Ch.P.) Strategic Wealth

The Chartered Professional Strategic Wealth is a leadership designation, offered by the Canadian Securities Institute, designed to change the wealth management sector. It has been designed with extensive industry input and focuses on building comprehensive expertise. A Ch.P. Strategic Wealth is an unrivalled leader, capable of offering comprehensive service that connects every aspect of a client's financial life.

Canadian Investment Manager (CIM)

A designation granted by the Canadian Securities Institute to graduates of its advanced CIM program in portfolio management. This program meets the educational requirements from the Investment Industry Regulatory Organization of Canada for licensing as an associate or full portfolio manager.

Chartered Life Underwriter (CLU)

An individual who has passed exams administered by the Canadian Association of Insurance and Financial Advisors (CAIFA), indicating that he or she is a qualified life insurance agent.

Certified Management Accountant (CMA)

An accountant who has successfully completed the education, examination and experience requirements of the Society of Management Accountants and is a member in good standing of his or her provincial society. Members are subject to a code of professional ethics/conduct, mandatory continuing education and mandatory professional liability insurance in respect of any public accounting practice.

Derivatives Market Specialist (DMS)

As a qualified Derivatives Market Specialist, an individual is recognized for his or her specialized knowledge in the advanced concepts of derivative investments and risk management.

Fellow of the Canadian Securities Institute (FCSI)

The highest designation conferred by the Canadian Securities Institute. FCSIs must satisfy educational requirements and have a minimum of five years' experience in the securities industry. In order to maintain the designation, FCSIs must meet high standards for ongoing professional development and ethical practice.

Financial Management Advisor (FMA)

A designation granted by the Canadian Securities Institute to graduates of its FMA program in advanced financial planning and wealth management. Graduates of the FMA program are able to provide advanced financial planning advice to sophisticated and high–net worth investors.

Personal Financial Planner (PFP)

The banking industry's equivalent of CFP. To earn this designation, administered by the Institute of Canadian Bankers (ICB), bank/financial institution employees must complete a financial planning educational program and have a minimum of six months' work experience.

Registered Financial Planner (RFP)

A designation administered by the Canadian Association of Financial Planners (CAFP), a non-regulatory, voluntary membership body. No educational program is necessary, but passing an exam is required.

Registered Health Underwriter (RHU)

An individual who has passed exams administered by the Canadian Association of Insurance and Financial Advisors (CAIFA), indicating that he or she is an insurance/financial advisor with advanced knowledge of disability insurance underwriting.

Specialist in Financial Counselling (SFC)

A designation administered by the Institute of Canadian Bankers, for bank/financial institution employees and a counselling-focused supplement to the PFP.

Courses

Branch Managers' Examination Course (BM)

A self-study program offered by the Investment Funds Institute of Canada (IFIC) that provides managers with information to ensure that the business activities of a branch comply with both the organization's policies and provincial securities commission regulations.

Branch Managers Course (BMC)

A self-study course offered by the Canadian Securities Institute that prepares senior financial professionals for the challenges of running a branch office. BMC meets regulatory requirements and provides the skills and knowledge that branch managers require to effectively supervise staff and branch activities.

Canadian Investment Funds Course (CIFC)

A self-study program offered by the Investment Funds Institute of Canada (IFIC), covering the role of the salesperson, economic and financial environment, mutual funds, portfolio management, taxation, pensions and competitive products. The CIFC is typically taken by bank and trust company advisors, mutual fund representatives, professional accountants, insurance agents, business students and individual investors.

Canadian Securities Course (CSC)

A self-study program, offered by the Canadian Securities Institute, covering the financial services industry, fixed income securities, equities, mutual funds, derivatives, factors influencing market process of securities and the economy. The CSC is typically taken by bank and trust company advisors, mutual fund advisors, professional accountants, insurance agents, business students and individual investors.

Derivatives Fundamentals Course (DFC)

A self-study course offered by the Canadian Securities Institute that provides students with an overview of how futures and options work, how they are priced and how to choose an appropriate strategy for clients or a personal portfolio.

Officers', Partners' and Directors' Course (OPD)

A self-study program offered by the Investment Funds Institute of Canada (IFIC), which provides policy and regulatory knowledge that is needed to understand the securities and compliance requirements of a province or territory.

Partners, Directors and Senior Officers Course (PDO)

A self-study course offered by the Canadian Securities Institute that helps senior management comprehend and deal with the complex issues and responsibilities associated with the management of an investment firm.

Professional Financial Planning Course (PFPC)

A self-study course offered by the Canadian Securities Institute that helps students gain a thorough understanding of financial planning issues and investment management.

Technical Analysis Course

Helps public investors and financial professionals learn how to determine probable future price trends through the analysis of historical market information. Complements fundamental analysis and helps improve the quality of investment decisions. Available as a self-study course and individual modules or through in-class seminars by the Canadian Securities Institute.

Associations and Agencies

Advocis
1-800-563-5822
http://www.advocis.ca

Canada Deposit Insurance Corporation
1-800-461-2342
http://www.cdic.ca

Canada Revenue Agency
http://www.cra-arc.gc.ca

Canadian Investor Protection Fund
1-866-243-6981
http://www.cipf.ca

Canadian Securities Institute (CSI)
1-866-866-2601
https://www.csi.ca

Financial Advisors Association of Canada
(see **Advocis**)

Financial Planners Standards Council (FPSC)
1-800-305-9886
http://www.cfp-ca.org

Institute of Advanced Financial Planners (IAFP)
1-888-298-3292
http://www.iafp.ca

Institute of Canadian Bankers (ICB)
1-800-361-7339
http://www.icb.org

Office of the Superintendent of Financial Institutions (OSFI)
1-800-385-8647
http://www.osfi-bsif.gc.ca

OmbudsServices

Canadian Life and Health Insurance OmbudService (CLHIO)
1-888-295-8112
http://www.clhio.ca

Financial Consumers Agency of Canada (FCAC)
1-866-461-3222
http://www.fcac-acfc.gc.ca

Financial Services OmbudsNetwork (FSON)
1-866-538-3766
http://www.fson.org

Investment Industry Regulatory Organization of Canada (IIROC)
416-364-6133
http://www.iiroc.ca

General Insurance OmbudService (GIO)
1-888-421-4212
http://www.giocananda.org

Ombudsman for Banking Services and Investments (OBSI)
1-888-451-4519
http://www.obsi.ca

Index

Glossary

A

Annuity: a sum of money paid in a series of regular payments

Asset Allocation: a representation of how a portfolio is invested among the various available asset classes

Asset Class: in investments, the general type or category into which an investment falls

B

Bank: an establishment that keeps, lends, transfers, and issues money and other financial services

Bond: an interest-bearing certificate of private or public indebtedness

Brokerage: a business to arrange the purchase, sale and transfer of securities

C

Canada Pension Plan: A Canadian government administered scheme to provide funds to retired workers, and financial benefits to their surviving dependents (http://www.hrsdc.gc.ca)

Cash Flow: measure of a business or organisation's cash generated from operations

Codicil: a legal modification to an existing will

Commercial Paper: a fixed income instrument that is an unsecured, short-term loan to a credit-worthy corporation

Commission-based Compensation: a system whereby an investment advisor is paid a fee for each financial transactions he or she arranges

Common Shares: a security representing ownership of a corporation, conferring the right to vote on policy and elect company directors. Owners of common shares have the lowest priority in the event of liquidation

Credit Rating: an assessment of an individual or business's ability to borrow and repay funds

D

Defined Benefit Pension Plan: a scheme whereby an individual will receive a predetermined amount of money during his or her retirement

Defined Contribution Pension Plan: a scheme whereby an individual deposits a fixed amount into a retirement plan, but the amount of money available upon retirement is determined by market conditions thereby making the benefit unknown

Deposit Insurance: a scheme whereby an investor or saver's money is protected by a government agency in the event of a financial institution going bankrupt

Discretionary Management Contract: an agreement between an individual and a portfolio manager, giving him or her the right to buy and sell stocks on behalf of the investor without prior consultation

Dividend: a share of surplus funds distributed to the shareholders of a public or private company

E

Employee Share Purchase Plan: a scheme whereby employees of a company are allowed to buy stock in the company typically at a reduced price

Estate Planning: legal work to ensure the distribution of an individual's assets after death in the most tax-efficient manner

Executor: a named individual responsible for carrying out a deceased person's wishes as outlined in a will

F

Fee-based Compensation: a system of remuneration whereby a financial professional is paid a set amount, often based on a percentage of assets or on hours worked or tasks undertaken

Financial Needs Pyramid: a five-level "pyramid" diagram used to outline the stages of an individual's financial life, culminating in the preservation and distribution of his or her estate

Financial Planner: an individual who assists clients in establishing and implementing a prudent strategy for managing their financial or money-related needs

Financial Plan: the long-term plan or strategy developed by a financial planner

Financial Services Industry: the collective term for all the institutions dealing with money, insurance, banking and other related matters

G

Gross Income: an individual's total earnings, before the deduction of taxes and other expenses

Guaranteed Investment Certificate (GIC): a security providing a low-risk, fixed rate of return

I

Inflation Rate: the rate at which the price of goods and services rises

Insurance: a contract whereby an institution offers to protect an individual or business against financial loss, sometimes as caused by specific events

Interest Rate: the percentage of a sum borrowed which a borrower must pay to a lender, usually monthly, semi-annually or annually

Investment Advisor: an individual who is licensed to offer advice on stocks, bonds and a other similar securities to an individual or corporation

Investment Personality: the general level of financial risk an investor is prepared to accept

Investment Policy Statement: a contract between an individual and his or her investment counsellor or portfolio manager's discretionary powers

L

Life Annuity: an insurance product offering a fixed, regular payment, usually taking effect after an individual retires from paid employment

Life Income Fund: a registered account created for various locked-in registered plans that is designed to provide an individual with income during his or her retirement

Limited Partnership: an arrangement whereby one or more general partners in a business is liable for losses limited by the amount of money they have invested

Locked-In Retirement Income Fund: see Life Income Fund above

M

Marginal Tax Rate: the amount of tax payable on income over an amount set by the government

Mortgage: a financial instrument whereby money is lent by a financial institution for the purchase of property in return for an interest in that property, which expires when the loan is repaid

Mutual Fund: a financial product whereby money from a group of investors is pooled together and invested in a wide range of securities

N

Net Income: an individual's income after the deduction of taxes and other expenses (see gross income)

Net Worth Statement: an individual's financial worth, arrived at by deducting liabilities from assets

Non-registered Securities: securities that are held outside of a registered account and are therefore considered taxable assets

P

Pension Adjustment: The amount that an employer or employee contributes annually to a registered pension plan and subsequently reduces the allowable contribution limit to an RRSP

Portfolio Management: a service whereby an institution or a qualified professional manages an individual's investments in accordance with their investment objectives

Power of Attorney: an agreement whereby one individual acts for another in financial matters

Preferred Shares: a class of ownership of a corporation whereby holders of these shares are paid their dividends first

Probate: the legal process of authenticating and administering a will

R

Rate of Return: the gain or loss made on an invested sum of money over a period of time

Registered Educational Savings Plan (RESP): a registered account wherein money saved for a child's future post secondary education costs is sheltered from taxation

Registered Retirement Income Fund (RRIF): a registered account that provides a stream of income to a retired individual

Registered Retirement Savings Plan (RRSP): a registered account wherein money saved for an individual's retirement is sheltered from taxation until it is withdrawn

Retirement Planning: the process whereby an individual plans, saves and invests money to be used to provide an income during his or her retirement

S

Security: an investment instrument that is purchased by the holder for investment purposes

Spousal RRSP: a retirement savings plan established by one spouse for the financial benefit of the other

Stock Exchange: an exchange where shares and other financial instruments are traded

Stock Option Plan: an arrangement whereby employees of a corporation are entitled to buy shares at a predetermined price that are exercisable for a predetermined amount of time

T

T-2033 Form: a government document used to transfer investments from an RRSP or RRIF to another between different financial institutions

T-4 Slip: a government document provided to an individual from his or her employer detailing annual earned income and deductions

Term to 100 Life Insurance Policy: an insurance policy providing a guaranteed sum of money to a named individual upon the death of another

Term Deposit: a sum of money held by a financial institution for a fixed period of time that earns interest

Total Debt Service Ratio: the amount of debt an individual is allowed to assume, based on his or her assets, liabilities and income

Treasury Bill: a short-term debt obligation backed by the government, bought at a "discount rate" and surrendered for its face value

Trust Company: a legal entity that administers assets on behalf of individuals and companies

U

Universal Life Insurance Policy: a life insurance policy with a savings element and a cash surrender value

V

Vesting Schedule: the rules governing the exercise of an employee's stock options

W

Will: a legal document detailing an individual's specific wishes in regards to the distribution of his or her property after death